BIRKIE FEVER

*A
10-Year
History
Of The
American
Birkebeiner*

TOM KELLY

PHOTO CREDITS

All photos used in this book are courtesy of the American Birkebeiner. Photographers include: Tom Bieber, Jim Burt, Bruce Cutting, Bob Davenport, John Dunster, Bill Fritsch, Bruce Fritz, Budd Hagen, Lynn Howell, Tom Kelly, Michael Kienitz, Robert McCoy, Fred Morgan, Ted Nagel, Rick Olivo, Ginny Peifer, Pam Penfold, Mark Perlstein, Tom Riles, Tom Rutlin, Hal Stoelzli, Barry Stott, Dick Taylor and others.

© Tom Kelly 1982

ISBN 0-933424-39-6

Library of Congress Catalog No. 82-16840

Published by Specialty Press Publishers & Wholesalers, Inc.
Box 426
Osceola, Wisconsin 54020
USA

Printed in the United States of America

Book and cover design by William F. Kosfeld

All rights reserved. No part of this publication may be reproduced, stored in a retrieval system or transmitted, in any form or by any means, electronic, mechanical photocopying, recording, or otherwise, without prior permission in writing from the publisher.

Library of Congress Cataloging in Publication Data

Kelly, Tom,
    Birkie fever.

    1. American Birkebeiner, Wis.—History.   I. Title.
GV855.4.K44   1982   796.93   82-16840
ISBN 0-933424-39-6

To my parents, who will see their first Birkebeiner in 1983, for their help throughout the years, and to Carole, for her persistence and patience to help make this book possible.

PREFACE

It was a brisk January evening in 1978. Bob Woodward, who was Telemark's cross country ski school director at the time, his wife-to-be Eileen, Norwegian Audun Endestad (who had been living with Woodward), and another Telemark employee, Lea Justice, who would years later become my public relations assistant for American Birkebeiner X, were headed back to Telemark from Duluth.

The foursome had just seen the latest sensation of the silver screen, *Saturday Night Fever*. All agreed, it was a pretty good movie. Audun didn't care for John Travolta that much, though. "I believe Audun didn't think Travolta did enough training," recalls Woodward.

Woodward had been working on a story for the *Birch Scroll* at the time, putting together his thoughts in anticipation of the race. Woodward, who was, and still is, a noted nordic author, was grasping for some theme for his short piece. His editor, myself in this case, was getting ready to call him for the story.

All of a sudden it hit! "Birkebeiner Fever." Audun and the others thought it was great—a catchy phrase.

The next day, Woodward threw his idea out to Lodge manager Dave Howard and me. It was fantastic! What a great catch-line, we all thought. While Woodward put it to use in his story, which appeared on page three of the February 1978 edition of the *Birch Scroll*, Howard put it to work as the name of the first-ever lodging package offered by Telemark for Birkebeiner Week.

Such was the birth of "Birkebeiner Fever." But like any exotic ailment, Birkebeiner Fever has deep roots. It has inflicted its symptoms on the many thousands who have had the opportunity to be part of the greatest ski event in America—the American Birkebeiner.

When publisher Tom Lebovsky and editor Bill Kosfeld (a Birkie skier since 1976) approached me in the summer of 1981 about this book, I thought the idea was excellent. Rolf Kjaernsli had written his book on the Norwegian Birkebeiner ten years earlier and I'm sure that Tony Wise had always hoped that someday a similar book would be written about our own race in America.

My first-hand Birkebeiner experience dates back to 1976. I had initially visited Telemark a few months earlier for a U.S. Ski Team camp and the Olympic Tryouts. My original cross country experience had only been a year earlier at the 1975 Junior Nordic Nationals at Ishpeming, Michigan, as a freelance reporter and photographer for *Ski Racing*.

I remember my first Birkebeiner like it was just yesterday! The huge size of the starting field, catching Jana Hlavaty and Chris Haines before the race for a photo of their bicentennial bibs, and watching the skiers climb up Morgedal towards me like a sea of centipedes.

In working on *Birkie Fever* I've come to learn a lot about the background of the American Birkebeiner. In the annals of the Birkebeiner there is more ski history than could ever be compiled. It's a history that takes skiing right down to its roots, and gives what is known as the citizen skier a serious role in competition.

In the course of these pages one couldn't begin to scratch the surface of all that has happened over the years. Each of the thousands of pages of results and notes researched for this book have uncovered hundreds of new stories—stories of Birkebeiners past, and Birkebeiners to come. And these pages will undoubtedly bring up countless more.

This book is for each and every skier who has ever dreamed of the challenge of the Birkie. For those who have met that challenge, I hope that it will conjure many new dreams. And, most of all, will rekindle the memories of their Birkebeiners. For those who have not been exposed to the "Fever," I hope that it will give you at least a small idea of just what this race has meant to the thousands who have taken the challenge.

I've made dozens of new friends in researching this book and finally met dozens of others I had known for years only as lines in result sheets or faces in photographs.

This is my first book. I had thought that it would be a lot like putting together a big *Birch Scroll*. Well, that was quite an underestimation! It's been a long year of research, tracking down long, lost skiers and trying to find the words that would record for history what the Birkebeiner is all about. I hope I have accomplished this in these pages.

With any project of this magnitude there are many thanks to be given—to the office staff at Telemark for their patient cooperation, for my own staff for the long hours assisting in researching data and photographs and for the patient editing of Bill Kosfeld. Dozens of Birkebeiner skiers gave up their time for interviews at all hours of the day and night and from many corners of the earth.

But a special thanks is owed to Tony Wise. His foresight (with a little prodding from Hayward's Swede Carl Hanson) and persistence have combined to put Cable and Hayward, Wisconsin, on the map, around the world, as the home of the greatest ski event in America, the American Birkebeiner.

On Saturday, February 24, 1973, Minneapolis skier Rufus Jefferson handed a little cannon to Birkebeiner Race Chairman Bob Treland. Treland didn't know Rufus at the time. And he didn't know just how many races that little cannon had started. At 9 a.m., Carl Hanson, who had dreamed of that day since witnessing the Swedish Vasaloppet in his childhood, pulled the string on the cannon. Just as Rufus had predicted, that little cannon belched out a cloud of smoke and a boom that sent skiing America booming ahead.

The American Birkebeiner had begun.

It's been quite a few years since Rufus skied the Birkie. He still has his little 1905-vintage 10-gauge Winchester cannon, though. And the Birkebeiner is still a part of his life. But while he doesn't step up to the starting line with thousands of others, Rufus never misses a Birkebeiner. Without fail, on the last Saturday in February, Rufus Jefferson goes skiing somewhere—just to be out on skis in the wilderness or in a nearby park, thinking back to that brisk morning in 1973.

As he silently breaks trail, his thoughts turn to Telemark. He can see them all clearly in his mind—thousands of skiers, climbing up the grueling hills, swooping down the long stretches of downhill. Every year, hundreds of new Birkebeiners experiencing the thrill of having that gold medallion draped around their neck.

Not a one of the original Birkebeiners will admit to even dreaming that the little race in 1973 would grow to what it is today. But deep down in their hearts, they had to know something! I hope this book will tell you a little about that something special which Birkebeiners like Rufus Jefferson found that morning back in 1973.

Birkebeiner Fever will be with us for a long, long time!

Tom Kelly
August 1982

FOREWORD

Birkebeiner Happiness!

The American Birkebeiner Race has brought much happiness to its participants, and that happiness has motivated Birkebeiner competitors to develop their physical and mental capacities to the nth degree in order to meet the challenge of this grueling race.

The competitors' happiness, in turn, motivated the Telemark race organizers to persevere during the growth of the American Birkebeiner race from only 53 finishers the first year to nearly 6,000 in its tenth year. The growth occurred because the Telemark organization wanted to put on not only a world class race, but also a world class *happening* that would be both athletic and social in nature. It has accomplished these goals because it accepts constructive criticism and gives cross country skiers the kind of athletic and social event they dream of attending.

I am happy Tom Kelly has written a book about the American Birkebeiner so that all participants connected with the race the past ten years will get reflective pleasure out of reading about the struggles involved in promoting and competing in one of the world's great athletic events. I also hope the book will motivate many other Americans to take up cross country skiing as a lifetime sport, so that they, too, can get happiness from pushing themselves to their highest level of physical and mental fitness.

Many American people in the past twenty years have changed their lifestyle from sitting to exercising. However, most people can't stand the boredom of calisthenics or jogging, per se, over a long period of time. They need frequent competitive events to motivate them to try new techniques and attain higher degrees of skill, physical fitness and mental toughness. Participants in the American Birkebeiner, and other Worldloppet races, have developed a keen desire to survive and achieve.

The mottos of two Worldloppet races seem to sum up the motivational reasons that cause cross country ski racers to train, train, train. The Austrian motto is "Jeder ein Sieger, uber sich selbst" ("Every one a victor over oneself"); the Swedish motto is "I fäders spår för framtids segrar" ("In our fathers' tracks for future victory").

The personal victory of finishing North America's largest ski race, in which a large segment of the world's cross country citizen racers have at one time competed, motivates snow-belt people to take up cross country skiing and enjoy the sport all of their life. What other sport has a happy 107-year-old man as its guru—a man who is still physically fit and mentally alert after a century of cross country skiing. Jack Rabbit Johanssen is living proof that Birkebeiners of all ages have pointed their skis down the right tracks to a lifetime of happiness.

Tony Wise
Telemark, USA

The Norwegian Birkebeiner-Rennet, where skiers must carry a 12-pound pack up and over a mountain on the 55-kilometer course between Rena and Lillehammer.

INTRODUCTION

"... I remember as I moved along the trail in the very first Birkie race, among the snow-clad pines of the beautiful Telemark forests. I said to myself: 'This is just like skiing in the Drammensmarka.' This is an area in Norway where many years ago I had spent countless happy hours on my wooden skis. So this Birkie race was a reunion with my past." — Karl Andresen, Founder.

Without a doubt, there are endless numbers of stories which can be told about the ten years of the American Birkebeiner. Certainly the memories which we may have about it can more than fill all the hot summer nights that we spend dreaming about snow.

There is one memory which I shall not forget. It has become my own personal inspiration and has made me realize the true meaning of the American Birkebeiner. During the past ten years, I have heard the national anthems of America and Norway played many times during Birkebeiner week. But never have I been so moved as when I sat near Karl Andresen and watched him, a very proud American, share his Norwegian heritage by singing in Norwegian. I believe it was then that I finally realized the Birkebeiner is so much more than just skiing 55 kilometers.

I consider myself very lucky that Tony Wise and so many other people were willing to put forth so much effort so that we might experience and feel that, for a short time, we also are just a bit Norwegian. I would not trade these experiences for any other, nor the friendships I have made. Perhaps for that brief time we are more than individuals representing different nations, states and cities, but are more a culture within ourselves, known as the Birkebeiner culture.

The Birkebeiner is many things to many people. Perhaps the greatest benefit from it is that once we have the "fever," it tends to keep us on a year-round program of physical activity, convincing us that there really is no reason for growing old. There may be many of us who no longer count the years in birthdays, but in Birkebeiners. It seems that much of our yearly physical activity is done with the Birkie in mind.

John Kotar trains for road races and marathons such as Grandma's Marathon in Duluth and the Paavo Nurmi Marathon in Hurley, Wisconsin. Dave Landgraf and Karl Andresen compete in road runs and canoe races during the summer months. Always in the back of these Founders' minds is the February Birkebeiner. Fred Constalie has changed his lifestyle saying that, "the former Fred suffered too much in February." Now his entire family has joined him in cross country skiing and he looks forward to one day having all four members of his family ski the Birkie.

The Birkebeiner is definitely an important part of the growth in awareness of the value of physical fitness and nutrition in America. As more and more people become aware of these things, we see noticeable changes and improvements in skiers' abilities and techniques, especially in the past five years. As a nordic ski instructor at Telemark in the seventies I had the opportunity to give lessons to many beginners, only to see them pass me by in later Birkebeiners.

But isn't training for the Birkie a mere symptom of the "fever?" All that we need to do is jog, hike, bike, roller ski, canoe and generally enjoy ourselves while waiting for the next Birkebeiner to happen. But what would skiing 55 kilometers be without the hours upon hours of planning and preparation spent to bring us all together in February? That so many people have the desire to train for this race is truly a tribute to the people who have made the Birkebeiner an international festival, bringing so many people together to share the experience.

I am always proud to be able to say that I am part of a group of ten skiers who skied the first ten Birkebeiners. I am also as proud, if not more, to be a friend of people like Karl Andresen and the many others who have made the Birkebeiner an event to look forward to each year. *Birkie Fever*, by Tom Kelly, has allowed me to relive the special events and to remember all the good friends I have made at the Birkebeiner.

Ernie St. Germaine, Founder

CONTENTS

I	*A Little Bit Of Norway Comes to Wisconsin*	page 8
II	*Quinn Brothers Make Their Birkebeiner Mark*	page 19
III	*Birkebeiners Join Hands Across The Ocean*	page 27
IV	*American Olympians Take On Norwegian Elite*	page 36
V	*Where Were You When . . . ?*	page 48
VI	*The Closest Birkie*	page 62
VII	*Year Of The Mystery Champion*	page 74
VIII	*A Trail For The Future*	page 90
IX	*Sixty-Five Degrees And Sunny?*	page 107
X	*Greatest Birkie So Far*	page 134
	Results 1973-1982	page 154

CHAPTER I

A Little Bit Of Norway Comes To Wisconsin

February 24, 1973 dawned bitter cold in Hayward, Wisconsin. It was a typical northwoods winter Saturday as wisps of smoke streamed from chimneys into the cold northwestern Wisconsin air and piping hot cups of coffee helped locals greet the day.

Most of the town was oblivious to the commotion over at Historyland, a summer tourist attraction just east of town. After all, it was still four months before the summer tourist season would begin. Resorts on nearby Round Lake, the Chippewa Flowage and others were boarded up for the winter. Ice fishermen watched their tipups on Nelson Lake and snowmobiles sat ready for an afternoon ride.

But while Hayward went about its usual weekend business, things were beginning to stir at Historyland.

The familiar aroma of Esther Pfister's German apple pancakes, a popular summertime specialty at Historyland's Wannigan Pancake House, was replaced by a strange new odor—a curious combination of chef Bill Hotze's blueberry soup and the pungent scent of burning pine tar.

In a few months the Pancake House deck would be buzzing with tourists sipping lemonade and iced tea while watching the Namekagon Queen steam

Although not everyone appears in this historic photograph (at least one skier was late for the start), 35 skiers started the first Birkebeiner on the ice of Lumberjack Bowl. Spectators on the Wannigan Pancake House deck included a number of entrants in the women's and junior's race, which began an hour later on County OO. Sven Wiik, who helped lay out the trail, and eventual champion Eric Ersson are on the side closest to the Pancake House deck.

out of Lumberjack Bowl. But today, the umbrella tables were replaced by skiers dabbing goopy pine tar and wax on the bottom of their wooden skis.

It was an odd collection that gathered on the frozen ice of Lumberjack Bowl—35 Birkebeiner cross country ski racers, bundled up in woolen sweaters and strange looking knickers. Many of them wondered why they were there at all and each was anxious to find out what it would really be like. But not a one gave much serious thought to what the Telemark-Birkebeiner (the name American-Birkebeiner was not universally adopted until 1974, although 1973 medallions did use the American-Birkebeiner name) would someday become. Few realized that they were about to make skiing history.

One of those watching from the deck of the Wannigan Pancake House was long-time Haywardite Tony Wise, owner of the Telemark ski area at Cable, the final destination for the intrepid group of Birkebeiner skiers. Wise's Telemark resort was celebrating its 25th anniversary that year.

Admittedly, the first Birkebeiner was not a big affair in itself, claims Wise. But deep in his mind, and in the minds of skiers like Sven Wiik, the former American Olympic coach who had designed Telemark's new cross country ski trails, and Samuel Eric Ersson, Telemark's Swedish nordic director, there was a vision of something grand in the future—something that Hayward's resident Swede, Carl Hanson, had been trying to tell Tony for years!

Just what their expectations were seems somewhat clouded. Cross country skiing in America had not even reached its infancy by 1973. And although the famous Swedish Vasaloppet was over 50 years old, races such as the prestigious Finlandia Hiihto and others hadn't even begun!

The history of the American Birkebeiner actually began with the creation of the Telemark ski area in Cable. Following his service in World War II, Wise returned to Hayward in 1947 with an MBA from Harvard and an idea he had after experiencing skiing at Garmisch-Partenkirchen in Germany; he decided to add a new dimension to the already popular summer tourist region. That new dimension was skiing!

Mt. Telemark, a 300-foot-plus alpine ski hill near Cable, opened on December 13, 1947. The name "Telemark" was suggested by Wise's Norwegian roommate at Harvard. Telemark was the province in Norway where skiing began and was close to the home of Wise's grandmother, who was born in nearby Rendal.

Even as early as 1947, when Telemark began, Wise thought how spectacular it would be to be able to put on a pair of skis at Telemark and ski to Hayward.

"When I started Telemark I was looking for a Norwegian shield theme for our logo," recalled Wise. "I ran across a little booklet sent by the Norwegian Information Service which had a painting of two Viking warriors. A rendition of that picture became our Telemark shield."

The historic origins of cross country skiing in America are generally attributed to the era of Snowshoe Thompson, who carried the mail across the high Sierras on skis as early as 1856. Ironically, though, earlier reports of man on skis have surfaced from parts of southern Wisconsin.

Through its first 25 years, Telemark grew to become one of the leading resorts in mid-America—a popular alpine ski area, but one never destined to attain the status of the Vails or Aspens that were popping up out of the Rockies.

Telemark's tiny base chalet was quite a luxury back in 1947. No one could have dreamed of how it would grow in the next 30 years before a fire would level it to rubble. But four-and-a-half years before that 1977 fire, a massive $6-million, 200-room hotel, the Telemark Lodge, was erected. The design and architecture were unique not only for the midwest, but it was a lodge unlike any other in the nation. On its dedication, Olympic alpine medalist Billy Kidd said, "Telemark is the only ski area in the country where the Lodge is bigger than the ski hill!"

The Lodge was a necessary step in the evolution of Telemark. The sixties saw a boom in downhill skiing. But slowly skiers began flocking to the Rockies. Whole resort cities grew to become oasis' in the snow and mountains. Telemark needed a change, said Wise, to make it competitive against the mountain resorts. The striking lodge was a big part of that change, but even more was in store.

Looking ahead, Wise asked Duluth, Minnesota, skier George Hovland and Rick Scott of Superior, Wisconsin, to produce a feasibility study on cross country skiing. Both were more noted regionally as downhill skiers and instructors, although Hovland had been a member of the 1952 U.S. Olympic Cross Country Team, along with nordic authority John Caldwell of Putney, Vermont.

"Looking back, it's interesting to note how well some of our predictions came true," said Scott, one of those 35 adventurers at Lumberjack Bowl who continued on to become one of the ten skiers to complete the first ten Birkebeiners. "We looked at figures for ski imports to determine how the sport would grow in America."

"I had never thought that cross country skiing could be a profitable business venture," said Wise, "so I never really gave it that much thought. But every spring, Carl Hanson would bring me a copy of the Mora (Sweden) newspaper showing the thousands of skiers that competed in their Vasaloppet."

Hanson was persistent in his efforts—too persistent, his wife often told him. But he had his convictions and if anyone had a dream in his mind, it was Carl Hanson.

"Finally, in 1972, I sent Jerry Berard (general manager) and Fred Goold (assistant manager) out to Colorado to look at some nordic centers," added Wise. "They came back with a positive response and in September 1972, Sven Wiik came out to design our touring center trails."

"We had lunch with Sven," recalled Berard, "and that was all it took to know that he was the man we were looking for!"

At that time cross country skiing was still very limited in the United States. Wiik was one of a handful of nordic experts in America, with his background as American cross country coach at the 1960 Squaw Valley Olympics.

"Nordic was just becoming popular and Tony wanted to become *the* area in the country," recalled Wiik. "But I backed him up. I told him, 'you have everything that any touring center would want in terms of terrain and snow.' And we pursued it with that in mind."

One of Wiik's suggestions was to hold a symbolic race, something that would generate special interest in the new cross country ski trails.

So armed with Wiik's support and Carl Hanson's newspaper clippings of the Swedish Vasaloppet, Wise set out to create the event.

In continuing the Norwegian heritage of Telemark, Wise chose to pattern his race after the famous Norwegian Birkebeiner-Rennet, first run in 1932. As legend has it, Viking soldiers Torstein Skevla and Skjervald Skrukka, nicknamed "Birkebeiners" for the birch bark leggings they wore, carried the child prince Haakon Haakonssøn 55 kilometers to safety in the Norwegian civil war of 1206.

Their heroic rescue was commemorated in a painting by Norwegian K. Bergslien in 1853 which hangs today in the famed Holmenkollen Ski Museum in Oslo. That beautiful painting had become the symbol of the Norwegian race—the same symbol Wise had discovered in his search for a Telemark logo in 1947.

"Ola Stormoen (Telemark's first ski instructor in 1947) came here for our 25th anniversary December 13, 1972, and told me more about the Norwegian Birkebeiner," said Wise. "When he returned home, he sent me a book on the race written by Rolf Kjaernsli. I had never realized the significance of the painting of the Viking warriors until that point."

But Telemark's Birkebeiner was not the first Birkebeiner in America. A year earlier the Sons of Norway chapter in Bemidji, Minnesota, started a short race called the Bemidji Birkebeiner. Officials even obtained a letter from the Lillehammer Ski Klub in Norway granting them permission to use the name. The emergence of another Birkebeiner at Telemark did cause some concern, especially since Bemidji already had permission to use the name.

Nothing more ever arose between the two Birkebeiners. The Bemidji Birkebeiner continued, although it never reached the scope of the Norwegian event. It remained a 16-kilometer event and is still held today.

It's hard to imagine today just how simple the race was in the beginning. Bob Treland, an assistant ski area manager at Telemark, was assigned the task of putting the race together. He had no title, no big budget to work with, but then he really didn't even need that much help!

Fred Morgan, Telemark's part-time publicity man, got the word out on the race. Basically that consisted of media and skier notices a few weeks before the event. Some posters were sent to area ski shops but most of the publicity was by word of mouth and visits to other area races.

Race Chairman Bob Treland (left) and Telemark instructor Dave Riechel go over plans for the first Birkebeiner.

Bob McClelland, a Telemark bartender who had worked on the trails the previous fall, put together the food stations on the course. He began collecting items just two weeks before the race.

Chef Hotze claimed to be an expert on blueberry soup. "I've made plenty of that before!" But his strange mixture of blueberries and sugar left a lot to be desired and was probably the sweetest thing ever served in any ski race to this very day.

There was little precedence with which to work; only a handful of sizeable races existed across the country. The 160-kilometer Canadian Ski Marathon, a two-day untimed trek though the Quebec brush, was one of the most well-known long-distance skiing events of the day. The several-year-old Rabbit Ears Race in Steamboat Springs, Colorado, the Glacier Stampede in Alaska, the Washington's Birthday Race in Vermont and the Frisco Gold Rush were also on the scene. The new Telemark-Birkebeiner was billed as "the longest cross country ski race in mid-America."

"I don't even remember just how I first heard about Telemark," said Duncan McLean. "It was the first year I ever skiied. Barry Bolich and I came down from Ironwood about three weeks before the race out of curiosity and they really took care of us. They showed us the trails and really encouraged us to enter the race. Barry and I had been training for the UP [Michigan's Upper Peninsula] Winter Games which had everything from ping pong to skiing."

Some ideas on the race were exchanged with Sven Wiik the previous fall, but most work fell in place closer to the race.

In late January, Treland met with Haywardite Ward Williamson and other local snowmobilers. They pored over topographical maps of the area, locating an odd assortment of logging roads, snowmobile trails, railroad beds and wilderness paths—a trail that has never been accurately measured, and one that would never quite do by today's standards. But it was a start.

"The first two years we marked the trail with red and blue crepe paper," said Treland. "We really moved up the third year when we used plastic tape!" The course started in Lumberjack Bowl, went out onto Lake Hayward and across the property of John and Mary Duffy, east of the Namekagon River, very much as it did in later years. It was quite a thrill for the Duffy children to be able to sit in their living room and watch the race go by on Saturday mornings each year.

Famous painting of the rescue of the Norwegian prince by "Birkebeiners."

Before reaching Wheeler Road, it swung north to Airport Road, proceeding north across Highway 77, running along the west side of the runway, over the Namekagon River bridge and onto the railroad bed alongside town roads. The course then followed the railroad right-of-way to Phipps, past the Phipps Tavern, and east to the Phipps Firelane. At this point, about a quarter of the way into the race, it was just east of the present course at Mosquito Brook Road. The Phipps Firelane closely parallels the course today. At County Highway OO, it continued north, connecting with the Seeley Fire Tower Road.

As the course neared Telemark, crossing from Sawyer to Bayfield County, it headed north on Randysek Road, then east on McNaught Road, connecting with a back trail to Telemark, behind the newly-built Telemark Lodge.

The course was far from ideal. "There was not much to do in terms of the trail design or layout," said Wiik. The course itself was measured with a snowmobile odometer and calculated at 50 kilometers, although some estimates put it at around 45. For historic purposes, later re-estimates of the trail put it at 48 kilometers, which is now considered the official distance of the race.

There were four food stations on the route, each about 15 kilometers apart, including one at the finish. Ersson had told officials about blueberry soup which was used at the Vasaloppet. Telemark added donuts and pastries from its own bakery, along with oranges and water. "I remember we had a lot of donuts left over," recalled McClelland.

Rod Lundberg, athletic director at Hayward High School, provided football warmup jackets to be used to warm skiers at aid stations. The local National Guard battalion provided cots, while rental skis and wax came from Telemark.

Sawyer County Sheriff Don Primley, a nationally certified emergency medical technician (EMT), organized an EMT team to provide emergency care at points along the course. The initial development of an emergency crew was certainly a noteworthy achievement. Primley's crew would grow even bigger and more sophisticated with each passing race.

Medallions were given to everyone completing the course, whether the Birkebeiner or shorter women's race. They were a brightly-painted red, white and blue rendition of the Birkebeiner Viking logo on a stock medal. Original medals were recalled the next year for renumbering. Today those original medals, which were the same for the first three years, have become true collector's items.

The field for the first Birkebeiner was virtually devoid of elite skiers. If there was a favorite, it was certainly Ersson.

Ersson came to Telemark in late November, 1972. Before coming to Wisconsin he spent two weeks with Wiik at his Scandinavian Lodge touring center in Steamboat Springs, Colorado—learning the techniques he would teach the new cross country skiers at Telemark. Bob McClelland, a newcomer to cross country skiing like virtually all Telemark employees, drew the task of showing Ersson the trails when he arrived.

Ersson was known to many as Sam, his real first name. Wise, however, preferred his middle name of Eric, which was more Scandinavian-sounding than Sam. Ersson was very popular with Telemark employees and by the end of February he had picked up quite a cheering section.

"We all hoped Sam would win," said Treland, "but we didn't know how good Sven Wiik would be."

Among the skiers that first year were Wayne and Jacque Lindskoog of Minneapolis. "We were charter members of the North Star Ski Touring Club so we probably had as much skiing experience as anyone," Jacque recalled. "We were probably among the first 200 skiers in the Twin Cities and had only been skiing for a few years."

The Lindskoogs were introduced to the concept of long distance mass start races when they saw a film on the Vasaloppet at a club meeting.

"We basically thought it would be fun," she added. "We had done a lot of skiing in the Porkies [Porcupine Mountains, Michigan] in the past and some long distance ski touring. The Birkebeiner was a culmination of the things we had been doing."

No one really gave it much thought when Jacque decided to ski the 50-kilometer Birkebeiner instead of the 22-kilometer women's race. No one really thought that a woman could actually ski that far, which is why the shorter race was

Sven Wiik was instrumental in designing the first and subsequent Birkebeiner trails.
1975-23

set up. In fact, it wasn't until 1975 that women could officially enter the Birkebeiner. (Women were not permitted in the Boston Marathon until 1972.) The Vasaloppet in Sweden and German König Ludwig Lauf did not lift their ban until the 1980's!

"There was never an intent to crash the race or to liberate it," Jacque said. "I just picked up my bib and raced. I didn't even think about it. In fact, I probably never would have said anything, but after the race my friends said that something should be done to recognize women!"

"I'm not really sure how many people even knew she was in the race," said Treland. Although she did not receive an official time, she was later credited with a 4:33:35, and is today listed in the official award listings of the race. An asterik indicates that her finish was unofficial as women were not allowed.

The remainder of the field were also simply citizen skiers, by today's standards. There were no U.S. Ski Team members or foreign stars. Just a handful of enthusiasts from a couple of midwestern states, out to try something new. Many of the entrants were on cross country skis for the first season—some for the first time!

Fred Albright, Telemark's personnel director, was one of those first-timers. Ersson had talked him into it and he used his one day off to ski the race.

Dave Landgraf, a Hayward native who was teaching school in Bloomington, Minnesota, was one of those who had never been on cross country skis. His lifelong Chippewa Indian friend from Northwoods Beach, near Hayward, Ernie St. Germaine, talked Dave into skiing the Birkebeiner.

"My entire training consisted of skiing in the parking lot at Met Stadium in Bloomington," recalled Landgraf. "I'd never skied up or down a hill in my life."

In a 1973 publicity photo, Telemark Public Relations Director Fred Morgan (right) takes a few strides on Lumberjack Bowl in Hayward under the watchful eyes of Carl Hanson (left) of Hayward and ski school director Eric Ersson of Telemark. Note the long skis and huge poles held by Hanson, a Swedish native who had been suggesting the idea of a race similar to his nation's own Vasaloppet to Telemark's Tony Wise for many years.

Although St. Germaine had pursuaded Landgraf to enter, he was as much a rookie himself. Just a week earlier, he was just another alpine skier, or an "uhlpeener" as Ernie's old friend Lyman Williamson of Hayward called the breed. In the course of a Saturday afternoon, Lyman changed his good friend Ernie's outlook.

"Lyman may seem to some as a real character and maybe even slightly eccentric for the truly unusual things he has done," said St. Germaine, "but to me he was and still is someone that I truly admired. I have often hoped that I might turn out to be half the man that he has been."

On that fateful Saturday, just a week before the Birkebeiner, Williamson let his good friend really have it. "Those 'uhlpeeners' aren't really skiing," he said. "They ride up in a chair and just ski down—that's only half skiing! Here, try this." With that, St. Germaine was led out into the driveway, put onto a pair of ridiculous-looking skinny skis and sent out into the woods.

"I scrambled up the driveway, did a fancy jump turn, took off in a wild run and crashed into a snowbank," said St. Germaine. All Williamson could mutter was, "damn fool Indian!"

But that was enough of an introduction. Williamson was sufficiently pleased with his pupil's progress that he hit him with a big offer. "You can represent me next Saturday in the race Tony is having," Lyman said. "I'll even sponsor you."

On Friday, less than 24 hours before the Birkebeiner, Tom Polaski of Bayfield, Wisconsin, was out on the trail with a group of friends. Cross country skiing was something new to this veteran of the Mt. Telemark alpine runs. In fact, he was giving serious thought to skiing the race in alpine skis and boots. "We skied about ten miles the day before and found that it just wouldn't work," recalled Polaski. "So we decided to go with cross country skis."

Later that evening, with the lights of St. Paul glittering in the moonlight, 17-year-old St. Paul Academy students Bruce Derauf and Peter Alden carefully applied layer after layer of wax on their Norwegian Madshus skis. All the while they were thinking about the rest of their group who were winter camping up in Hayward in anticipation of the Birkebeiner Saturday morning. At 3 a.m., Derauf and Alden rose in the cold morning air for the three-hour drive up to Hayward.

Race officials awoke "early" at 6 a.m. to prepare for the start. As the sun crept up over the frozen lakes east of Hayward, chef Hotze mixed his first vat of blueberry soup, a far cry from the french onion soup he would delicately season that evening at the Telemark Lodge. Out on the trail, Ward Williamson and his crew pulled Robin Williamson and Steve Maznio on alpine skis behind snowmobiles and track-setters. The tracks were rough that year, and rather deep. A number of skiers had problems with the sides of their ski boots chafing against the walls of the deep tracks.

As 8 a.m. came around, entrants began to file into Lumberjack Bowl—adorned with an unusual assortment of knickers, bamboo poles, wooden skis and pine tar. Registration workers scurried with last-minute entrants. Tony Wise typically paced the ice of Lumberjack Bowl, waiting for the start. Bob Treland, meanwhile, wound the springs of the four Westclox clocks that had been purchased in town to time the race.

Wax experts dabbed a mixture of blue, purple and red wax on top of their pine-tar encrusted ski bottoms, hoping they would not lose their wax across the abrasive ice of Lake Hayward. The wet wood bottoms of the skis would prove troublesome to many skiers that day.

St. Germaine and Lyman Williamson arrived at 8:45 a.m.—plenty of time, as St. Germaine recalled. "I'll pick you up at Telemark," shouted Lyman to his star racer.

As 9 a.m. ticked ever closer, Charles Weydt, an instructor at the Indianhead Vocational Technical Institute in nearby Rice Lake, was trying to get back on the right road to Hayward. Weydt, who hadn't a great deal of skiing background, had read about the race in the St. Paul *Pioneer Press*. He thought he would give it a try—in an old pair of downhill skis, with strap bindings. About 10 to 15 minutes after the start, he finally made it to Lumberjack Bowl.

So, from around the midwest they gathered: There were 54 in all, 34 men and one lone woman on the line for the 50-kilometer Telemark-Birkebeiner, plus 19 women and juniors watching from the sidelines, awaiting the bus ride to

Telemark instructor Dave Reichel warms up at Telemark in the days before the race.

Waxing changed immensely through the first ten years of the Birkebeiner. In 1973 skiers waxed their wooden skis on the Wannigan Pancake House deck before the Birkebeiner. Notice the 75-mm bindings that were used almost exclusively in the early days of the race.

their own start an hour later on County OO near Seeley. (Official race records indicate 34 men and one woman starting the race; one entrant, Terry Marshall of Chippewa Falls, Wisconsin, is not shown as finishing although he does appear in pictures of the start.)

One by one, the skiers ventured out onto the frozen Bowl. At the starting line, St. Paul Academy coach Kenyon King persuaded race officials that his high school racers, while only 17, were strong and capable of skiing the entire 50-kilometer race instead of the shorter event. It took some talking, but Derauf, Alden and Bob Levin were able to step up to the starting line.

As 9 a.m. approached, Minneapolis entrant Rufus Jefferson handed a miniature cannon to Treland. "Here, maybe you can use this!"

Rufus' 1905-vintage Winchester 10-gauge cannon has probably started more skiers on their way than any cannon in North America, claimed Wayne Lindskoog. "A Twin Cities race just wasn't complete without Rufus' smoke-belching Winchester."

After a few words of instruction and encouragement, Treland gave a sign to Carl Hanson. Hanson had lived nearly three-quarters of a century for that moment when he could, right here in little Hayward, Wisconsin, relive the most prestigious sporting event in his own Sweden.

With the pull of a string, Hanson set off a cannon shot that would be felt for years to come, on ski tracks around the globe—it was the beginning of the American Birkebeiner!

As the cannon sounded, nearly every one of the starters stood in awe as the Swede Eric Ersson literally flew across the lake. It was the proudest moment of old Swede Carl Hanson's life! Some of the photographers on the sidelines even missed Ersson in their start photos since he sprinted out from the start so fast. "We had never seen skiing like that before," recalled Derauf.

"I don't care what the competition would have been, even the U.S. team, Sam (Ersson) would have won anyway," said Wiik. "He was a great skier."

A few kilometers across Lake Hayward, Lyman Williamson's parting words finally hit home to St. Germaine. "There I was, almost to the end of Lake Hayward and the finish line wasn't even in sight," said St. Germaine. "I was totally exhausted and all I could think about was what Lyman had said, 'I'll pick you up at Telemark.'"

It was lonely on the course that gray winter morning—hardly what it is today! It took only a few kilometers along the snowmobile routes and makeshift ski trails for the 'pack' to thin itself out. No one, save the several dozen on-course workers, even saw Ersson after the start, or even Sven Wiik for that matter.

The mixture of sand and snow on the logging roads and railroad bed took its toll on skis and wax. Halfway into the race, St. Germaine pulled up alongside another skier who was rubbing the bottoms of his skis. Not wanting to let on his innocence, St. Germaine did the same. "Here," said the unknown skier, "try some of this." He tossed him a tube of purple klister and Ernie applied it as best he could to the cold wood. "It probably won't hold that well, but it'll work for a while," said the wax expert across the track.

St. Germaine watched the skier glide effortlessly down the trail and continued his first solo attempt at waxing—right in the heat of the race. Soon, another skier came up the trail and asked Ernie about the wax. "Does it help?" the new skier asked. "Sure," said St. Germaine, trying to keep a straight face as he passed on his new-found expertise in the art of waxing. "It may not hold for long, but it'll work for a while." He tossed him the tube and hit the trail. "Keep it!" he shouted as he strided away, his head held high and his form probably better than it is even today!

At the second food station, near OO, Bruce Derauf passed up a summer sausage sandwich offered by a friend in favor of some piping hot blueberry soup. A couple cups of blueberry soup, washed down with a cup of water was the perfect combination, especially with the high sugar content of that year's batch.

Food station attendants hadn't become that well versed on the proper serving procedure, though, and many skiers found that they had to pour their own blueberry soup.

Derauf had long since parted company from his St. Paul Academy companions and, like most Birkebeiners that year, had no one to share the experience with along the trail. At the last food stop, around 42 kilometers, he finally caught up to Alden, who was talking with the local girls and sipping a cup of blueberry soup. "I think he thought I was farther back," said Derauf.

Meanwhile, Dave Landgraf found out what hills were really like. Dave was quite an athlete, and only that saved him the first year. "Most of the race I skied alone not knowing if I was lost or not since trail markings were sparse and snowmobiles were very prevalent," he said.

A little before noon, 2:48:16 into the race, Eric Ersson crossed the finish line at Telemark to become the first Birkebeiner champion. Frances Wise, the oldest daughter of Tony and Sheila Wise, put the laurel wreath around his neck. Sven Wiik came across nearly a half hour later in 3:15:03.

Meanwhile, just a kilometer from the finish, Oshkosh, Wisconsin, skier Nils Meland was finding out what exhaustion was really like. "I had a muscle spasm in my right thigh," he recalled. "In my misery I took a wrong track. Some weekend skiers made me aware of my mistake. I backtracked and found that I had been overtaken by another racer." Meland caught up to Kenyon King, the coach from St. Paul Academy, and the two fought it out right down to the finish line—both of them ready to drop at any instant. As the duo slid across the bunny hill of Mt. Telemark, King skated ahead, winning the first Birkie mini-battle by only a second in 3:33:10.

Meanwhile, Derauf and Alden kept pushing each other along the wooded track. Finally, the music from the Chalet began echoing in their ears. At last, the woods opened up onto Mt. Telemark where surprised alpine skiers tried to figure just what it was emerging from the forest. Together, Derauf and Alden crossed the finish line, in an impressive 3:58:04.

Skiers finished all afternoon in front of the Base Chalet, with downhillers watching in wonder. One Birkebeiner made it across on his hands and knees! Timers and record keepers kept a dutiful eye on the Westclox', recording each and every time.

Back in the forest, Dave Landgraf struggled up yet another hill—a far cry from his training ground in the Met Stadium parking lot. About five kilometers from the end he ran into Ernie St. Germaine—two rookies, two friends taking on a challenge they thought would never end!

Landgraf's form at that point had been reduced to a modified crawl, half herringbone going up and half colorful crashes at every downhill. Less than half a kilometer from the finish, the two skiers pointed straight downhill. At the bottom

35 Birkebeiner skiers await the start of the first race.

Top skiers in the 22-kilometer women's race in 1973 included, from left, Bebe Hanson, champion Carol Duffy and Marlene Tremblay—all of Hayward. In the first ten years of the race, Carol Duffy was the top Hayward woman all seven times she raced (missing only 1974, 1975 and 1979 races).

each decided to turn—right into the other. As they lay moaning in the snow Ojibwa curses filled the air. And to their utter embarassment, another skier came gliding effortlessly past them, made a neat parallel turn and headed to the finish line.

Earlier that morning, shortly before 10 a.m., the bus with entrants in the shorter 22-kilometer race pulled up to the starting line on County OO south of Seeley. A handful of skiers stepped off with their skis, joining others that had driven to the start.

Hayward was well represented in the women's race. Among the ladies were Bebe Hanson, who hadn't raced since her childhood in Sweden 25 years earlier, Marlene Tremblay, who had ridden up to the start with her friend Bebe, Adie Weber and Carol Duffy.

The driving force behind the Hayward ladies was, without question, Ersson. He had begun a ladies day program at Telemark, introducing women like Carol Duffy to cross country skiing. The program itself was very typical of ladies day programs, including a short ski outing to a cabin where hot wine was served.

But Ersson went a lot further. He felt that the new Birkebeiner race was something that the women should take part in, too. "I had never been a competitor in my life," recalled Carol Duffy. "I had no idea what racing was all about. In the race I skied with Marlene most of the way, skiing, I think, right on the tails of her skis. Finally I said to her, 'Marlene, excuse me but I'm going to have to pass you.' I had figured that to ski that distance (22 kilometers) I would have to ski that far three times in training. So in the weeks before the race, I would go up to Telemark with my cranberry juice and ski the Birkie loop."

There wasn't much thought by the women, at the time, about skiing the longer race. "They just said that this was the women's race so that's what we skied," said Carol. "We had never heard of Jacque and didn't even know that a woman was skiing the long race."

The starting area for the 22-kilometer race was nothing fancy, just a cleared-out section of the Birkebeiner trail. It would still be a half hour or so before the first Birkebeiner racers would be through. At 10 a.m., they were off—a mere 19

1973 Birkebeiner champion Eric Ersson, Telemark's first cross country ski school director, chats with Telemark Public Relations Director Fred Morgan at the finish.

racers, mostly women and boys under 20, also heading for the finish line at Telemark.

Duncan McLean, who was later to go on to win both a citizen's and American elite championship in the Birkebeiner, won the 22-kilometer event that year, despite the fact that it was his first year on skis. Because he was 18, he was not allowed to race the Birkebeiner itself. He won in 1:08:33, even passing the tracksetters and groomers, and was actually the first across the finish line at Telemark—40 minutes before Ersson.

"I've always been kind of sorry about not being in the long race the first two years," he reminisced. "But the Birkebeiner became very, very important to me. I made a vow that first year that I would ski the Birkie for 50 years. All the kids at school laughed. I know that someday I'll have to ski the Finlandia [Finnish race usually held the same weekend as American Birkebeiner] to complete my Worldloppet series, but I just hope that either the dates change or I can charter a Learjet and ski both on the same weekend."

Meanwhile, the women continued their quest for the finish. Much as expected, it was Carol Duffy taking the title in 1:56:21, just two and a half minutes ahead of Marlene Tremblay. Bebe Hanson wasn't far behind, even though she had passed up a few food stations not realizing how important they were! The win marked the beginning of quite a ski career for Carol, who missed the next two races due to the birth of her eleventh child.

Ed Van Mullen of Winter, Wisconsin, who was the first to register for the race, came striding across the finish line at 3:34 p.m., 6:34:07 after he had started. Although officials didn't know it at the time, one skier who had been late for the start was still on the course.

Late in the afternoon racers and officials alike gathered in the Telemark Lodge's Laukka Theater. It wasn't much of a party that year, a nice low-key awards presentation and cheese fondue. Telemark veterans, like Polaski, headed for the ever-popular Rathskeller to show off their medallions to their downhilling buddies.

"We had stayed up until 5 a.m. that morning just talking about the race," said Polaski, a well-known and popular figure around Telemark for many years. "After the race we took a dip in the pool and headed for the Rathskeller. I remember doing a Russian dance, heading to Metro's for dinner and falling dead asleep by 8:30 that night."

But the Birkebeiner wasn't over. As dusk settled and darkness closed in, Charles Weydt, who had been lost more than once that day, finally struggled across the finish line, searching frantically for someone to record his time of around nine-and-a-half hours.

"I sort of half-expected no one to be there," Weydt recalled years later. "I told Bob [Treland] what had happened. He gave me my award and something to eat." Weydt returned, though, skiing either the Kortelopet or Birkebeiner for years to come.

The Birkebeiner was a dream come true, especially for Carl Hanson. Imagine having a race like his old Vasaloppet right in his home town in America. And to top that, having a Swede win it!

The American Birkebeiner had begun. There were dreams alright that first year. But those dreams were best put in perspective by an account in Hayward's *Sawyer County Record*. "At 9 a.m. Saturday the 24th, a gun shot will be heard throughout the midwest to start a cross country ski event that promises to become one of the big winter events of the region. . . . In Minneapolis last weekend there were 850 skiers in the Jonathon Tour (VJC Race) event. . . . Won't that look like something on Lake Hayward a year or two from now."

Indeed, it would!

CHAPTER II

Quinn Brothers Make Their Birkebeiner Mark

64 Birkebeiner skiers stormed out of Lumberjack Bowl on a bitterly cold morning to start American-Birkebeiner II.

For all intents and purposes there was little major change between Birkebeiners I and II. The name was changed from Telemark-Birkebeiner to American-Birkebeiner with little fanfare, and the number of entrants in both the long and short races jumped from 54 to 98. That was about it.

But a pair of 25-year-old twins from Cloquet, Minnesota, a city just west of Duluth, left an indelible mark that year. It was a tremendous performance by both and was the only time in the first ten years of the race that American skiers have finished first and second.

The race itself remained fairly low key, almost totally the same as a year before. There was something in the air, though, that indicated big things were in store for the Birkebeiner. Perhaps it was a certain mystique about the Birkebeiner, skiing 50 kilometers through the frozen forest, which struck the heart of cross country skiers across the Upper Midwest.

At this time in history, national and divisional sanctioning through the United States Ski Association (USSA) was an important factor for any race. The USSA controlled schedules and races, and events such as the Birkebeiner were very unusual.

On the same weekend as the Birkebeiner, a much shorter sanctioned race was held in Cloquet. It was a well-established race, attracting many of the serious skiers from the Upper Midwest.

Telemark also had a USSA-sanctioned race, the Telemark Nordic Invitational, held the day after the Birkebeiner in 1973, 1974 and 1975. Typically, USSA racers would compete in Cloquet on Birkebeiner day and then come down to Telemark on Sunday for the Invitational.

At first, the USSA Central Division officials weren't too concerned—this 50-kilometer event called the Birkebeiner wasn't a sanctioned race.

There was concern about losing racers from already sanctioned races, like the Cloquet event the same weekend. But the Birkebeiner began to raise some eyebrows in 1974. Several important names were appearing on the start list that hadn't been there a year before. Many of those who missed the race in 1973 knew in the back of their minds that the Birkebeiner would not be just a passing phenomenon. All of a sudden, skiing veterans like George Hovland and Charlie Banks of Duluth, John Burton of Minneapolis and others were in the Birkebeiner. Banks, for one, had never skied a 50-kilometer race.

"I thought it would be kinda' fun," he said. "And it really was." He hasn't missed a Birkie since.

"I would have given anything to be in that first race," said Hovland years later. "I was all set to go. I had known Tony for years and was well aware of the first Birkebeiner. I remember John Kotar from the Duluth Touring Club calling me up and telling me that I should race. I was in the process of a divorce at the time and my wife's attorney called a Saturday meeting. If I had known then what I know now about the Birkebeiner, you can be sure I would have been there!"

Hovland was a member of the 1952 U.S. Olympic Team that competed in Falun, Sweden. Burton was also on that team.

"Twenty years after I came back from the (Swedish) Vasaloppet, I started this touring club (Duluth Touring Club, 1972)," said Hovland. "I always had in the back of my mind to put on a race like the Vasaloppet. Finally, the year before the Birkebeiner, I had a race lined up from Cloquet to Duluth. It finally fell apart when we couldn't get land permission."

The early to mid-seventies was a time when the Eastern, Rocky Mountain and Alaskan Divisions of USSA were producing the best racers in the country. The Central Division was far from a hotbed of racing.

Dave and Don Quinn grew up in Cloquet, Minnesota. Of all the midwestern states, Minnesota alone had a strong youth ski program at the time. In fact, interscholastic skiing in the state high school system was excellent.

Mike Marciniak, who had skied competitively in the late fifties, began coaching in Cloquet during the sixties working primarily with the Cloquet Ski Club but also assisting head coach Joe Novak of Cloquet High School. The two top skiers on that team were Dave and Don Quinn.

On the high school circuit the Quinns were among the best in the state. In 1966, the year they were graduated, Dave won the Minnesota state championship. Don was fifth.

"Skiing was just not a big thing back then," recalled Don Quinn. "People thought it was crazy!"

Crazy or not, the Quinns racked up quite a record. In their senior year, Don won their first four races and David won the last five. At the USSA Central Junior Championships the duo was never defeated, finishing first or second every year. After high school they headed west for Gunnison, Colorado, to ski for Sven Wiik, who was culminating an illustrious career as coach at Western State College. It was a tough time to head into collegiate racing with the likes of Easterners Mike Gallagher, Clark Matis, Mike Elliott and others burning up the ski tracks at the National Collegiate Athletic Association (NCAA) Championships.

In their four years of competition at Western State, Dave's best finish was a ninth in the NCAA championships, while Don was 16th. In 1971 the twins graduated and went to work for their coach at Scandinavian Lodge in Steamboat Springs, Colorado.

Each of the twins had his eyes set on coaching, something both managed quite successfully after their competitive careers. But after college, there was still plenty of time for racing.

It was bitter cold the morning of American-Birkebeiner II as skiers packed their bags and finished waxing skis on the deck of the Wannigan Pancake House.

It was a cold, cold morning as skiers await the start.

The field quickly thinned out after the start.

Three skiers, using various techniques, stride across Lake Hayward shortly after the start of the 1974 race.

Dave had been on either the U.S. Ski Team's developmental or B squad since 1969. In 1972, he was named to the Olympic Training Squad. In January of 1974 he went to Alaska, hoping to make the U.S. Team that would compete in the International Ski Federation (FIS) World Championships that February in Falun, Sweden.

The summer before, the Quinns had moved in with U.S. Ski Team member Mike Gallagher at his Pittsfield, Vermont, home. For six months, they trained and lived together in the hills of Vermont.

Nearing the peak of his career, David had been expected to make the FIS team at the Anchorage tryouts. Sadly, he narrowly missed a berth. Many of his old college nemeses were on that FIS team which included Gene Morgan, Bob Gray, Mike Gallagher, Joe McNulty, Larry Martin, Ron Yeager and a couple of youngsters, Bill Koch and Tim Caldwell.

"I was really disappointed for David," recalled Gallagher. "He had trained so very hard to make that team!"

Although disappointed at missing the squad, David was in good spirits and headed back home to Cloquet to spend some time on midwestern snow before returning to Steamboat. At the same time, Don was returning after trying to find some good skiing in the snow-starved East.

"We saw a poster, I think at Pine Valley [ski area] in Cloquet," recalled Don. "We thought it would be a great race to ski in. We really trained for it, too. I think we were skiing 30, 40 or 50 kilometers a day. Some days we went up to ski Charlie Banks' course [near Duluth]. It was very important to us and we really looked forward to doing well."

Meanwhile at Telemark, preparations were proceeding for the second Birkebeiner. Like the race a year before, it involved few workers and not a lot of time. Much of what Bob Treland had learned in 1973 was effectively put into action for 1974.

The course was virtually the same, winding its way from Hayward to Telemark on an assortment of logging roads, town roads and railroad beds—nearly all of which were used by snowmobilers.

Entry fees held at $10 for men in the 50 kilometer and $8 for women and juniors under 20 who would be skiing the shorter race from Seeley to Telemark. There was a $2 late fee for entries received after February 19.

Duluth skier Charlie Banks won the men's 50 and over age class in 1974 in his first Birkebeiner.

John Burton, Minneapolis, a member of the 1952 U.S. Olympic Team, was second to Charlie Banks in the men's 50 and over competition.

Don Quinn leads brother Dave past a farmhouse on the first half of the course.

There wasn't much of a ski track as skiers plod along the edge of the railroad bed near Phipps in the early part of the course.

Although repair stations weren't added until 1976, race officials did remind skiers in their pre-race bulletin to double check their equipment. "A binding can work itself loose over this long distance if you don't have those screws set in with epoxy."

Bus transportation was provided from Telemark to the start in Hayward. A system was setup for tagging clothing at the start for pickup at the finish. Four food stations were setup on the course. Donuts and rolls were ordered for the start area from the Telemark Lodge bakery. Start time was set for 9:30 a.m., a half hour later than a year earlier, with the short race beginning near Seeley at 10 a.m. With that, American-Birkebeiner II was ready to go.

Dave and Don Quinn drove down to Telemark from Cloquet on Friday. They pulled into Dave Reichel's driveway and hauled their Splitkein racing skis into the house. Reichel, who was nicknamed "wheat germ" by his fellow employees for his health food habits, was a Telemark cross country ski instructor. When the Quinns rolled in, he gave them a hand as they talked about the next day's race.

Friday was a brisk day with temperatures in the teens and a light snow falling. It would clear by Saturday morning, though, as the area braced for an expected cold snap. That night, as the temperature plummeted, Reichel and the Quinns torched binder into their synthetic-bottomed wood skis so their wax would hold over the abrasive surface of Lake Hayward.

Just as predicted, Saturday dawned cold and clear. The mercury had dipped to 21 below zero fahrenheit during the night.

"The conditions were excellent, other than the weather," said Quinn. "But we knew how to dress. We wore long johns and knickers, earbands, caps and wool socks over our boots. It really wasn't that bad!"

But for a lot of skiers, it was a pretty miserable morning. "I don't think I've ever seen skiers so bundled up," recalled Dan Danielson of Wayzata, Minneso-

Dave Quinn, a native of Cloquet, Minnesota, leads his twin brother Don down the track in the 1974 American-Birkebeiner. As can be readily seen, tracking of the course has changed considerably from this race.

A giant poster advertised Telemark's late-February cross country events.

A skier rounds a turn in front of Phipps Tavern in the first half of the race.

Skiers stride alongside a roadway in a single track.

Julie (front) and Jill Hubbell of Hayward lead a string of skiers in the women's race—all bundled up warmly against the cold. Jill finished second in the women's 19 and under division; Julie was third.

Champions of American-Birkebeiner II gather at the finish line including, from left, second-place Don Quinn, third-place Lars Arnesson and champion Dave Quinn, who is holding a bottle of Aquavit given him by an unknown spectator when he finished. Notice the socks around the boots to keep feet warm on the bitter cold morning.

Jacque Lindskoog, the first woman to ski the Birkebeiner, proudly displays her medallion in front of the Base Chalet at Telemark following the 1974 race. Lindskoog completed the first two Birkebeiners even though women were not eligible to enter. Her efforts led to women's classes for the third and subsequent races.

ta. "They just didn't know how to dress back then. There were a lot of clothes tossed along the trail when the skiers got warmed up."

Although it was nearly 20 below at the start, the Quinns knew enough about midwest Februarys to know that it would warm up during the race. Even in the three hours they expected it to take to complete the race, they knew it wouldn't stay that cold.

"We were ready for a good race," said Don. "Lars Arnesson [Telemark's new Nordic Director] from Sweden had been winning all the races in the midwest. I think he had been 50th the year before at the [Swedish] Vasaloppet."

As 9:30 approached, David and Don rubbed in another layer of Rode special green on top of their binder, corking it in as curious newcomers looked on in the blistery cold.

Moments later, the gun went off and American-Birkebeiner II was underway. Just as expected, Arnesson and the Quinns burst from the starting field, leaving the remainder of the 64 Birkebeiner starters, including Sven Wiik who had been second a year earlier, in their tracks.

Stride for stride they skied across the lake—the Quinns, dressed in white racing suits, were like two white knights in a medieval fairytale. As they left Lake Hayward to head out onto Duffy's field and the trail to Telemark, David caught a quick glance behind him and discovered Arnesson was nowhere to be found. The abrasive lake had taken its toll and stripped the wax from his skis.

The twins took advantage of the situation, moving out fast and building a lead—a lead that Don would need later. Back and forth the twins skied, switching the lead as they broke through the light snow on the track. At about 35 kilometers, David pulled away. A few kilometers later, Don surged forward but couldn't catch his brother as he skied into the distance.

Spectators were sparse along the course. A few gathered beside the stretch of track near the airport and a few more at the Phipps Tavern further down the trail. Out on the course, it was cold.

"I thought I was going to die," said Hovland. "My hand froze, my toes froze, everything froze! I had picked up a tiger's milk bar at a health food store and stuck it in my pocket. When I really needed it I realized it was frozen solid. I think I chewed it for almost an hour hoping it would soften up."

For the leaders, the cold wasn't a problem. "We were really impressed with the course. It was a beautiful trail and in excellent condition," said Don.

But somewhere after 40 kilometers the tracks suddenly stopped. Seeing a group of snowmobilers nearby, David quickly realized what had happened. Somehow he managed to figure out which way the trail went and soon found himself back on track.

Don wasn't so fortunate. "There were about 10 or 15 guys on snowmobiles. They had erased part of the track in a tight corner section. David had asked them which way the trail went and they had laughed at him. They told me which way to go and I skied down the trail, but they had told me the wrong way. I skied back and went around a corner and finally, there was a perfect track. I knew I wouldn't catch my brother, but I just wanted to make sure I was second."

The conflicts between snowmobilers and skiers were commonplace in the early days of skiing, and especially in the Birkebeiner. That was to change dramatically over the coming years.

After David picked the correct trail leading to the finish, it was little problem for him as he glided in past gawking downhill skiers in 2:59:47. His brother arrived in 3:08:43, immediately inquiring about Arnesson and much relieved when he learned that he was indeed second. But he didn't make it by much. The Swede came in about a minute and a half later in 3:10:14.

David beamed from ear-to-ear as he stood proudly along side his brother and Arnesson for photographs. Flashy red, white and blue Birkebeiner medallions hung around their necks, plus a laurel wreath around David's. In his hand was a bottle of Aquavit from an unknown spectator.

All afternoon racers came across the finish line, each and every one anxiously heading for the warmth of the Lodge, a hot shower and a dip in the pool. The marks of battle from bloodied bibs to blueberry soup icicles hanging from hair and beards, left the alpiners shaking their heads that day.

Just as the year before, Duncan McLean crossed the finish line first, winning the 20-kilometer junior men's race in 1:06:50, four minutes ahead of Tony Hartmann of Madison, Wisconsin. Frances Wise was the women's champion with a time of 1:35:45 on the same course. Marlene Tremblay of Hayward, was 15 seconds back.

Even in 1974, there was still no women's division in the 50-kilometer Birkebeiner. But this year, race officials gave Jacque Lindskoog more official status, listing her in the men's 20-34 year class where she finished 18th in 4:53:30, which actually put her in the top half overall!

Lyle Lund of Westby, Wisconsin, had the distinct honor of bringing up the rear — his 7:33:50 was the fastest trail sweeping time in the first ten years.

Norwegian Consul to Wisconsin Byron Ostby added another international flair at the awards ceremony as trophies were presented to the top three skiers in every class.

The following week, under a page one headline that read: "American-Birkebeiner race may become a national event," the local *Sawyer County Record* heralded the start of bigger things to come.

"It was a very important race for my brother," recalled Don Quinn years later. "We were both so impressed with the race, especially the hospitality and the awards. We knew then that it was a premier event!"

David missed the Birkebeiner the next year, he had been having trouble breathing after races and after much testing it was found that he had cancer. In looking back, that might have been one of the reasons Dave didn't quite make the 1972 FIS team.

But while he wasn't on the track the next few years with skis, he was there in spirit and in 1976 wrote: "I really appreciated the large board of signatures of some of the competitors from Birkebeiner IV. Really have missed the x-c skiing this year, however, I am looking forward to next season, as I really love this sport. Congratulations to you and the people who made Birkebeiner IV such a tremendous success. I really enjoyed the course and the trails at Telemark when I last skied there. Your excellent support for the sport of x-c skiing is greatly appreciated."

On Christmas Day, 1977, David Quinn died. But in his 29 years, he gave more to the sport than could be asked of anyone in one lifetime. And one of the most important moments of his life was standing like a white knight in the sun in front of the Telemark Base Chalet, with the laurel wreath around his neck, beaming with pride at becoming a Birkebeiner champion.

Frances Wise posed proudly between her parents, Sheila and Tony Wise, after accepting the laurels as women's champion.

Duluth skier George Hovland relates his experiences to Race Chairman Bob Treland following his first Birkebeiner. Hovland was second in his class.

A brightly-colored red, white and blue medallion, actually made of plastic, was awarded to finishers in both the short and long races in 1973 and 1974. In 1975, only finishers in the 55-kilometer Birkebeiner received the medallion. The modern-day medallion was introduced in 1976.

25-year-old David Quinn is half smiling and half grimacing as he poses for photographers following his victory in the 1974 Birkebeiner. Just behind Quinn is Byron Ostby, Norwegian consul from Madison, Wisconsin.

CHAPTER III
Birkebeiners Join Hands Across The Ocean

The crowd on the Birkebeiner starting line had grown considerably—324 skiers now stood ready for the 55 kilometers ahead. There wasn't much problem being back in the pack as the wide starting line afforded skiers the opportunity to string out into just a few rows.

Twenty-three-year-old Chris Haines trudged up the hill from Lillehammer's Breiseth Hotel to the starting line of the Norwegian Birkebeiner-Rennet. The towering climb seemed to take as much effort as would the race ahead. At the top, he found himself among the multitudes—over 1,000 skiers in his 20-34 year-old class alone!

It was the first trip overseas for the Anchorage, Alaska, skier. Norway was quite a change from the good old U.S.A. Skiing was a way of life in Norway, as he had seen just a week earlier competing in the Holmenkollen Festival in Oslo.

Haines and Wausau, Wisconsin, skier Asbjørn Snekkevik, a Norwegian native, had the honor in 1975 of being the first representatives of the American-Birkebeiner to compete in Norway. For Snekkevik, it meant returning to his homeland—the land where he now lives. For Haines, it was an eye-opening experience, as it would be for dozens of other Americans who would stand proudly on the starting lines in Lillehammer and Rena for years to come.

It was ten minutes until race time and already not a spot was to be found on the front line of Haines' group. Somewhere in the crowd was Dag Anmarkrud, Norwegian Birkebeiner champion the year before—the skier Haines had upset three weeks earlier in the hills of northern Wisconsin. But Anmarkrud was on his home turf this time around.

"You're either in a position to sprint to the front or you get trapped," recalled Haines. "That's what happened to me." It seemed like an eternity before the U.S. Ski Team member managed to break free, giving the leaders a 15 to 20 minute head start.

Haines finished 98th overall that day, in a field of 2,200. Anmarkrud, who was over four minutes behind Haines in the American race, was seventh. But the doors that were opened that year have drawn the two nations even closer together. And the two sister races have had closer ties ever since.

If there was ever a turning point or a Birkebeiner landmark race, American-Birkebeiner III was the one. By yesterday's and today's standards alike, it was certainly not a classic race. A lot of things did not go well in American-Birkebeiner III, but many new avenues were paved.

In a sense, the third Birkebeiner drew the line between modern days and old. Interestingly enough, much the same was happening in cross country skiing around the world that year.

A year before, at the World Championships in Falun, Sweden, the ski industry was taken by storm with a new fiberglas ski introduced by Kneissl. "It will never work," scorned the skeptics. But when Swede Thomas Magnuson, on a pair of fiberglas skis, upset Finland's Juha Mieto, still on wood, even the most skeptical skiers knew that something big was in store for the sport.

When the Birkebeiner began in 1973, US cross country skiing was not even in its infancy. Only a very small group of persons even knew what the sport was all about. Slowly that began to change.

The Birkebeiner itself was even scorned in 1973 and 1974 as being a novelty. USSA competitors laughed at the distance and stuck to their schedules of 15 to 30 kilometer races. And as Birkebeiner officials found out that year, the popularity of long distance racing was something the USSA was reluctant to admit.

"I think it was just the time," said Tony Wise. "The time was just right—for the Birkebeiner and for cross country skiing."

After two years of being a low-key event, the Birkebeiner was finally attracting fields of hundreds of skiers—many skiing for the first time in their lives. The Birkebeiner suddenly took on a new significance. And now Telemark and Tony Wise set out to make the Birkebeiner the granddaddy of skiing in North America, and one of the biggest races in the world!

Sven Wiik, who had put together the first Birkebeiner in 1973, returned to plot out a new trail—this one 55 kilometers long, exactly the same as the Norwegian race. The new trail, which combined an array of logging roads and snowmobile trails, took the track off the town roads and railroad beds of 1973 and 1974, and put it into the much more rugged terrain of the county forestland between Hayward and Telemark. The week of the race, the course was measured with a 300-foot rope towed behind a snowmobile.

The addition of the more rolling terrain increased the overall vertical climb, again attempting to be more like its Norwegian counterpart.

The general route itself was quite similar to the permanent trail which was built several years later, although it lacked the vertical climb that the course has today. All of the trails used for Birkebeiner III still exist today as major snowmobile routes through the picturesque northwoods.

As in the first two events, the race began at Historyland near Hayward. But this year, to accommodate the larger crowds that were expected, the line was moved out of the Lumberjack Bowl bay and onto the open spaces of Lake Hayward. The new positioning allowed racers to take advantage of the bigger facilities at the Logging Camp Cook Shanty, which was used as the registration and gathering spot before the race.

"We really had to change the trail," said Wise. "We just couldn't continue to go down ditch lines and railroad beds any longer.

"The problem was that the race was growing so fast that even our change from the Lumberjack Bowl site to the ice behind the Cook Shanty didn't work. In order to get 55 kilometers we had to make a figure eight loop around the western end of the lake. We still had a bottleneck at the point where the trail came off the lake at John Duffy's.

"And even with our improved trail that year, we knew that we would have to have a better trail in the future."

One of the original ideas for the 1975 course was to run the race underneath the Highway 77 bridge—where the Namekagon River enters Lake Hayward. Telemark cross country director Ingemar Sundberg stands on a snow bank alongside the bridge. The idea was eventually scratched because of the unpredictability of ice conditions and the low passage under the bridge.

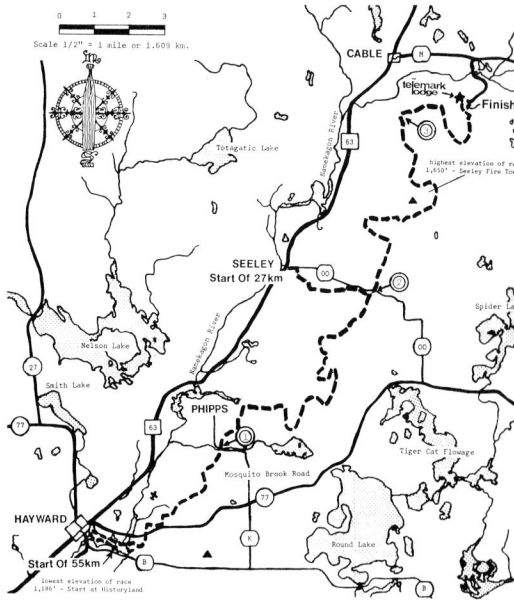

A course map for American-Birkebeiner III.

Tony Wise chats with Wausau, Wisconsin, skier Asbjørn Snekkevik, a Norwegian native, prior to the race. Snikkevik was the fastest touring division skier and won a trip to Norway along with elite champion Chris Haines.

From the beginning it was evident that Birkebeiner III was a milestone. News releases went nationwide weekly, posters were sent to ski shops across the midwest and by the time early February rolled around, there was hardly a serious skier in the three-state area who hadn't at least heard of the Birkebeiner.

A goal of 500 entrants was set. And although entries fell short of the specific goal that year, it was just a year before the *long-range* goal of 1,000 was nearly hit. Registration fees remained at $10 for the 55-kilometer race and $8 for the 27.5-kilometer race for women and juniors. There was a $2 late entry fee for entries after February 17, with registrations being accepted up to 8:30 a.m.—just an hour before the February 22 starting gun.

The idea for a Norwegian-American racer exchange was conceived in January, just six weeks before the Birkebeiner. Wise contacted Lillehammer Ski Klub president Arne Myhren to extend an invitation to 1974 Norwegian Birkebeiner Rennet champion Dag Anmarkrud to attend the 1975 American Birkebeiner. Wise, in turn, would then send the top American citizen and USSA competitive skier from the American-Birkebeiner to Norway.

An exchange of this nature was certainly unusual for the Norwegians, whose race had existed for over 40 years with hardly an entry from outside their borders. But Myhren and club associate Karl Snilsberg, owner of the Breiseth Hotel in Lillehammer, thought it was an excellent idea.

The invitation was conveyed to Anmarkrud, from Hernes, Norway, and he accepted whole-heartedly. In addition, former Telemark Nordic Director Lars Arnesson decided to return from Sweden, making it truly an international field.

The next step, thought Wise, was to generate some stiff competition from the United States. At this point in time, the U.S. Ski Team was really unaware of Telemark and the American-Birkebeiner race. While 1974 champion Dave Quinn had been a member of the developmental squad, no active U.S. Ski Team member had competed in the race.

"Jim Balfanz was nordic director of the U.S. Ski Team at the time," said Wise. "I gave him a call in January to try to persuade him to send some skiers to the race. He was only mildly interested at first but he was going to be up at Ironwood [Michigan] for a ski jump so I offered to fly him down to see the course and talk about the race. That he agreed to do. It was our first big breakthrough."

Balfanz was indeed impressed by what he saw and heard on his short trip to Telemark. "I think he felt in his bones that the race was going to be big. He said he would have several skiers at the race. He mentioned a skier by the name of Koch, who I had never even heard of. In fact, when I wrote down his name I wrote 'Coke.' " At the time, Bill Koch was a 19-year-old junior who was tearing up the European racing circuit. A year earlier he had won a bronze at the European Junior Championships. In December and January of the current season he had won five of seven starts in European junior races, before returning with lung problems and a badly cut finger.

At the sound of the cannon, the field is off—the last time the Birkebeiner started on Lake Hayward.

Skiers stride in a pack across the ice of Lake Hayward at the start of American-Birkebeiner III.

U.S. Ski Team member Chris Haines leads Norwegian Dag Anmarkrud through the woods not far into the race. Haines' teammate Larry Martin is about 50 meters behind the two.

Gary Larson of Duluth, later to become a U.S. Ski Team coach, grabs a cup of Gatorade from Hayward's Linda Wickland at a food station.

With his ski tips seemingly hooked together in a snowplow, Dave Landgraf slows up for a food station.

Hayward skier Dennis Tremblay snowplows up to a food station along the course.

Charles Dionne, Eden Prairie, Minnesota, crosses a snow-covered roadway. Dionne skied every Birkebeiner through 1979.

A line of ladies, led by Sharon Nelson (80) of Westby, Wisconsin, ski single file down a lone track in the 27.5-kilometer event.

Kochie didn't make it to the Birkebeiner that year. Instead, he went back to Europe to win the first major gold medal in American cross country history, taking the junior 15 kilometer at the Finnish Ski Games February 28, and finishing second to a promising Swedish junior, Thomas Wassberg, at the Holmenkollen.

"Looking back now it would have really been something to have had Kochie here that year," said Wise. "But it was a tremendous thrill to have Balfanz arrange for Chris Haines and Larry Martin, both from the A Team, compete in the Birkebeiner."

"Both racers will be racing the longest race of their lives," read a mid-February news release.

Pete Brucato of Milwaukee had been a skier most of his life and attended Dartmouth College in the ski pioneer era of Dick Durrance, the first American world-class downhill skier. Although Brucato had done a great deal of cross country skiing in his college days, in recent years he had pretty much stuck to downhilling at his club's private runs on Holy Hill, west of Milwaukee. Brucato had always been a big supporter of the U.S. Ski Team and, in addition to his tremendous fund raising efforts in the metropolitan Milwaukee area, he offered a home-a-way-from-home for ski team members.

"I had read about the Birkebeiner but I didn't even know how to pronounce it," recalled Brucato. "I remember reading something in a ski magazine about George Hovland from Duluth, who I knew, skiing it. I said to my wife, 'If George can ski it, I can ski it.'"

Although his wife, Martha, was not that optimistic, Pete received all the encouragement he needed when Balfanz called one day. "Jimmie called to tell me that he was sending a couple kids up to the race and asked if I could go up to take care of them. I told him I would and asked him about racing myself. He said, 'Pete, you don't have to race it, just ski it.' At the time I had these old Gröswold hickory skis, which were made by a famous Denver ski maker. Jimmie said those wouldn't do at all and he said he had a pair of skis in his garage he would send me."

A few weeks before the Birkebeiner, Brucato returned home one afternoon to a brand new pair of Splitkein plastic-bottomed skis—the beginning of the fiberglas revolution.

Brucato considers himself one of the lucky few to this day. Although the fiberglas revolution was underway, only about 2,000 pairs were reportedly imported that year into the United States. Only Lovett in Colorado was producing any fiberglas in the States and those were only available to U.S. Ski Team members. As with any new product, there were plenty of bugs to be worked out. Breakage was the biggest problem.

Although Brucato's new skis weren't completely fiberglas, they were certainly a step in the right direction.

Several other skiers jumped on the fiberglas bandwagon that year as well, many regretting it at first. Paul Vesterstein, a longtime midwestern ski rep who owns the Continental Ski Shop in Duluth, Minnesota, had landed a shipment of plastic-bottomed Köngsbergs from Norway. The skis were imported by Olav Uland of O-U Sport in Seattle. Cross country skiers, like any serious athletes, are always anxious to be the first to try anything new and improved. Naturally, Vesterstein sold a lot of the skis.

But waxing technology, both on the part of manufacturers and skiers alike, was far from what it would later become. The hard plastic bottoms were very, very fast, but getting wax to adhere was tricky.

"Boy, it was awful," recalled Birkie founder John Kotar. "I think they held wax for about half a kilometer. I held off buying a pair until right before the 1974 Birkie when I finally decided that I had to have some." With time things improved.

From the factories and racing circuits in Europe, U.S. coach Marty Hall brought the news back to America. "Everything I've seen and heard in Europe indicates that the wood ski is dead," Hall said in a magazine interview in 1975. "No more gunk and goo, the mystery of waxing is gone!"

Already, in the first year of fiberglas production, klister and powder cambers were being produced. Even waxless patterns were being turned out by the factories. Kneissl, which had produced only 8,000 pairs of cross country skis a few seasons earlier, was gearing up for an 80,000 run for the coming season.

Hall's comments, which were published in the March 19, 1975 issue of *Ski Racing*, were the first solid evidence that cross country skiing was exploding.

There had been a couple snowless years and warehouses were finally emptying from a surplus of wooden skis.

"There's no great racing market right now," Hall said, "but it should grow as the sport of touring continues to grow. Once they recognize the advantages of the new skis, tourers will be jumping on them."

All in all it was a hot year for cross country skiing. And it was evident to race officials that the Birkebeiner was going to continue to grow. In an attempt to get more competitive skiers in the race, it was decided to obtain USSA sanctioning, something which had not been done for the Birkebeiner the previous two years.

"In the early days the USSA was not too thrilled about us skiing in the Birkebeiner," said Ironwood, Michigan, skier Roger Pekuri. "I was a marathon runner and the Birkebeiner just sounded like so much fun. And it was! But there just weren't many races that long."

As the seventies rolled on, Wise and Telemark would learn a lot more about the operation of the USSA and the FIS. But in 1975, it was a relatively new experience.

In his entire development of Telemark, and for his entire life, for that matter, Wise has been a doer. When something needs to be done, it is done—no questions asked! With that in mind, Wise and Bob Treland set out to obtain USSA sanctioning for the Birkebeiner.

In January, during his discussions with Balfanz about U.S. Ski Team members skiing in the Birkebeiner, Wise talked about sanctioning. A request for sanction was sent to the national USSA offices in Denver on January 19.

Assuming from his discussions with Balfanz that everything was in order, Wise publicly announced the USSA sanction just a few days after applying. The announcement also included the offering of a prize of a trip to Norway for the winner of the newly-created "USSA Competitor's Class," plus a trip for the winner of the "Touring Class." Wise also retained the service of Sven Wiik as technical director for the race, to review the race organization and supervise the handling of any rule interpretations or disputes.

Although a request for sanctioning had been filed with USSA Central Division in Chicago, officials weren't too happy about the way the entire matter was being handled. Most of the Birkebeiner's efforts had been funneled through the national office. Through an apparent mis-communication at the Central office in Chicago, cross country committee chairman Lars Kindem of Minneapolis had not been informed of the request.

Kindem, who was later to play a major role in the development of ski racing at Telemark, effectively rejected the sanction through his refusal to give divisional approval, which was needed.

"The Central Division Cross-Country Committee does not and will not sanction a race of this distance for its classified members," stated Kindem in a letter

Chris Haines skates across the finish to become the third Birkebeiner champion.

Norwegian Consul Byron Ostby (left) poses with American-Birkebeiner III champion Chris Haines.

Norwegian Dag Anmarkrud, the first Norwegian exchange racer to ski in the American event.

to race officials. Kindem then cited problems over the expense-paid trip to Norway in regard to its effect on amateur status, and also the "bolting" of senior racers to ski the Birkebeiner instead of racing in the previously sanctioned race in Cloquet, Minnesota, the same day.

Additionally, the division already had a rule on its books that specifically prohibited another race in the same area receiving sanction on the same day as a previously approved race, such as the Cloquet event.

Kindem also advised officials that if they were to award an expense-paid trip, that a disclaimer must be issued to all USSA classified racers informing them they may be placing their amateur status in jeopardy if they participated in the race. It was a tough blow for race officials. But while there was little question that the sanctioning could not be obtained, Wise was insistent the expense-paid trip not effect amateur standing.

In a memorandum issued to all competition class skiers before the February 22 race, Wise outlined the status of the trip and its effect on amateur status. After researching the question with Balfanz and Byron Nisbien, American chairman of the FIS eligibility committee, Birkebeiner officials concluded that the expenses as a representative of the American-Birkebeiner did not constitute a prize that jeopardized amateur status. Wise also advised skiers that an attorney in Minneapolis had been retained to protect that position should it be questioned.

Kindem and the USSA never budged from their position, but also never forced the issue when the race went as planned.

Those problems temporarily aside, officials prepared for what would be the biggest Birkebeiner to date—over 300 starters, more than three times the number of a year before. It was the biggest percentage increase in the race's first ten years and will be forever!

Nineteen seventy-five also marked the first move toward a Birkebeiner Week, with live entertainment in the Lodge Thursday night to kickoff the weekend. Jim Cullum's Happy Jazz Band from San Antonio, Texas, performed that night in the Telemark Nite Club. Special Scandinavian menus were developed for the Telemark dining room and coffee shop and a Norwegian folk troupe was arranged to instill yet another nordic touch to the weekend's festivities.

In Hayward's *Sawyer County Record* that week, a course map and spectator information was provided along with an announcement requesting snowmobilers to stay clear of the course on Saturday. A map detailed the snowmobile trails that would be closed beginning at 2 p.m. on Friday when tracks would be set for the race.

Local citizens were enlisted to help, as well, although it wasn't until 1978 that an organized community volunteer effort was undertaken.

The night before the race, Haines and Martin prepared a strange energy drink concoction, boiling down Coca-Cola to a syrupy base—something race officials found quite unusual. The special energy drink would keep them going the next day.

Early Saturday morning, Chief of Course Jerry Berard drove Sven Wiik and his wife to the start in Hayward. Around 8 a.m. skiers began to congregate at Historyland. Coffee and donuts were served at the Cook Shanty, as had become tradition, and the smell of klister, wax and pine tar filled the air.

"I didn't know what to use for wax," said Brucato. "I remember we went to Historyland and they had a bunch of waxes on the counter. We just kinda' looked over shoulders and tried whatever looked best. I think that John Burton helped us with some klister and we put some hard wax over it."

Purple or silver klister, with a layer of blue hard wax, was the wax of the day. But, like the previous races, skiers would find that the combination of an abrasive track and wooden or plastic-bottomed skis that didn't hold wax well, would spell doom before they would reach Telemark.

It was especially bad in 1975. With the exception of the national team, no one really knew enough about applying wax to the new plastic-bottomed skis. And even if they did, the skis were nothing like the sophisticated P-tex bottoms that would sweep the nation in the coming years. By almost all accounts, it was the worst year for waxing in the first ten years of the race!

With the firing of the gun at 9:30 a.m., American-Birkebeiner III was underway. Everyone who had stood in awe of the Quinn brothers streaking across the lake a year before, couldn't believe their eyes this time either. What a sight it was—Haines, Anmarkrud, Martin, Arnesson and a host of others—gliding, stride for stride, across Lake Hayward. It was the last any of the masses saw of them.

"I started out with them but fell flat on my face on the lake," said Pekuri. "After that, I was pretty much on my own."

On Friday, just a day before the race, rain put a glaze on the course that left officials concerned. But that night, temperatures dipped below freezing across northern Wisconsin turning the course to ice. Temperature at racetime was around 20 degrees fahrenheit. But before the day was out, it would warm up to the low 40's. Much as expected, the glazed trails took a big toll on the wax.

There wasn't much of a pack that year. Haines, Anmarkrud and Martin sprinted away from the start leaving the rest, including Arnesson, in the lurch. Like most early Birkebeiners, everyone from leaders to trailsweepers skied alone. Haines broke away shortly after the start and wasn't seen until the finish. Anmarkrud hung a few minutes back with Martin most of the way before the Norwegian moved out to try to catch Haines.

The still unnamed 27.5-kilometer race began at 10 a.m. right in Seeley, just off Highway 63. Few of the contestants in that race had reached the Birkebeiner trail itself before Haines came skating through in the lead.

"The most impressive thing for me that year was to see these guys skating," said Wise. "We had never seen that before. When Haines came through at OO he was skating just like on ice, which is pretty much what the trail was like at that point because of the rain the day before."

As Haines wound his way around Mt. Telemark, skiing across the flats of the Telemark Golf Club, he knew that victory was his. At the finish line, his win was met with surprise by race officials who had seriously felt that Anmarkrud could not be beaten.

"I remember our surprise that an American had won," said Wise years later, "but at the same time we were incredibly proud!" Not until 1981, when Tim Caldwell won the postponed Birkebeiner, has another American crossed the finish line first.

Haines' 3:00:34 was less than a minute slower than Dave Quinn's time a year before, on a course that was five kilometers longer. It was two hours later when Vigdis Snekkevik, a native of Norway, came across in at 5:00:57 to become the first "official" women's winner ever. Her husband, touring division winner Asbjørn Snekkevik, finished in 3:44:46.

Vigdis, who was 29 at the time, would get a rude introduction to her own nation's Birkebeiner a few weeks later. Women were still not eligible and it took a special dispensation to allow her and several other women to race. And even though they received permission to race, they weren't treated all that well during the event. Much has changed since then, even in Norway!

Back on the course, Twin Cities skiers Pat Richards and Jean Dick clicked off the kilometers. This was the first year a women's class had been established for the Birkebeiner itself but only seven women took up the challenge, most

Jeannette Vortanz hangs a medallion around the neck of U.S. Ski Team racer Larry Martin.

Steve Maznio of Cable ended up fourth in the 27.5-kilometer race for skiers 19 and under. Maznio's first introduction to the race was in the role of a human tracksetter, being towed behind a snowmobile with alpine skis in races the years before.

Ironwood, Michigan, skier Roger Pekuri skis into the finish under the watchful eye of curious spectators at Telemark.

Linda Strande of Minneapolis had an easy time winning the 27.5-kilometer women's race from Seeley to Telemark.

Hayward skier Libby Morgan gets a helping hand near the finish line of the 27.5-kilometer race.

of them friends of Jacque Lindskoog who had taken part in the first two Birkebeiners on her own.

"Jacque had warned us of a big hill at Mosquito Creek," recalled Richards. "Jean was ahead of me and out of sight when I reached the hill. I remember thinking I was going much too fast as I sped down the hill, trying to snowplow on the ice. Halfway down I heard a soft little 'track.' Vigdis Snekkevik, who won that year, skated around me in her tuck and rapidly disappeared from view. How she ever came to be behind me I'll never know!"

Jean Dick and her husband Terry, both members of the North Star Touring Club, had really planned ahead for the race. Jean had told Tony Wise about an energy drink called ERG, which was suggested for an energy replacement at the food stations. Birkebeiner officials added ERG to the stations for the first time in 1975. But like many of the plans for Birkebeiner III, there wasn't quite enough ERG for the number of racers. Anticipating this in advance, the Dicks had pre-arranged that their personal plastic bottles with their names on be taken to each of the five food stations. Just as expected, when stations four and five rolled around, these bottles of ERG turned out to be all that was left for the enterprising North Star skiers.

Conditions were generally awful that year. The rain on Friday, bitter cold that night and considerable warming during the race forced skiers, one by one, to stop by the trailside to scrape their wax and apply some red klister, or whatever else they had that might work.

At one point, Dave Landgraf came upon a skier lying in the snow and moaning loudly from a cramped leg. Landgraf did what he could to help the skier work out the cramp. Soon, both were on their way, Dave skiing ahead. A few kilometers later, the victim tracked the good samaritan, heading over the next hill on his way to the finish.

But regardless of conditions, they pressed on—each skier fighting a battle with himself. Coming into the finish, Pete Brucato had begun his own little race with a pair of twins, Jon and Joel Malkerson of Edina, Minnesota. "One was ahead of me and the other behind," said Brucato. "But I wouldn't give in. We came crashing into the finish line and I went straight into a net. I remember the first aid crew coming up to me and asking me if I was okay. I told them I was alive, anyway. The ski patrol took one look at me and took me right into the first aid room. I had hypothermia."

John Moody, White Bear Lake, Minnesota, won the 27.5-kilometer race in 2:07:47; Linda Strande, Minneapolis, was the top woman in 2:29:07.

Slowly, the Birkebeiner drew to a close. Ed Van Mullen, Winter, Wisconsin, brought up the tail end of the race in 8:14:30. In every official's mind were new ideas, "This is what we're going to do next year." Within days, notes were made for the 1976 race. Letters from skiers were analyzed and filed. Not until the great trail congestion of 1979 was critiquing so important.

"One of the most important things you can do is to critique yourself and to act on the needs and requests of those affected," said Wise.

At the awards ceremony that evening in the Laukka Theatre, Brucato had recovered to say a few words in support of the U.S. Ski Team. Chris Haines held his birch bark leggings high—the first time the now traditional prize was awarded.

As trophies were presented, Wise spoke of a special pin or award that would be presented someday to those who had completed ten races. Of the original 34 Birkebeiner finishers 16 still had a perfect record through the third race.

Twenty-seven skiers received a similar honor that year for having completed the first three Birkebeiners—short race included. Three small laurel wreath medallions (one for each of the three years they had completed the race) hung on short ribbons from a pin, with a colorful Telemark logo in the center of the wreath, were awarded.

Despite its growing pains, American-Birkebeiner III was a true milestone in cross country skiing. The sport as a whole was growing more rapidly than could ever be imagined. It was just two years before that the local newspaper, the *Sawyer County Record,* talked about the dream of having as many as 800 skiers in the Birkebeiner someday. Officials knew that that someday was here!

For Chris Haines and Asbjørn Snekkevik, Norway seemed like a long way away. But in just three weeks, the American Birkebeiner skiing ambassadors would bring the two races and two nations even closer together.

And skiing in America would never be the same.

CHAPTER IV
American Olympians Take On Norwegian Elite

It was a bright, sunny Saturday morning, February 21, 1976. America was looking ahead to a summer full of fireworks and bicentennial celebrations. On a snow-covered golf fairway near the Telemark Lodge, over 700 skiers stood waiting anxiously for the 9:30 and 9:35 a.m. cannon shots that would send them through 55 kilometers of forested northwoods from Telemark to Hayward, the opposite direction from the first three races. (There were separate starts for elite and citizen racers.) Another 300 were waxing in preparation for the 27.5-kilometer race start near Seeley.

On the starting line, one of the newest Americans in the race, Jana Hlavaty, proudly wore bib number 1976. Jana, who had just returned from the Innsbruck Olympic Games, stood prouder than ever that morning. A native of Czechoslovakia, her application for citizenship in America originally wasn't scheduled to be accepted for several weeks. But backed by the enthusiastic support of the ski world, Congress passed a special bill to speed up her naturalization in time to have her named to the 1976 U.S. Olympic Team. The Birkebeiner was her first major race since returning from Innsbruck. Next to her, previous year's champion

1976 was the first really big starting field for the Birkebeiner, still far less than the coming years would bring. As the cannon sounds, start line workers hold up pennant ropes separating the starting lines.

1976 marked the introduction of a new Birkebeiner medallion, available only to skiers completing the 55-kilometer race. The new medallion was given to all first-year finishers and was also made available for $10 to any previous finisher who had received the old red, white and blue medallion.

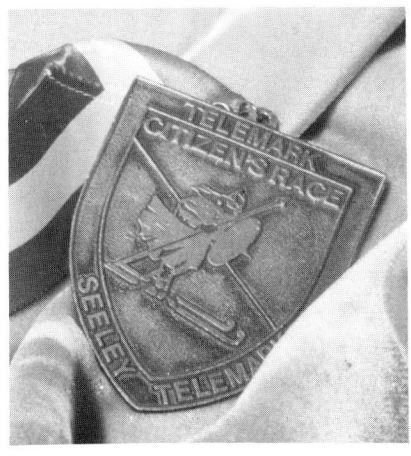

A new medallion for the shorter women's and junior's event, which had been dubbed the Telemark Citizen's Race, was inaugurated following the 1975 race. Medallions were sent out after that race and were given to all skiers completing the 27.5-kilometer course in 1976.

Chris Haines rounded out the bicentennial bib combination wearing 1776. Haines, too, was returning from Innsbruck, and eager to defend his Birkebeiner crown.

Across each bib were the words: American-Birkebeiner. In it's fourth running, it was the first time that the bibs had recorded the name of the race. A new medallion was also introduced, an Olympic-like cast medal which is still used today.

This was a pivotal year for cross country skiing in America. Virtually everything on the sport was rewritten in the months between the 1975 Birkebeiner, when Haines held off the challenge from Dag Anmarkrud, to the moment in 1976 when 993 skiers gathered for the fourth American-Birkebeiner.

Not all of the changes were good, at least not initially. But the results of what happened during that year are still the major force behind the sport in America today.

In the offices of the Sawyer County courthouse in Hayward and the halls of the Wisconsin state capitol in Madison, Tony Wise was spearheading an effort to build a ski and recreation trail through the Sawyer County forestland between Hayward and Telemark—a trail that could someday handle a race with as many as 2,000 skiers!

This was also the season that Telemark made it into the annals of the U.S. Ski Team. With only a week's notice, Telemark played host to an early-December training camp and became an instant hit with coaches and athletes who had initially come to the resort only because they couldn't find snow elsewhere.

And when snow was still scarce around the country, Telemark stepped in with a week's notice to hold the 1976 Olympic Tryouts, sending Bill Koch off to Innsbruck to win the silver.

Looking down the starting line on that bright Saturday morning, you could just see the change. Few wore bulky sweaters and parkas. In their place were streamlined knickers and brightly-colored racing suits. Under skiers' feet were plenty of fiberglas skis, just another indication of the dramatic change the sport had seen in the past 12 months.

Race officials had learned a lot in the 1975 race. Comments from workers and letters from skiers, many of which were highlighted in the first issue of the *Birch Scroll*, April 1, 1975, became an integral part of planning for 1976.

One of the biggest areas of concern was the trail itself. Even after moving from the railroad beds to logging roads, the trail between Hayward and Telemark was just not capable of handling the race.

Work on the new trail began in earnest almost before the last skier had crossed the finish line at Telemark in 1975. Sven Wiik, technical director of the 1975 race, had been instrumental in developing both Telemark's cross country trail network and the first three Birkebeiner trails. His aid was enlisted in designing a permanent Birkebeiner trail to run between Hayward and Telemark. Shortly after Birkebeiner III Wise sent Wiik a complete set of topographical maps of the area. Sven then sat down and began using his years of experience to design a trail from scratch, stretching from near Lake Hayward to the Bayfield county line near Telemark.

Wiik spent much of March and April plotting a trail that would cut through the heavily-wooded Sawyer County Forest, over eskers and across glacial moraines. Although Wiik was a resident of the mountains of Colorado, he knew it was no secret that the terrain of northern Wisconsin was better suited to cross country skiing than almost anywhere in the country, and as good as anywhere in the world.

On May 7, 1975, the Sawyer County Board's Forestry Committee held a hearing on the proposed trail. Wise knew there was a long road ahead before the first track could be set, and it had to begin in that meeting.

As Wise explained to the committee, the trail would be the longest publicly-owned ski trail in the state and would serve as a pilot program for other such recreational trails. The trail would be constructed to be of sufficient width and length to be used for the Birkebeiner and other races. In the summer months it would double as a hiking trail and would be available for hunters in the fall. No motorized vehicles would be permitted.

One of the key tasks ahead was obtaining funding. Wise knew that from the start. But the mid-seventies were a time when there was money to be found in both state and federal governments for such purposes.

Little action was actually taken at the meeting, but committee members were favorably impressed as to the potential of the project and recommended that the matter be brought up at a special meeting of the entire Sawyer County Board on May 20.

Between those meetings, Wiik and Race Chairman Bob Treland spent eight days walking the woods, marking trees and determining the proposed route of the trail. The work required long days in the woods—a somewhat tedious job, but brightened by the feeling of working so close to nature.

As the May 20 meeting approached, the Birkebeiner Trail was beginning to take shape—but only in the form of cloth ribbons on trees along the proposed route. Wise drew up a game plan detailing virtually every aspect of the trail's cost, design needs and benefits to the region.

"One thing that we found out right away was that there definitely was federal money available for projects of this type," said Wise. "And we felt that it was very important that Sawyer County not lose this money to some other part of the region as had happened so often in the past."

In the early planning Wise spoke of the millions of future recreational dollars that such a trail could bring into the region, historically considered as an economically depressed region of Wisconsin. It could be the key to promoting year-round tourism in the northwestern part of the state.

An extensive report was prepared by the Sawyer County Conservation Committee in advance of the May 20 meeting. Complete trail guidelines and cost outlines were included. The grand total came to $96,534.00. The project soon attracted the whole-hearted support of the county.

With the backing of Sawyer County, officials enlisted the assistance of the Wisconsin Department of Local Affairs and Development in Madison. Bill Bechtel, a former aid to Wisconsin Senator Gaylord Nelson, went to work to find the necessary funding. Bechtel found several leads, the most promising through the Upper Great Lakes Regional Commission, a federal commission which was created to work with states bordering the Great Lakes to funnel federal funds into projects to develop the economies of the states.

Plans were still set for construction of the trail that summer. Workers were even lined up through the Wisconsin Manpower Council. But the paperwork and bureaucracy proved to be too time consuming. Although it was clearly evident that the trail would become a reality, by the time fall came around, it was also obvious that it would not be in time for the 1975-76 winter.

At the same time, officials were working on the race itself. One of the initial ideas, which was announced in the second edition of the *Birch Scroll* on May 12, 1975, was to start the race on the far west end of Lake Hayward, closest to the city. As it was planned, skiers would congregate at the National Guard Armory and a half hour before the race, march together down Hayward's Iowa Avenue to the lake, in an Olympic-like parade.

The start would have more tracks than ever before and would proceed across the lake, under the Highway 77 bridge and onto the trail. Food stations would be enlarged and improved and the finish area made more comfortable for spectators. Results would be improved by use of separate finish chutes to match color-coded bibs for each class.

Top Olympic racers would take part, along with more competitors as a result of hopeful sanctioning through the USSA and FIS. It was even hoped that national television would cover the race.

Although not all of the ideas presented in that May *Birch Scroll* came to pass exactly as planned, all did contribute in a major way of making American-Birkebeiner IV the beginning of the modern era of Birkebeiners.

The *Birch Scroll* quickly became the official publication of the race. For the first time since its inception, the race had a regular publication to let skiers know what was being planned. The *Birch Scroll* was to go on to become one of the biggest nordic publications in America, its circulation hitting 20,000 within just a few years. And the little four page newsletter soon became a full-fledged newspaper.

Probably the most significant change was the move of the start from Hayward to Telemark. The new start was announced in the September, 1975 *Birch Scroll*.

No longer could Lumberjack Bowl or Lake Hayward handle the start. The race had long outgrown the Wannigan Pancake House and now the Logging Camp Cook Shanty.

1976 marked the first time that the words "American Birkebeiner" appeared on racing bibs. NorTur, Inc., a new Minneapolis-based distributor of Norwegian ski products, provided the bibs as the first full-fledged race sponsor. Bibs bore the names of NorTur's products, including Epoke skis.

The new start and finish of the 1976 race are outlined on maps.

Minnesota Vikings mascot Hub Meades made his Birkebeiner debut in 1976.

1976 was the first year of major U.S. Ski Team participation in the Birkebeiner. Among the entrants were John-Mike Downey (left) and Randy Kerr, who are headed for the start.

The new course began at Telemark and finished where the first race had begun. It provided more spectator viewing at the finish and added vertical climb to the course, which was needed to meet FIS course requirements.

After the USSA sanctioning problems encountered in the 1975 race, Treland went right to work to secure the sanctioning for 1976, within days after American-Birkebeiner III had ended. Despite the problems of the season past, USSA was very cooperative.

In early April, while race officials were still working with representatives of the Central Division of USSA, Jim Balfanz was abruptly fired. The firing was never fully explained but reportedly came over his vociferous comments regarding nordic budget cuts.

Balfanz' leaving was anything but amicable and the shock waves over the entire incident were felt in nordic circles from coast to coast. His firing prompted the resignation of the top jumping coaches, several top jumpers and resulted in a reorganization of the cross country staff under new Nordic Director John Bower.

At the time of Balfanz' dismissal, race officials had begun to work on sanctioning in earnest. It was felt that this was an important step in the development of the race. Lars Kindem, chairman of the Central Division's cross country committee, made his first trip to Telemark in April. Earlier he had met with Sven Wiik and Wise in Chicago to discuss sanctioning of the Birkebeiner. The date of February 21, 1976 was reserved for American-Birkebeiner IV, and the sanctioning was approved by the Central Division in May.

The sanctioning by the USSA established stricter rules for the so-called elite division. Skiers in that division had to be registered racers with their national association. A separate starting time also had to be established for this elite group to insure that they were alone on the course—something that was unique to the 1976 race. Keep in mind that it was quite unusual, at the time, for such a race to be sanctioned. Previous USSA races were, for the most part, strictly USSA-classified events and did not have mass starts. The Birkebeiner represented somewhat of a milestone in what was to be known as citizen racing.

While only the elite race was officially sanctioned, for all intents and purposes, the elite and citizen's races were one, even if they did start five minutes apart! The terminology "citizen racing" was relatively new. The USSA official who probably had the most foresight into this new breed of competition was Chicagoan John Lindstrom. Lindstrom was the chairman of the USSA's Citizen Cross-Country Committee at the time. He was one of the few Americans who had actually skied, or really even heard of, many of the races in Europe that would eventually become the Worldloppet.

In April of 1975, Lindstrom published the first draft of the Citizen's Racing Handbook. The draft strongly encouraged USSA involvement in this new type of racing and set up procedures for sanctioning and organizing citizen races. A proposed national bicentennial series was even suggested, something which, unfortunately, did not come to be.

As the summer went on and work on the race and trail project progressed, Wise felt that more involvement with the national association and national team skiers was needed. "To develop the sport we needed some stars," said Wise. "Every sport has to have some names for people to key on, someone to look up to and emulate. We knew we needed to have a strong involvement in the Birkebeiner with skiers of national and world-class stature."

In early October, officials of the U.S. Ski Team and USSA were holding a coaches clinic in Minneapolis. All of the top officials were present and Wise felt this to be a perfect opportunity to introduce everyone to Telemark first-hand.

"We were working through Lars Kindem at the time," recalled Wise. "I had talked to him in advance but he just didn't think there was time to bring the group up. We finally got them to agree to fly up for dinner one evening at the Lodge."

So Wise picked up the phone and called Midstate Airlines, the small commuter airline which served Hayward and a handful of other midwestern towns. A Midstate Beech 99 was chartered to bring the entire entourage to Telemark.

Among the guests that evening were nordic coach Marty Hall, Lindstrom, Kindem and others. Bower, who had been at the Minneapolis meeting, didn't make the trip up to Telemark. Without question, it was a quick introduction to Telemark, but one that would eventually open their eyes to what the new touring center had to offer.

"We didn't have much time to show them the trails," said Wise. "We showed them a little back on the golf course and some of the trails behind the Lodge. Then we looked at some of our ABC Wide World of Sports coverage of the Lumberjack World Championships in Hayward. For dinner, we gave them the specialty of the house, the Telemark Extraordinaire (a huge helping of virtually everything on the Telemark menu). At the time, I think that impressed them the most."

The purpose of the visit was to let them know Telemark was ready to help the U.S. Ski Team and American skiing in general. Just over six weeks later, the visit paid off.

Bower, who hadn't made the trip to Telemark but had heard the good comments from the others, called Wise on Thanksgiving Eve to ask a favor. The team had been training in Cooke City, Montana, and was on its way back east. Snow conditions weren't favorable in the east, but they were terrific in northern Wisconsin. Bower asked if the team could spend a few days at Telemark.

When the team arrived at the airport in Duluth, they were greeted by local television and newspapers, plus a welcoming crew from Telemark. It took most of them by total surprise.

In his comments to the Duluth media, Hall, who hadn't had a chance to see much of the terrain in his October visit, said the team appreciated the hospitality of Telemark but added that the terrain was pretty flat and they would be heading out east after a few days.

However, after Hall finally had a chance to get out and ski the next morning he came in quite impressed by the trails. "He hadn't thought that much about the terrain at first," recalled Wise, "but I remember when he came in that first day on the trails. He was impressed!"

"It was a tremendous experience for both us and the team," said Wise. "The kids all liked it—it was the first time they had ever been treated first class! We even had all of their pictures up on the wall. We were sincerely honored to have them staying with us."

After their training week at Telemark the team was supposed to go east to prepare for the Olympic Tryouts in Lake Placid. But around Christmastime, Wise got another call from Bower. The snow still hadn't arrived and Bower wanted to know if Telemark could step in to hold the tryouts over New Year.

With just a week's notice, Telemark put on its first truly national ski race. Right down to the final racer, it was an event successful beyond anyone's dreams. Media attention focused on the Telemark Nordic Center and a collection of no-name skiers, despite at least one that should have already been in the limelight worldwide.

A few months before the Birkebeiner, an act of Congress gave Jana Hlavaty her American citizenship just in time for the Innsbruck Olympic Games. Jana returned from Innsbruck to take part in American-Birkebeiner IV.

As starting time approaches, the field of citizen skiers readies for the first Birkebeiner start at Telemark. The line of elite racers had left five minutes earlier.

Some skiers actually wondered whether they were really going up the ski hill or not. Their question was answered quickly as the pack ascended the top of Morgedal for the first time.

Skiers break out the herringbones as they begin their ascent of the Morgedal headwall for the first time.

Although the elite skiers climbed straight up and over, most everyone else had to herringbone their way up the steep headwall of Morgedal. Over the next three years, the climb up and over Mt. Telemark would become a trademark for the Birkebeiner.

Bill Koch, who had been tearing up the junior circuit in Europe, was certainly the favorite and won all three Olympic Tryout races he entered at Telemark. But just how good he really was, no one actually understood. Certainly, no one ever really expected him to go on to Innsbruck and bring home a silver, or that six years later he would beat the best skiers on the globe to win the Nordic World Cup.

The Innsbruck Olympic Games were set for the first two weeks in February, which allowed time for top skiers to make it back for the Birkebeiner. Wise wanted an international field and set out to bring it to America.

Nineteen seventy-six marked the second year for the Norwegian/American Birkebeiner exchange. Ivar Formo, one of the top racers in Norwegian history, had won the Norwegian Birkebeiner the year before. As champion, he was invited to America. Along with Formo, Wise sent invitations to a host of other top Norwegians including Oddvar Braa, Magne Myrmo and Odd Martinsen—definitely the cream of the crop in Norway.

But communications were slow. By the time Innsbruck arrived, there had still been no word back. Wise was persistent, however, and kept placing calls to Innsbruck until finally reaching Formo.

"We had a very nice conversation," recalled Wise. "He was very sorry that he could not come this year but hoped that he could in the future."

Despite the inability to land the top Norwegians, Wise pressed on. The appearance of Norwegian Birkebeiner champion Dag Anmarkrud at the American race the year before had stirred some interest back in Norway. In fact, a group of 15 members of the SAS Ski Club was already planning on coming over for the 1976 race. Among this group was Bjørn Arvnes, who had won the 1971 Norwegian Birkebeiner.

Norwegian Bjørn Arvnes, who would win the following year, leads countryman Jan Vidar Skaug and American John-Mike Downey through the snowcovered northwoods.

The SAS Ski Club was the first foreign group ever at the Birkebeiner and set the stage for years to come. It was a unique experience for residents of the isolated northwoods towns of Cable and Hayward. Local skiers had an inside look at some of the finest athletes in the world.

"Their waxing help was so good for me that I came in a whole hour before my father began looking for me," said Wise's daughter Frances.

Through his contacts at Epoke in Norway, Finn Haug (who had started a Norwegian ski product importing company called NorTur, Inc. a few months earlier) arranged for several other top skiers to ski the Birkebeiner. Among this group was Audun Kolstad and Tore Gullen. Gullen, in fact, was on the Norwegian Olympic Team, giving the Birkebeiner at least one Olympian from Norway in addition to the Americans who were expected.

On February 17, the roster was sweetened a bit more when the Norwegian Ski Association cabled Wise that Gjermund Eggen, who had won three golds at the 1966 FIS Championships in Innsbruck, and Johs Harvicken, who had a bronze and a silver from Sapporo, would be competing.

Citizen skiers in the Birkebeiner move out on the trails behind Telemark.

"The difficulty we had getting the top Olympians that year had some future benefit," said Wise. "First of all, we realized that in order to showcase the top skiers in the world we had to have a different event; namely what became the Gitchi Gami Games. But, even more importantly, to give races like the Birkebeiner enough prestige and international recognition, we had to develop some sort of worldwide series of races. If I had to pick a birthdate for the concept of the Worldloppet, the Birkebeiner in 1976 was the date."

One of the happiest with the 1976 race field was Haug. The Norwegians would make a big impression that year, and the next. It was perfect timing for his new company's involvement with the race.

Haug had moved to America from Norway in 1969 and had been involved in ski importing in Minneapolis during that time. He had been aware of the Birkebeiner and wanted very much to be involved.

"I had started working with the U.S. Ski Team through our supplier agreement with Janoy (his former company)," said Haug. "The first time I had met Tony was at the training camp for the team that December.

"In Norway, Epoke was very big in racing. We needed something here, though, to get that same recognition. I felt that we should get involved in the Birkebeiner. I saw it as becoming a tremendous race."

Norwegian Olympian Johs Harvicken grabs a cup of liquid on the course.

With that idea and the price of the race bibs, NorTur, Inc. became the first sponsor of the Birkebeiner. For the next two years, the now familiar black and yellow of Epoke would become almost a symbol of the American-Birkebeiner itself.

The events over the past year leading up to the 1976 race, combined with Bill Koch's Olympic silver, all jelled as the race approached. For the first time in history, media attention was focused on cross country skiing. The *Chicago Daily News, Chicago Tribune, Newsweek, Time, The New York Times* and even a journalist from SAS' *Scanorama* in-flight magazine from Oslo were at Telemark for the Birkebeiner.

One of the things that really caught the interest of the media gathered for the Birkebeiner was the start, where skiers would climb the 370-foot-high Mt. Telemark to start the race.

"I think, at first, people were pretty scared of what the hill would do to them," said veteran racer Dan Danielson, "so everyone took it pretty easy going up. People were also pretty excited about it—it added another element to the challenge of the sport!"

Some skiers hadn't understood that the course *really* did go up and over Mt. Telemark. One first-year skier looked up and wondered about the fencing that seemed to funnel up that big hill!

The racers themselves found a highly-organized system at Telemark that year. Gone was the last-minute registration and bib pickup rush in the Pancake House and Logging Camp Cook Shanty. Instead, an entire registration staff greeted entrants in the Red Arrow Ballroom of the Lodge.

A well-coordinated bus system was developed to move racers from the finish back to Telemark, and also to get entrants in the 27.5-kilometer race to the Camp Wismer National Guard Rifle Range starting area south of Seeley.

Although a combined Birkebeiner and Citizen's Race start had been suggested a year before, it would be yet another year before the two would start together. At the finish in Hayward, skiers would also find showers waiting for them at the Hayward Elementary School.

A lot of work had gone into the planning of American-Birkebeiner IV. Many lessons had been learned the year before. And all of it showed as race time neared.

An hour before midnight Friday, the phone rang in U.S. Ski Team assistant coach Tom Upham's room at Telemark. Upham, who had been named women's coach before the season, was coaching the American contingent at the Birkebeiner. When he reached the phone he was surprised to hear the voice on the other end. It was John-Mike Downey.

Downey, who had narrowly missed the Olympic team, hadn't really been expected to make it out to the Birkebeiner. But he had left his home in Butte, Montana, early that morning hopping a real milk-run flight to Duluth—stopping in Bozeman, Billings, Bismark and Minneapolis before finally reaching Duluth.

It would be about an hour or two, Upham told him, before a ride could make it up to meet him. With his skis at his side and his backpack under his head, John-Mike stretched out on a terminal bench to catch some sleep.

Finally, at about 1:30 a.m., he arrived at the Lodge and was in bed by 2 a.m.—just seven hours before race time.

"Sometimes I do really well without much sleep," the red-haired, freckled-faced racer told the press after the race. "It was one of the most enjoyable races I've ever entered."

The sun came up brightly at dawn, creeping over the woods to the east of the Lodge and reaching through the windows into the lobby, which was soon buzzing with activity. It was a beautiful day—a little chilly, not cold, but sunny and inviting, especially for skiing 55 kilometers.

In the Lodge, Arvnes, Kolstad and the other Norwegians put the finishing touches of blue skare on their Epoke skis. Temperatures were in the mid-20's, but warming and cooling during the week had left the course crusty and abrasive. Skare and klister were the order of the day.

Finn Haug made the last checks with his company salesmen who would man the new wax and repair stations on the course. Snowmobiles and four-wheel drive trucks hauled ERG and oranges to the food stations, while Don Primley went over last-minute details with his crew of EMTs.

Jerry Berard, who had been chief of race for the Olympic Tryouts and was now chief of race for the Birkebeiner, surveyed the start area along with technical delegate Lars Kindem. Chief of Course Bob Treland sent a crew of forerunners out on the track.

The 9:30 start rapidly approached. On the sidelines, skiers went through the ski marking gates, adjusted the strings on their bibs and took a few deep breaths. All eyes were on the hill ahead and to the left—370 feet straight up Valhalla and Morgedal!

At exactly 9:30, following a countdown by announcer Bob Davenport, Haywardite Carl Hanson pulled the string on the cannon and sent the first wave of 141 elite entrants off and running—literally flying up the hill. It was a sight to behold for the touring skiers still waiting on the line. Kolstad broke away right at the start, Arvnes hot on his heels, and the rest of the Norwegians and U.S. Ski Team racers hot in pursuit. As the black and yellow suits of the Epoke racers crested the hill they looked like they actually had wings on their feet. The sight was enough to give Finn Haug the idea for his new company slogan, "The Wings of Winter."

Back on the start line, the remaining 617 skiers rubbed their skis back and forth, waiting in breathless anticipation for their shot—well over half of them attempting the challenge of the Birkebeiner for the very first time! After the first wave, the citizen skiers were cautiously instructed to move up to the front line. At 9:35, they were off, a huge mass of skis and poles creeping and crawling up the hill.

For years, thousands of alpine skiers had thrilled to take a few turns down Morgedal and Valhalla. Now, it was time for somebody to try it the other way. Madison, Wisconsin, skier Bonnie Albright got to know the hill better than most. Trying to herringbone up, she slipped and fell, deciding right then that she could do better by crawling, her skis stretched out behind her.

With the elite racers already five kilometers out on the course, the touring skiers were ready for their next challenge—the downhill on the other side. In the four years that the race went up and over Mt. Telemark, it was the downhill on Stormoen that was the most exciting part of the course. Unfortunately, it was also the most hazardous, prompting officials to eliminate the hill beginning with the 1980 race.

Virtually every Birkebeiner skier from 1976 through 1979 has a story to tell about Stormoen. And there were plenty in 1976! Some, like Pete Brucato, had excellent downhill training and found it a joy. Pat Richards, a pretty good skier in her own right, knew how to handle herself on a downhill too. Naturally, she took the shortest, and fastest, route, but ended up crashing and dislocating a thumb trying to avoid another fallen skier.

There were thrills, and there were spills. But the "hill" had become a trademark of the race, even though for many it was a love-hate relationship!

The 1976 trail was very similar to the 1975 course, only run in the other direction. The use of logging roads and snowmobile trails, which in most cases had been cut from the woods over the easiest terrain possible, made for quite a flat course. Compared to the eventual permanent Birkebeiner Trail, it was flat as a pancake after going up and over Mt. Telemark.

The race, to this day, still ranks as one of the closest in history. The lead changed back and forth constantly. At the midway point, the U.S. skiers were in the lead but Downey and his teammates knew that the Norwegians were right behind.

"We had figured they'd make their move about 15 kilometers from the finish," said Downey, "but with about 20 kilometers to go Kolstad took off. We just jumped in behind and stayed with him." At about 41 kilometers, near the Mosquito Brook crossing, Arvnes and Haines were battling for the lead but it was still anyone's race.

But somewhere just after the food station, something went awry. At the time there was a group of nine to ten racers in a pack bidding for the lead. The skiers came to a fork in the trail and somehow managed to get off on the wrong track, taking them to the south toward Highway 77.

Arvnes was reportedly leading at the time. With his head down, he missed the trail marker and headed off in the wrong direction. The others followed close behind.

When the skiers reach Highway 77 at O'Brien's hill, they knew right away that something wasn't right. A police officer who noticed the skiers quickly

In a fight to the finish, Norwegian Audun Kolstad comes across the line first to become the champion of American-Birkebeiner IV in a thrilling two-second victory over John-Mike Downey of the U.S. Ski Team.

Just seconds behind Kolstad and Downey, Bjørn Arvnes (right) and Jan Vidar Skaug come across the finish.

U.S. Ski Team members Chris Haines (left) and Larry Martin exchange a handshake at the finish.

radioed to the finish line to alert race officials. Meanwhile, the officer directed the skiers down another snowmobile trail to the south, hoping they could eventually meet up with the trail.

While the skiers were heading off towards the south, Kindem drove out to Mosquito Brook Road and took a snowmobile into the area where the skiers had supposedly gone astray. Everything appeared to be in order.

Treland, meanwhile, hopped on a snowmobile and headed out to where he hoped the group would come out of the woods. He was in luck. His hopes came true almost to the second as he met the skiers heading out of the woods onto a town road—about four or five kilometers away from where they left the track, but still in good order to get back on course.

He quickly told them to follow behind and led them for another kilometer or two, connecting back on the trail near Wheeler Road.

The irony of the whole episode was that as far as the group had skied off the tracked trail, their route through snowmobile trails and back roads came out almost exactly, to the meter, the distance they actually missed on the trail!

The lead group had no trouble following the trail on Lake Hayward and coming down the track into Lumberjack Bowl it was a five-man battle. Kolstad had the lead with Downey right behind him. Hot on Downey's skis was Arvnes who was being pursued by Jan Vidar Skaug. Bringing up the tail on the first pack was Randy Kerr of the U.S. Ski Team.

Warm weather that week had forced officials to keep the finish off the soggy snow on Lumberjack Bowl. Instead, the final few hundred meters snaked around the huge lumberjack climbing poles on the shore, winding its way in front of the bleachers and into the finish line. Nearby stood a chain saw ice carving of a Viking ship created by local resident Art Moe.

Kolstad was smart. He effectively moved to the inside on the corners and boxed out Downey from passing. It was a fight to the finish line, with Kolstad finally crossing the line in 2:40:44.14—exactly two seconds ahead of Downey who had only two and a half seconds on Arvnes. Haines, the pre-race local favorite from his win the year before, was seventh, two minutes back.

Just 23 minutes later, Jana Hlavaty, proudly displaying number 1976, came sprinting across the finish line in 3:05:31.12. Jana hadn't had as good an Olympics as she would have liked, but she couldn't have asked for better at the Birkebeiner. "It was a dessert," she said, "so easy after Seefeld!"

Long distance racing was very, very new to women. This was the first year that women were *even allowed* in the Norwegian race. And the women's 20-kilometer wasn't even scheduled for world championship competition until the 1982 FIS Championships in Oslo, Norway.

Hundreds of spectators look on as skier after skier battles each other coming into the Lumberjack Bowl finish.

"The girls were very apprehensive, except for Jana," said Upham. "They all did very well and none felt totally exhausted. And I couldn't believe Jana! I skied with her for a little after 50 kilometers to see if she was okay, and I couldn't even keep up with her."

Hlavaty's Olympic teammate Lynn VonderHeide was second, while Terry Porter and Margie Mahoney of the U.S. Ski Team were third and fourth, followed by Tammy Valentine.

It was the first time for Valentine in the Birkebeiner, and the only time she skied the race in its first ten years. She had been skiing fairly closely with another racer for quite a few k's. As they headed into the finish, Tammy had a slight lead. Suddenly over the loudspeaker came those words familar to many skiers as they near the finish. "Now coming into the finish, number 1957, Tammy Valentine of the U.S. Ski Team."

His eyes open wide, Jon Tofte, of Duluth, Minnesota, turned to see that it was a woman he had been skiing against! With every ounce of energy he had left, he lunged forward at the finish line trying to get ahead of Tammy. She thought he made it, but race records have Valentine with a couple tenths of a second edge.

As skiers continued to stride into Lumberjack Bowl, Race Secretary Cheryl Poppe was nearly beside herself trying to calculate and collate results in the tiny Indian Museum next to the Wannigan Pancake House. It was a horrid task that year, trying to do the work that computers would do every year after that.

One of the proudest to come across the line that day was Duncan McLean. McLean, who had won the short race in its first two years, was second in the touring division behind Telemark Nordic Director Ingemar Sundberg, coming across in 3:07:44.49. McLean was then awarded the touring division trip to Norway when officials determined that Sundberg, by virtue of his professional employment at Telemark and the fact that he was from Sweden, was not eligible.

McLean went to Norway that year, along with Downey, to stir the hearts of the Norwegians. McLean was quite a media attraction, while Downey made the Norwegians shutter by coming in third overall, something quite unheard of then, and for some years after.

Eyes closed in relief after the grueling 55 kilometers, Ironwood, Michigan, skier Duncan McLean crosses the finish—winning a trip to Norway as the top citizen racer.

Jon Tofte (left) of Duluth makes a valiant attempt to overcome U.S. Ski Team racer Tammy Valentine at the finish, winding up on the snow as Tammy barely edges him out.

Champion Audun Kolstad (left) and second-place John-Mike Downey pose for photographers on top of a picnic table on the Wannigan Pancake House deck. Just a few years earlier less than three dozen racers had waxed on the same deck in anticipation of the first Birkebeiner.

It was quite an experience for both of them in Norway. Downey even had the service help of U.S. Ski Team coach Marty Hall in Norway. Bill Koch and Doug Peterson were there also, but didn't ski.

The 27.5-kilometer Citizen's Race, as it was called in 1976, was won by Bloomington, Minnesota, skier Francis Koch. He came across the finish line at Hayward in 1:39:37.31. Golden Valley, Minnesota, racer Bonnie Fuller won the women's division in 2:00:04.97.

It was nearly 7 p.m., though, before it was all over. Gary Haddock, of Pittsfield, Illinois, brought up the rear of the pack in 9:14:51.91. Haddock, greatly advanced his skiing career after that, though, taking on challenges like the Worldloppet in years to come.

That evening the Lodge was alive with activity. But this year it wasn't with downhillers who happened to be at the Lodge the same weekend as the race. It was cross country skiers and racers feasting at a special skier's smorgasbord and the first Birkebeiner Awards Banquet. Even later that evening skiers danced and listened to the high-tempo sound of Jim Cullum's Happy Jazz Band, hardly noticing a little sag in the 'oomp-pa-pa' from the tuba player who experienced cross country skiing for the first time that day by skiing in the Birkie, as everyone began to call it (he didn't finish).

There were trophies, trophies and more trophies that year. Birch bark leggings were given to Audun Kolstad and a new SAS Scandinavian Airlines Trophy, brought by the SAS Ski Club from Norway, was presented to the fastest American touring division skier, Duncan McLean.

A new award was also presented in 1976 by Carl Hanson. Carl had wanted to give something to the race, and decided that it would be appropriate to reward the top woman from Hayward in the race every year. So he carved a wooden goblet, which is on permanent display in the Birkebeiner awards showcase today at Telemark.

Carol Duffy, who had won the women's division in 1973 before taking a few years off with her eleventh child, came back in 1976 to win the first Carl Hanson trophy—Carl presented the trophy himself.

Prior to her first Birkebeiner in 1973, Carol had never competed in any athletic event. Within just a few years, running and skiing had become a major part of her and her husband's lives. When she decided to enter the 55-kilometer Birkebeiner many of her friends said she was biting off more than she could chew and that only the finest conditioned athletes could attempt the Birkebeiner. "It's amazing to look back now and to really see that there was no reason not to ski that far," said Carol. "But at the time, I wasn't sure. But I just thought that I would give it a shot and just try to finish."

Members in the new 25% Club were initiated, despite some controversey over the qualifications. Originally it was listed as a 20% Club, which was simply an error in not matching the Norwegian 25% equivalent.

Then, there was question of whether elite skiers should be mixed with tourers. In 1976, skiers were separated into elite and touring divisions. Age breakdowns within the two groups did not match. For example, within the touring men's 18 year, 9 month to 34 group there were three different elite age groups.

Twenty-five percent Club times were then figured for touring skiers by also adding in the elite skiers within the respective age breakdowns—making it quite a challenge to make the 25% Club that year.

That evening, Wise announced that beginning the following year, skiers would no longer have to contend with sharing a trail with snowmobilers. A new Birkebeiner Ski Trail appeared to becoming a reality.

Within the next few months after the race, the long hard hours of lobbying the summer before would become fruitful. The final grants needed for the new Birkebeiner Ski Trail would come through.

But still, as the dawn of a new era of skiing arose, no one really dreamed of what was ahead.

"I certainly envy future American-Birkebeiner winners," wrote McLean when he returned from Norway. "To me this has realized dreams of visiting the birthplace of skiing and has tied me closely to the Norwegians. I hope that the boost to cross-country provided by Tony Wise will set off a chain of trail building—an 'awakening' of sorts to what the Norwegians have known for a few millenia. Winter can mean a lot more than shoveling walks. Ask a Norwegian!"

The Americans would learn that lesson first-hand in 1977!

CHAPTER V
Where Were You When...?

It was about ten minutes until 9 a.m., Saturday, February 26, 1977. Chief of Race Jerry Berard was pacing in front of the starting area just off the second hole of the Telemark Golf Course. Behind him were nearly 2,000 skiers, all anxiously awaiting the boom of the cannon to send them scurrying up and over Mt. Telemark. Their goal, 55 kilometers to Hayward or 27.5 kilometers to Seeley.

It was the first year the shorter race started together with the Birkebeiner. In previous years, the two had started separately and finished together, creating confusion at the finish line. The short race even had its own name in 1977, the Telemark Kortelopet.

The new name Kortelopet was derived from the Scandinavian words for short and race. Haakon Randar, a Norwegian native now living in Elm Grove, Wisconsin, put the two words together to form the race title which finally gave the shorter event a specific title.

Although the total number of entries was only about doubled over the previous year, because of the combined start there were more than *three* times the number of skiers on the starting line than ever before!

The combined mass of Birkebeiner and Kortelopet skiers (see far back line) ready for the starting cannon. It was the first time that the two races had started together—a combined total of 1,936 in the starting field.

Just days before the 1977 Birkebeiner, American and Norwegian dignitaries dedicated the new public Birkebeiner Trail at the finish line on Hayward's Lumberjack Bowl. Pictured are, from left, Hayward Mayor Robert Anderson, Tony Wise and Rena, Norway, Mayor Kare Halvorsen.

For the second year in a row, the product names of the sponsoring NorTur company appeared on racing bibs, this year along with "Telemark, U.S.A."

Berard's concerns turned towards the Telemark Road, where the traffic flow was snarled from cars parked alongside the road. The traffic was a mess. Cars were parked everywhere. Skiers were literally crawling out of bus windows trying to get to the start.

As time ticked away, Berard glanced at his watch. It was just under nine minutes until the start. Along the start line, nearly 400 Norwegians were sliding their new Epoke skis back and forth on the snow, impatient for the shot of the cannon.

"I'll never forget it," recalled Berard years later. "I was out in front of the field, right in the middle of the track ahead of the starting line. All of a sudden I heard this whooshing sound. I turned around and there they came—hundreds of skiers charging out of the start. I looked around for Lars [Kindem, technical delegate]. I finally spotted him, swearing at the top of his lungs in Norwegian. We just threw up our arms and told them to fire the cannon!"

In the history of the Birkebeiner there will probably be two races remembered more than any others. One will be the snowless race(s) of 1981, and the other, the historic early start of 1977. No one will ever know for fact exactly what or who started the masses. A number of skiers jokingly took credit for the 8½-minute early start.

The night before, at the Telemark Lobby Bar, Kindem, who had spent several years studying and teaching in Norway, was conversing with some old Norwegians. "They were talking about breaking early at the start the next day," recalled Kindem. "They were using the Norwegian word which translates into 'thief start.' I told them they weren't."

The field that year was divided, for the first time, into three lines. The front line was very small—limited only to national team or international-caliber skiers. The second line were members of the 25% Club, which had been instituted a year before. Behind them were all the remaining skiers in both the Birkebeiner and Kortelopet.

According to Bjørn Arvnes, who later went on to win, skiers in the third rank began moving up front and mixing with racers in the second rank. In turn, skiers in this rank began pushing their way to the front.

Kindem had a plan, though. Expecting the skiers would try to head off the line only a minute or so early he intentionally called out the wrong time over the loudspeaker.

At 8:51 a.m. Kindem called out "ten minutes to go," in English and Norwegian. There were actually only nine minutes to go, but Kindem had fully expected everyone to synchronize their watches with his starting time. While they would be getting ready to go a minute early, the cannon would fire—exactly at 9 a.m. "I was ready for a one minute early start," he said later, "but I never expected them to go *ten* minutes early!"

As things got rougher and rougher along the line, Arvnes, along with teammate Kjell Pettersen and 1976 champion Audun Kolstad, decided to ski out to the right to avoid the confusion. About this time, former top-ranked U.S. Ski Team member Mike Gallagher was getting his skis ready on the sidelines.

"The only thing that saved me was that I knew a little Norwegian," he said later. "I heard them talking in Norwegian about starting early. I grabbed my skis and ran to the line." Seconds later, someone shouted "Let's Go!" and let out a war whoop. The race was on.

Although the final decision of Birkebeiner officials was that the false start was not planned, Kindem insisted that the start had been sabotaged. "At least 20 Norwegians edged ahead," he told the *Minneapolis Tribune*, "then someone let out a whoop and they surged past the first line of national team racers. It was planned. They were cheating, and if I could have spotted some bib numbers I would have disqualified them."

Kindem's comments later prompted an apology letter from one Norwegian who insisted that his countryman did not stage the early start and was very sorry that it had happened.

If 1975 and 1976 were the dawning of a new era in cross country skiing, 1977 was definitely its full-fledged arrival in America. This was especially true at the American-Birkebeiner.

While American-Birkebeiner V will be most remembered for the early start, it was also the inaugural for the new Birkebeiner Trail between Cable and

Hayward. And it was the first year for computerization of results, now commonplace in races even much smaller than the Birkebeiner. Plus this was the year the Birkebeiner became recognized as a premier nordic event—coast-to-coast and around the globe.

One of the biggest projects in Birkebeiner history was the planning and funding search to build the public Birkebeiner Trail. The ordeal, which had begun immediately following American-Birkebeiner III in 1975, dragged on through the summer and fall of 1975 and well into the winter of 1976 before Sawyer County was finally awarded a $30,000 grant by the Upper Great Lakes Regional Commission in March of 1976, just after Birkebeiner IV.

That grant, which was obtained through the persistence of Bill Bechtel, then of the State of Wisconsin's Local Affairs and Development Department, was contingent upon another grant from the U.S. Bureau of Outdoor Recreation, which was to come through the Wisconsin Department of Natural Resources, plus $20,000 from Sawyer County. Construction was to begin in May.

"We simply couldn't have done it without Bechtel's help," said Wise. "When we first began working with Sawyer County we did a lot of checking around Washington to find out who could help us locate grants. Everyone we talked to suggested Bechtel."

The approval of the $50,000 was quick to come in April, followed by final action by the Sawyer County Board on May 3 to seal the deal. The 25-mile trail would run between the area of the Fish Hatchery, east of Hayward, to the Sawyer/Bayfield County line, about nine miles from Telemark. Telemark would then construct a connecting trail to meet the public portion.

The segment from the county line to Telemark was one problem that Wise had to deal with himself. Bayfield County was not as interested as Sawyer in putting money into the project. Without Bayfield County's support, additional federal funds for the section in that county could not be made available.

The original construction of that segment was paid for by Telemark, which was able to receive an easement from the Bayfield County Board's Forestry Committee for use of the county forestland for the trail, provided Telemark pay for construction costs.

Eventually, in an effort to save money, only the one-kilometer segment from the county line to a town road, which connected to the Telemark trail system, was constructed by Wise. The originally-planned connection, which was

There were still 8½ minutes until race time when the skiers broke from the start and American-Birkebeiner V was underway—victimized by what the Norwegians called a "thief start."

shown by a dotted line on early trail maps, was not cut until the trail-widening project in 1979 when Bayfield County did provide supporting funds.

The actual trail itself had been plotted and marked a year earlier by Sven Wiik. Originally, officials had been hopeful that the trail could have been built in 1976, but delays in funding bumped that by a year.

During his visits to Telemark in 1975-76 for a training camp and Olympic Tryouts, U.S. Cross Country Ski Team coach Marty Hall had spoken to Tony Wise about Telemark playing host to a world-class ski race—not the Birkebeiner, but a race that would be part of the unofficial World Cup schedule the following season.

Wise was enthusiastic about the idea, especially after the difficulties he experienced in getting world-class skiers to compete in the Birkebeiner. In anticipation of that new event, Wise invited Hall back to Telemark in early May to begin laying out the new competition trails that would be necessary for a world-class race.

When Hall arrived at Telemark in the spring, he found yet another project—to finalize the planning of the Birkebeiner Trail for construction that summer. On the first Saturday in May, Wise sat down with Hall and Chief of Course Bob Treland on the deck of the Pancake House at Historyland in Hayward. Over a plate of German apple pancakes, Wise went over Wiik's already marked trail with Hall.

Treland, who had accompanied Wiik during his original planning a year before, went over the topographical maps with Hall, pointing out landmarks and getting his opinion on the course itself. With maps in hand, Hall and Treland headed out to the woods.

"The biggest problem we had at first was finding the trail itself," said Hall. "The leaves were beginning to bud and it was hard to spot the yellow flags that Sven and Bob had tied to the trees."

Hall went over the trail from beginning to end, carefully marking each and every tree for the crews that would be in later to do the cutting. "The hardest thing was to visualize the trail through the trees and leaves," said Hall. "When you're planning a trail it's good to be able to look ahead 200 or 300 meters. It was so hard to see the markings that I usually just had to send Treland ahead and just watch where he went."

Hall worked with Wiik's design, adding a few contributions of his own—including quite a bit more vertical climb, something Wiik noticed when he finally skied the trail for the first time in 1982. Many changes were necessitated because Wiik had planned the trail from Hayward to Telemark.

As the pack climbs up and over Morgedal, Philip Hoffer of Kandiyohi, Minnesota, hurries back down after running into ski problems on the hill.

"One of my biggest areas of concern was design to alleviate erosion problems," said Hall. "On a trail that long, you just can't provide the regular checking and maintenance that you normally should. It's not unusual for some small erosion problem to become a big problem before it's noticed. For that reason, I tried to eliminate as many sidehills as possible, choosing instead to go either on top of a ridge or down below."

By Hall's estimate, about 70-80% of the trail remained as Wiik had planned, with Hall adding the remaining 20-30% on his own.

The new trail was tough, according to Hall. "I'd be willing to guarantee that you'll never see another 2:40 on this trail." In actuality, Hall wasn't that far off. Only Per Knotten's 2:24 on the 53-kilometer 1980 course and Tim Caldwell's 2:34 in 1981 have eclipsed that mark.

While Hall and Treland were carefully plotting out the route that would take literally tens of thousands of skiers through the Sawyer and Bayfield County forests for years to come, the wheels of bureaucracy were spinning slowly. Although the project had received final approval, it wasn't until August that bids were finally approved for the beginning of construction. A completion date of November 1, 1976 was targeted—pretty close to the beginning of winter, but hopefully enough time to give American-Birkebeiner V skiers a new route between Telemark and Hayward.

Charles Barman of Superior, Wisconsin, takes the wide way down the far side of Stormoen as skier after skier crashes in front of him.

The trail itself was divided into nine segments, each being awarded to a local logging contractor. Each contractor could receive no more than three segments to insure a more labor-intensive project. Locally, the project was coordinated by Bob Kinney, a University of Wisconsin-Extension Resource Agent in Hayward.

What had amounted to two years of work by countless local, county, state and federal officials, came to a fitting triumph on Thursday, February 24, 1977—two days before American-Birkebeiner V.

Under the watchful eye of hundreds of American and Norwegian spectators, Hayward, Wisconsin, Mayor Robert Anderson and Rena, Norway, Mayor Kare Halvorson, skied through the finish line of the Birkebeiner in Hayward to officially dedicate the public trail.

Earlier that month the City of Hayward and the Town of Cable had issued resolutions extolling the virtues of the new trail linking their communities and furthering ties with the sister Birkebeiner in Norway. Hayward adopted Lillehammer as it's sister city, while Cable proclaimed Rena as it's sister in skiing.

"The trail gives the area the potential of becoming the cross country skiing center of the nation," stated Jack Revoyr of the Wisconsin Department of Business Development.

"This dedication represents the fulfillment of a dream to further expand the four seasons of recreational enjoyment available in Wisconsin," commented Farnum Alstrom, who was Wisconsin Governor Patrick Lucey's aid to the Great Lakes Regional Development Commission.

Gliding down Stormoen with a smile.

Nineteen seventy-seven was actually the closest race officials ever came to getting the Governor of the State of Wisconsin to the Birkebeiner in its first ten years. Lucey had been scheduled to be on hand at the dedication but was forced to cancel when weather problems grounded his plane in Madison. His complete ski outfit, all Norwegian in fact, sat neatly at Kinney's home, where the Governor was to have dressed.

The ties of the American-Birkebeiner to Norway were never stronger than they were in 1977. The sponsorship of NorTur the year before was strengthened that season, and the influx of around 400 Norwegians added a true international flair, in addition to making it the toughest year so far to make the 25% Club.

Although fiberglas skis had been introduced to the world at Falun in 1974, they really weren't available for recreational skiers in any great quantities until the winter of 1976-77. The new cross country ski had a dramatic effect on the ski market. One of the most enterprising promoters was Finn Haug of NorTur.

With a long trail ahead of them, skiers cautiously tuck down Stormoen.

Haug realized the tremendous potential of promotion that the Birkebeiner represented. His Epoke skis were one of the hottest fiberglas racing skis in Norway and were used by quite a few members of the U.S. Ski Team as well. But, like virtually all skis at that time, they were not that well known to the general skiing population of America.

Things were a little congested on the trails behind the Telemark Lodge as nearly 2,000 skiers vie for position just a few kilometers into the race.

One of Haug's most innovative promotions was to help to arrange a huge Norwegian tour group to the American-Birkebeiner, complete with Epoke skis and black and yellow suits supplied as part of their tour package.

The initial concept of the tour was actually presented over a year earlier by Knut Bordewick in a letter to Tony Wise. Bordewick Travel was one of Norway's leading agencies and handled cross county ski tours to a variety of races around the world. Bordewick proposed that Telemark work together with them to put together a charter flight of 180-200 persons.

Following the 1976 race, the small group of Norwegians from the SAS Ski Club brought back very favorable stories from their American tour. The 1976 race, which was won by Kolstad, picked up a great deal of media coverage in Norway, as did the American performances in the Norwegian Birkebeiner.

As the summer progressed, another agency became involved in promotion of a tour. Oslo's Bennett Travel, one of the world's most noted travel agencies, began working on a charter of its own. In the end, Pan Am also climbed on the bandwagon with a charter from Drammen, just outside of Oslo.

In November, both Arthur Iglum of Bennett and Einar Thu of Bordewick, visited Telemark and Hayward to lay the groundwork for their promotions. Both came in separate visits, going from motel to motel, meeting the townspeople and putting their plans together.

Keep in mind that this was quite a culture shock for local residents. Although the Hayward/Cable area has been one of the state's leading tourist areas for many years, the likes of a European tour group was more than most could comprehend. But Iglum was a master. His continental manner and very proper dress left an indelible impression on the people he met. "It didn't matter what kind of motel or resort he visited," said Wise. "He left them, especially the housewives, with a feeling that their resort was the nicest he had ever seen and how honored he would be to have some of his group stay with them. He made everybody feel like a million bucks!"

By mid-December nearly 400 skiers were booked on the three separate charter flights. American skiers were in for quite an experience that February.

For Haug, it was one of the most effective promotions in American skiing history. "We saw black and yellow everywhere," said Haug. "It was extremely effective in introducing the ski. We had dealers calling us through April asking how they could get the skis!"

On the trail. Notice the penned-in bib number on the left for a late entrant.

Countrymen Bjørn Arvnes and Kjell Pettersen battle it out on the course.

Few skiers will ever forget the face of 74-year-old Norwegian Sigvart Egge.

The charters had a tremendous effect on the race as well. The 400 Norwegians that year caused quite a stir. They introduced Americans to a new breed of skiing. Not everything was pleasant about the experience, though. The Americans learned quickly that winning was very important to the Norwegians. And the American skiers were literally in awe of the ability of the Norwegians—especially the women and older men! All in all, it was an eye-opening experience for all who took part in the race.

Among the Norwegians was 70-year-old Oscar Gjøslein, one of Norway's most celebrated skiers from the twenties and thirties, and his brother-in-law Sigvart Egge. Egge, whose wrinkled face made him look much older than his 74 years, left American skiers stuck in their tracks. And Gjøslein, who didn't look nearly 70, was even more unbelievable!

Gjøslein always had the upper hand. It wasn't until after each had skied in 40 Norwegian Birkebeiners that Sigvart finally beat Oscar in 1981.

Gjøslein, who won the Holmenkollen in 1935, has the honor of winning what is considered the most exciting Norwegian Birkebeiner in history. In the 1936 race, the fifth ever held, Gjøslein outsprinted Reidar Inglingstad to the finish line in 5:16:05, over the same course that is used today. And while Egge never won the race itself, he was a regular class winner until recent years.

The two were inseparable during their stay at Telemark. And that togetherness even included the Lodge's Lobby Bar, where they were often the last to leave at the end of the evening.

The most dramatic effect of the Norwegians was seen in Egge and Gjøslein's Class V, men 57 and over. There were 49 finishers in that class, a total which has never been matched since. Twenty-nine skiers made the 25% club, an unusually high ratio which was somewhat common in 1977 with the Norwegians crowding the fast end of the times in most classes.

Out of the 49 finishers, there were eight Americans and one Canadian. The Canadian, a legend in his own right, Rolf Hauge, was 12th. The top American was William Andberg, Anoka Minnesota, a perennial top finisher in the class, who had to settle for 41st that year!

Gjøslein was fifth in 4:07:57.80; Egge was 29th in 4:47:05.45—not bad for a couple of old gentlemen!

The Norwegian invasion of the Telemark-Cable-Hayward area was very complete. Hotels and motels, private homes and cabins, were filled with skiers. All the old Norwegians in Hayward brushed up on their Norwegian, which they

Craig Ward, later to join the U.S. Ski Team, leads Norwegians Hans Kvaloren (center) and Olaf Pedersen (right) down the trail. Pedersen, who was one of Lillehammer's best at the time, finished seventh.

would find very useful that week. Buses were lined up and travel arrangements coordinated to get each and every skier to the proper places at the proper times.

When the buses began pouring into Hayward on Thursday, Sheriff Ernie Lien, a second-generation Norwegian himself, met them at the Sawyer/Washburn County line, leading them into town with red lights flashing and siren wailing. That week Ernie showed them the town—even locking a few of them up in the county jail, all in good fun.

Hayward shop keepers were in for quite an experience as well. At Lindahl's, Indian headresses and other souvenirs went fast. "The next year I stocked up with even more Indian items," said Lindahl. "Then they crossed me up and bought Mexican rugs." At Lambert's Old Town Gift Shop, leather goods and more Indian souvenirs went quickly.

As race day approached, the weatherman was anything but cooperative. It hadn't been a bonus snow year. Warm temperatures, which began to melt snow on the course, were certainly unwelcome. To make matters worse, a freezing rain put a coat of ice on the track just a few days before the race. And then came the snow—about four inches, which put a nice topping on the slick, icy track.

Temperatures were chilly as racers woke up Saturday morning. A lot of skiers torched in some klister to hold their wax on the abrasive track. Arvnes, however, went with green and blue over a layer of orange binder.

By the hundreds they streamed out into the starting gates. Bus after bus brought Norwegians and Americans to the start. Registration in the Red Arrow Ballroom of the Lodge was buzzing with activity as bibs were given out to late-coming skiers.

In front of the Lodge, Minnesota Vikings mascot Hub Meades, who had made his inaugural Birkebeiner appearance a year before, posed for pictures with skiers. March music blared from speakers at the start, luring skiers to the line.

The cannon firing at around eight minutes before nine was one of those events where you'll always remember just where you were. For many that place was in front of the Lodge waxing. For others it was in portable toilets near the start and others maybe just off in the woods a ways. Some heard it as they drove in and others just saw the masses starting up the hill from their bus window. Founder John Holmquist and others were still in the old Base Chalet. Theirs was a rushed farewell to the chalet, which would burn to the ground a month later.

All instinctively looked at their watches, and all probably saw the same thing, 8:52 a.m. The first thought that goes through your mind is, "this darned watch is slow!" The next thought is to get into the race.

George Hovland had a relatively good start, compared to some. And he made it up Valhalla and Morgedal in good fashion—the same hills he had conquered in downhill races in previous years.

Stormoen wasn't too much of a problem either for the former national NASTAR champion. George, in fact, recalls passing about 300 skiers on Stormoen that morning. But when he hit the Birkebeiner Trail, snap went his new carbon fiber pole.

George is the type of person who doesn't think about decisions, he just reacts. His natural reaction was to simply turn around, ski back to the ski shop and buy a new pole!

By 1977, the Birkebeiner was big enough that you simply couldn't do that. There was no way to ski backwards on the trail. So George beat it though the brush, pushing limbs and branches aside as hundreds upon hundreds of skiers passed him by.

"Never will I ever forget it," recalled George later. "There he was, that 74-year old guy with the wrinkled face [Sigvart Egge] coming right at me heading for Hayward. I thought, 'My God!' I'll never forget that face."

It took a few minutes but Hovland finally made it to the Telemark Ski Shop, located in the old Base Chalet at the bottom of what was then the Exhibition Run. Ski shop manager Dave Blake was behind the counter. You probably would have a hard time finding a nicer, more softspoken and gentlemanly guy than Dave Blake. So it was natural that when George ran in screaming for a ski pole, Blake calmly excused himself from his customer who was trying to decide between some blue or red ski ties, and said, "Just a minute, George, I'll be right with you."

A thirsty skier reaches for a cup of Body Punch at an on-course food station.

Citizen winner Tom Haas of Duluth throws down a cup of Body Punch.

Kortelopet finishers proudly display their medallions. 1977 was the last year for this style.

"There I was, the whole race is going to Hayward and I had to wait for this woman to choose between red and blue ski ties," said Hovland.

A few minutes later, Hovland was back on the trail—new pole and all. "You know," recalled Hovland, "I had a great race that year, too!" He even made the 25% Club.

Meanwhile, Arvnes broke out in a pack of four or five skiers at the start, flying over Morgedal and out onto the trail. At three kilometers the tough, little Norwegian took the lead. At five k's, though, he fell on an icy downhill and was back in the lead pack. Soon, his countryman Kjell Pettersen took the lead and pulled away. But at around eight kilometers, Arvnes caught him and then led most of the rest of the way.

Race officials, though, still had a problem. What should be done about the early start? Kindem was mad enough about it to disqualify the Norwegians, although probably no one would have known where to begin. Some race officials wanted to just let it go. But, according to Wise, the only thing that really could be done was to adjust the times accordingly.

But it wasn't that easy. Electronic timing machines were already clicking off the minutes from their pre-determined and synchronized 9 a.m. start at the timing booth in Hayward. Later, as skiers began to come across the finish line, those times were fed into the Control Data computers until a final decision to re-calculate times and re-input the data was made.

"We really didn't know what to do," said Chief of Race Berard. "At the time we just wanted to let it go. But in retrospect, the only thing to do was to add 8½-minutes to everyone's time."

Arvnes came across the finish line alone shortly before noon. Try as he might, he just missed breaking the three-hour barrier, finishing in 3:00:03.44, his corrected time based on the early start. Pettersen came in a minute and 44 seconds later.

But while Arvnes didn't have much of a battle, a host of Americans certainly did. Despite the tough field of Norwegians, the U.S. skiers turned in spectacular performances. Don Nielsen, New London, New Hampshire, had been the top American most of the way. In fact, at Mosquito Brook he was still within shouting distance of Arvnes.

John Spencer, Anchorage, Alaska, had Bob Treadwell, Amherst, New Hampshire, nipping his tail at Mosquito Brook. Treadwell gave it his best, but just couldn't muster the energy to pass Spencer. About that time Nielsen also started to fade, paving the way for Spencer to take third overall.

Thanks in part to a letter from U.S. Ski Teamers Joanne Musolf, Pat Engberg and Terry Porter that January, Wise had decided that the time was right to also send a woman on the trip to Norway. So for the first time, there was more than just a trophy at stake for the ladies.

Soon, news flashed back on the course that Spencer had won the trip to Norway as the top American. Spencer's wife, Alison, (also on the U.S. Ski Team) was engaged in a tremendous battle with Porter. In fact, Porter even had a slim lead at the latter stage of the race. Alison hadn't really expected to turn in the best American finish. Long races were not here strong suit and she figured that Porter and Engberg would be too tough to beat.

John Kotar of Duluth, one of a dozen remaining Birkebeiner I veterans as of 1977, strides down the trail.

But about five kilometers from the finish, with Porter still holding a slight edge, Alison heard the news that John had just won the trip to Norway. "The good news really got me going," she said later. "But I wouldn't be surprised if Terry didn't give me a break so I could go [to Norway] with John."

At Lake Hayward, Alison really turned it on. She sprinted past Porter and skated across the finish line in 3:32:09.36—just two minutes behind champion Berit Mørdre Lammedal, Norway's Olympic medalist. As first American woman, she would join her husband in the Norwegian Birkebeiner.

Kortelopet skiers, for the final time, finished in Hayward with Norwegians dominating the race, as well. Bernt Lund of Oslo won in 1:35:46.31. Gina Regland of Lillehammer was the top woman in 2:18:04.85.

Out on the course, the nearly 2,000 skiers kept up their strides. Food stations dished out over 7,000 oranges while skiers consumed nearly 1,200 gallons of Body Punch, a new energy drink that was recommended that year by the U.S. Ski Team. Over 350 gallons of tea and honey was served at the finish line.

Mike Gallagher (right) was ending his career as a U.S. Ski Team racer when he won the 35-42 class in 1977. He greets Bill Estell of Alaska. Gallagher later went on to coach the U.S. Ski Team.

Norwegian Viggo Kampli (right) skates past another racer at the finish line.

Sten Fjeldheim, who was then skiing at Northern Michigan University in Marquette, crosses the finish line and collapses into the arms of technical delegate Lars Kindem. Kindem and Fjeldheim were very close, Kindem having trained Fjeldheim for many years in Minneapolis. The photo of Fjeldheim and Kindem embracing at the finish was used the next week by **Newsweek** magazine in a story on the Birkebeiner.

Skier after skier comes into the finish area, being routed through control gates for presentation of year pins and medallions.

Alison and John Spencer of Anchorage, Alaska, made it a husband/wife duo, each winning a trip to Norway as the top American man and woman. Both were skiing on Epoke skis, one of the best fiberglas racing skis in America at the time.

An icicle hangs from the hat of a Norwegian racer after finishing the 1977 Birkebeiner.

Despite a somewhat rugged course that year, injuries were relatively low. One, however, was the first rather serious injury in the history of the Birkebeiner. Forty-one-year-old Erkki Harju, a well-known Two Harbors, Minnesota, skier, was skiing in the Kortelopet that day along with his son, John, 19. On a downhill curve near the 21-kilometer mark, Harju went into the woods to avoid a fallen skier, hitting a large pine and breaking his right leg.

While lying in the snow, Harju sent his son ahead for help, hoping that someone else would stop to assist him. As John skied ahead for the nearest emergency station, skier after skier passed Erkki by. Enough skiers were falling on the turn that no one even realized that he had been badly hurt.

His position was so precarious on the trail that he was eventually forced to pull himself with branches into the protective cover of some saplings. Finally, after what seemed like 10 to 12 minutes, help arrived.

Chicago attorney Jim McCarthy was one of the first to stop, trying to shelter Harju from others that were still falling.

Dr. Jon Stephenson of Duluth, Minnesota, was enjoying a reasonably good race that day. But when he came by Harju, he stopped to help, as well. His stopping may have saved Harju's life. Stephenson went to work in what was a pretty unusual situation, he wrapped up Harju as best he could against the cold. Soon others stopped, including Bill Gitar, a medical student, and Ed Martin, a nurse, both from Duluth's St. Luke's Hospital.

McCarthy pleaded with skiers to give up their warm clothes to help keep Harju warm. "Once the skiers saw that he was hurt, the help was overwhelming. Everybody wanted to do what they could." One skier stripped down to a tee shirt, giving Harju his sweater.

At one point, McCarthy even stopped race traffic to keep skiers off the downhill while Harju was being moved. Harju had fallen at the bottom of a long, steep hill, in a blind right-angle turn. There was almost no way for skiers to see the trouble ahead. Some narrowly missed, including Twin Cities racer Ken Rykken who fell deliberately to miss the accident scene, flipping himself around and breaking a ski tip. He skied four kilometers with one ski until a spectator donated one of his skis for Rykken to finish the race.

According to McCarthy, "It wasn't the ideal location to break a leg, but it was far from the worst. At one point he was being attended by two doctors, a nurse, a lawyer and several others whose occupations were not revealed." Stephenson, along with McCarthy, had his finish time adjusted for his time-consuming efforts.

Harju, meanwhile, spent the better part of three weeks in the hospital and many more in a cast. John even brought home second place in his Kortelopet class—a position he might just have shared with his father that day.

The following few seasons Stephenson played another instrumental role in organizing doctors in the Birkebeiner, urging them to carry small medical packs and provide assistance to skiers in need. Harju, who told one newspaper reporter he would be back, kept his word. In fact, he has been a regular Birkebeiner skier ever since, and always near the top of his age class. Not bad after such a rugged introduction.

That afternoon, the Telemark Lodge began to take on the look it would have for many Birkebeiners to come. The Norwegian Dancers from Stoughton, Wisconsin, performed in the lobby, while officials and dignitaries began to file into the Red Arrow Ballroom for the second annual Awards Banquet.

Meanwhile, back in Hayward, quite a few skiers were still coming across the line. One thing you can be sure of, there weren't any Norwegians left on the course! Snow hadn't been too plentiful in Cedar Rapids, Iowa, that season, so 25-year-old Tom Carfrae didn't have much chance to try out his Christmas skis. That was too bad, since Carfrae had decided at the October ski show in Chicago to ski the Birekebeiner—despite having never skied before in his life!

Carfrae had made up his mind, though, and stuck to it. He had been working out regularly for the past 18 months to get in better shape, but had only a total of six miles on skis come Birkebeiner time.

About nine hours and four minutes after he left Telemark, Carfrae came across the finish line in Hayward. "People were always passing me," he said, "so I didn't get that many conversations going. I did a lot of daydreaming. A couple times I was really depressed. There were times when I didn't get a good talk going with anybody for ten miles and then it would really get bad, but seeing all those people doing the same thing I was doing but faster was an incentive to keep going."

Although the Bronzed Broom Award was not begun officially until 1978, Carfrae was the trailsweeper in 1977—following in a long line of fellow sweepers before him!

A few weeks later, Tony Wise had an opportunity to see Norway himself—for the first time. And his experiences reinforced what American-Birkebeiner skiers had learned that year. Skiing is the life in Norway! Wise was among 100,000 spectators at Oslo's Holmenkollen Festival, while his daughter Frances, who had won the citizen's race in 1974, skied in a field of over 5,000 in the Holmenkollen March.

One of the highlights of Wise's trip was an audience with King Olav V, the King of Norway. Wise had received the noted King Olav medal in the United States in 1975. The honor is bestowed on persons abroad who perform some service of help or support to Norway. According to tradition, recipients of the medal are entitled to an audience with the king.

Wise didn't really think much about it, but had brought his medal along—just in case. When his hosts, Pan Am representatives Derek Blix and Roy Kvenbøe found that out, they immediately made arrangements. Following a quick shopping spree for the proper black tie and shirt, plus a protocol briefing with an aide, Wise patiently waited for the Prime Minister of Bangladesh to finish his appointment before going to meet the king.

After exchanging formalities, the two spent about 15 to 20 minutes of conversation, shook hands and parted company. A brief, but important meeting to bring the two nations and races yet closer together.

There were plenty of handshakes across the ocean that year. At the awards banquet following the American-Birkebeiner, dignitary after dignitary spoke of the tremendous race that day. The new Birkebeiner Trail was praised by Arvnes

Hundreds of clothing bags are neatly lined up in the Pancake House parking lot.

Like most of his countrymen, this Norwegian skier earned a 25% Club pewter cup.

Ojibwa medicine man Chief Running Elk honors Rena, Norway, Mayor Kare Halvorsen (left) and Berit Mørdre Lammedal at the awards banquet Saturday night at the Telemark Lodge.

and others as the finest in the world. Einar Odden, a Norwegian journalist studying at the nearby University of Wisconsin-River Falls, helped translate two speeches from Rena Mayor Halvorsen to his new-found American friends. Side-by-side, Norwegians and Americans toasted their newfound friendships through skiing.

Later that night, several Norwegians came up to Sheriff Ernie Lien in Hayward after a night of celebration, and pinned their own awards from Norway on Ernie's uniform. One of the pins he received was Sigvart Egge's gold mark, one of the highest honors that can be received in the Norwegian Birkebeiner.

Ernie, in turn, reached into his pocket and pulled out a special deputy's badge, a badge reserved for just such honors, and pinned it on Egge's shirt. Years later, that deputy's badge was still pinned above all of the other awards on display in Egge's Norwegian home.

Such were the friendships of skiing.

John Spencer (left) and Bjørn Arvnes display their birch bark leggings as the top American and Norwegian skiers.

A March 24, 1977, fire completely leveled the historic, old Telemark Base Chalet, the site of the finish of the first three races, and a noted ski landmark in Wisconsin since 1947.

CHAPTER VI
The Closest Birkie

In the history of the Birkebeiner there will probably never be another race as close as American-Birkebeiner VI. The excitement of the finish was as stunning as Thomas Wassberg's slim hundreth of a second edge over Juha Mieto two years later in the Lake Placid Olympics.

American-Birkebeiner VI will also very likely go down as the slowest of the 55-kilometer events. Nearly a half foot of fresh powder greeted skiers on race morning. But the lovely new-fallen snow turned the Birkebeiner into a real horse-race, with the horses charging into Lumberjack Bowl like never before.

Alfred Kaelin, a Swiss who had excellent credentials but wasn't really expected to win, took the Birkebeiner title to central Europe for the first time, edging Italian Renzo Chiocchetti, Finland's superstar Pauli Siitonen and defending champion Bjørn Arvnes. Only six seconds separated the first four! And Sweden's Sune Asph and Switzerland's Albert Giger weren't more than a few seconds behind them.

The earlier races had seen the Birkebeiner grow into more than just an American event, but it was still basically Scandinavian-American. That changed dra-

The masses storm off the starting line, dwarfing the huge start banner in the middle of the Telemark Golf Club's number two fairway.

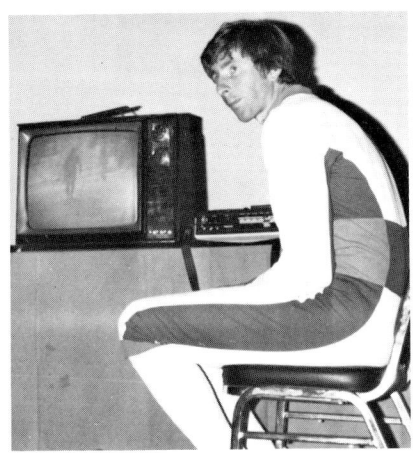

Telemark Academy Director Peter Davis goes over video tapes with skiers at the first Birkebeiner Training Weekend at Telemark.

Skiers pole past a snowgun at the first Birkebeiner Training Weekend in December 1977.

matically on Saturday, February 25, 1978—when the American-Birkebeiner became a truly international affair. Five nations were represented in just the first seven finishing places!

The famed 400 Norwegians a year before had braced everyone, but 1978 was truly a new experience for locals in the Hayward and Cable area. The novelty of Norwegian-speaking skiers gave way to a flow of German, Italian and Finnish, which was the one language which gave race officials fits!

When the Finns didn't speak English, there was simply no way to communicate. Not even the neighboring Swedes could help. More than once officials thanked the little town of Oulu, about 45 minutes northwest of Cable, for its Finnish-speaking natives!

Racewise, not much changed in 1978 other than the development, for the first time, of community group involvement in the food stations. But behind the scenes, a lot was happening. The interest of American skiers was reaching beyond anyone's expectations. No one had looked much beyond the couple hundred or thousand racers who had skied the few years before. It just seemed like all of a sudden there were more and more skiers each year catching what was coming to be known as "Birkebeiner Fever."

"Birkebeiner Fever." Like the term "citizen skier," Birkebeiner Fever came to be the catch phrase that flowed from the tips of skiers' tongues. Race officials used it in the *Birch Scroll* and in promotions, and skiers quickly picked it up. It was highly contagious!

Unbeknownst to many skiers, American-Birkebeiner VI ushered in a new era—the era of a ski series that was to become the World Loppet League (later shortened to World Loppet and then simply Worldloppet). Along the sidelines on race day were more than a dozen representatives from nine nations, all gathered at Telemark for the purpose of laying the groundwork for the organization that would link the world of skiing closer than it had ever been before.

The idea of the World Loppet League had been born several years earlier. In 1976, Wise saw that getting top world-class Olympians to compete in the Birkebeiner was fruitless. There was a definite need for an international ski series to attract top skiers to races like the Birkebeiner.

The concept of a long-distance ski series was not new in itself. In fact, two such series were already intertwined in Europe, the Alpentris and Euroloppet. The Alpentris—which included the Austrian Dolomitenlauf, Italian Marcialonga and German König Ludwig Lauf—was begun in 1971.

Like the Worldloppet, the Alpentris faced tough sledding in its formative stages. The idea was conceived by Dolomitenlauf president Robert Steiner,

Skiers do some last minute waxing in front of the Telemark Lodge.

who had more than his hands full trying to convince Marcialonga president Roberto Uggio of its importance.

Much the same problem was faced when the Swedish Vasaloppet and Finlandia Hiihto were aligned together with the Alpentris nations a year later to form the Euroloppet.

But both the Alpentris and Euroloppet had grown tremendously since their birth. The Euroloppet, especially, was looked on as one of the premier ski racing series in all of Europe. With the exception of the Vasaloppet, which was begun in 1926, all of the Euroloppet races were relatively new, having first begun in the late sixties or early seventies. The Finlandia, for example, did not start until 1974—one year after the American-Birkebeiner!

The names of the European races were known to few in the United States. Information was compiled from contacts such as American FIS representative John Lindstrom. During his 1977 visit to Scandinavia, Wise briefly met with Lars-Erik Larson of the Vasaloppet and Risto Rytokoski of the Finlandia Hiihto to lay the World Loppet groundwork.

Early response from the European nations had been mixed, but generally favorable. To all, dealing with Tony Wise and the American way of thinking was quite different from anything they had experienced before!

In January of 1978, Wise decided that the time was right to begin formation of the international ski circuit. Invitations to come to Telemark went out to representatives from the five Euroloppet races, plus three others—the Norwegian Birkebeiner, Swiss Engadin Skimarathon and Canadian Riviere Rouge Race, along with the American-Birkebeiner.

Invitations went not only to race officials from the eight other nations, but also to the top long-distance skier in each country. Without question, American-Birkebeiner VI would have one of the most prestigious racing fields in North America since Telemark's own nordic World Cup two seasons before.

One by one, each nation accepted the invitation to meet at Telemark U.S.A., a place of which they knew very, very little. Even Finland, which was playing host to the 1978 FIS Nordic World Championships in Lahti that week, sent a delegation including Siitonen himself, who was at the peak of his long-distance career at the time.

Norway, despite its close ties to Telemark, was one of the least receptive to the idea. Still, a corps of journalists, skiers and race officials made the trip to Cable. Amidst a host of special ceremonies and dignified functions for the Birkebeiner's foreign guests, two meetings were held to lay the groundwork for the World Loppet League.

Skiers and spectators move briskly in a light snowfall to the start of American-Birkebeiner VI.

Efforts to gain national television exposure on ABC's Wide World of Sports were in vain, despite a petition with over 2,000 names of Birkebeiner entrants and interested skiers in 1978.

On Thursday, even though the Finns had yet to arrive, the discussions began. Tony Wise took charge of the meeting, laying out his proposal for an international ski series—uniting skiers of the world in the name of world peace.

It was an interesting concept, no one disagreed! But many of the nations expressed their concern, each cautious not to take away anything from its own national race. Europeans tend to be extremely traditional and nationalistic—each nation very staunch about protecting its own customs and beliefs.

Most of the questions were raised over Canada and Norway. Although the Norwegian Birkebeiner was the second oldest race in the proposed series, the Norwegian tradition of wave starts and carrying a 12-pound pack were not met with open arms by the other Europeans. The Norwegians, ever conservative, were hesitant in their own right, as well. Such a concept as this was sure to meet with disapproval from their organization, they said.

Canada had the problem of being the youngest race—the first Riviere Rouge Race having been run just a year earlier. The Riviere Rouge was an offshoot of the Canadian Ski Marathon, a tremendous tradition among Canadians. Marathon purists weren't sure how to take the Riviere Rouge at first. The Marathon was almost sacred in Canada, and it took a great deal of fortitude for Riviere Rouge officials to carry forth their plan.

The triumvirate of Germany, Italy and Austria, the nations of the Alpentris, were the most vocal. Of the three, only Fritz Lang of Germany had enough command of English to totally understand the discussions. Fritz became their translator and may have even hedged enough on his back-and-forth translations to soothe their concerns and help make the World Loppet League a reality.

But Fritz, along with Italian Giulio Giovannini, had plenty of questions! After all, they were the fathers of the Alpentris and now, all of a sudden, this new concept was taking them by storm.

Most of the questions that were asked and objections that were raised reflected back on the fact that each nation wanted to have its way in the formation of such a new series. After all, they were the experts! And just who was this American entrepreneur that was trying to tell them how to organize such an idea as a World Loppet League?

But beyond all the discussions, questions and speculation, everyone knew that the World Loppet League was indeed the natural progression of what had already begun. After meetings on Thursday and Friday, interrupted only by a group photo in front of the Lodge, the representatives laid down 16 points of agreement which were to be the basis of the World Loppet League. All of the 16 points were to be taken back to the individual race committees and discussed. Comments were sent to temporary secretary Risto Rytokoski of the Finlandia Hiihto, who was secretary general of the Euroloppet at the time. A session to officially charter the World Loppet League was scheduled in conjunction with the annual Euroloppet meeting that Summer.

On June 10, 1978, at Uppsala, Sweden, the World Loppet League was officially formed by the nations of Austria, Italy, West Germany, Canada, the United States, Finland, Sweden and Switzerland. Norway did not attend.

But Norway was a key nation, thought Wise, especially with the already-existing ties between the American and Norwegian races. It would be like having a World Loppet League with only four of the five Euroloppet nations! And besides, Norway was the birthplace of modern skiing.

Undaunted, Wise headed for Lillehammer, meeting with representatives from both the Lillehammer and Rena ski clubs. After much friendly persuasion, helped greatly by Leif Norberg and Rolf Kjaernsli, Norway somewhat reluctantly joined.

In forming the organization officials noted: "The purpose of the World Loppet League is to make it possible to honor those citizen long distance cross country ski racers of the world who have completed the most outstanding long distance races in each member country. It is hoped that in future years, all skiing nations will be members of the World Loppet League."

The American-Birkebeiner the World Loppet League officials observed in 1978 was much the result of the 1977 event—one of the smoothest in history! Not a lot of things went wrong in 1977. Consequently there were few major race changes, unlike earlier years.

The traffic problems of 1977 were solved when Telemark security chief Dale Jensen put together a one-way traffic plan, routing skiers' cars in on Telemark Road and exiting on a logging road to Cable. Strict parking regulations were put into effect to avoid a maze of misparked cars on the roadway that had kept many skiers from the start a year before.

The downhill runout from Stormoen, on the backside of Mt. Telemark, was widened. It was already becoming evident to race officials that Stormoen would be a tricky area in years to come.

The festivities and ceremonies, which had already become so much a part of the Birkebeiner, were expanded again. Louise Mandrell, the then unknown younger sister of Barbara, came in for the whole week with her band. Wise had been looking for a Texas swing band, or something similar, for the Birkebeiner. Tandy Rice, the entrepreneurial agent who had made Billy Carter a national celebrity the previous fall (including an appearance at Telemark's Gitchi Gami Games) recommended Mandrell, who was still being managed by her father.

Audun Endestad, a popular Norwegian who was living at Telemark in 1978, led the elite pack up Morgedal, sprinting ahead at the start. Behind him were Sweden's Sune Asph, Italian Renzo Chiocchetti, Finland's Pauli Siitonen and 1976 champion Audun Kolstad of Norway.

Thousands herringbone up and over the Morgedal headwall.

Photographer Bill Stonecipher (center with beret) gets caught up in the pack going up Morgedal. A few years later, Stonecipher set his cameras aside and skied the Birkie instead.

The rush down Stormoen became more and more exciting with each passing year.

With the up and down of Mt. Telemark behind them, skiers head out onto the trail.

The popular Wisconsin band, Dr. Bop and His Nouveau Cabaret Orchestra, was also booked for Saturday night. The traditional Norwegian Dancers from Stoughton, Wisconsin, and LeRoy Larson's Norwegian Band were lined up to add a little bit of Scandinavia to the festivities.

The age class system, which had seen considerable change through the early years, was also changed for 1978 to parallel a similar move in Norway. The new divisions broke men down into five-year classes all the way up to the 60 and over category. Women were still relegated to only two classes, 19-34 and 35 and over.

In November of 1977, the first Birkebeiner Training Weekend was held. Peter Davis, who had just begun the new Telemark Academy that fall, put together a weekend of on-snow training, complete with expert coaching and video tape analysis. Eighteen skiers, including a handful of locals, showed up.

"It was very much like the training clinics today," said Davis. "We basically foresaw that it was becoming increasingly important to extend the Birkebeiner beyond just one weekend in February. So many skiers were finding that they couldn't tackle an event like that in an enjoyable way unless they trained properly."

Serious skiers were also getting serious about training. John Kotar has always been one of the strongest skiers among the Birkebeiner founders. His training log is typical of skier/athletes of the time.

In 1973, the first year of the race, Kotar's training consisted of about 400 kilometers on snow—no dryland work. A year later, he added about 15 kilometers of running and biking a week, plus 700 kilometers of skiing. By 1976, roller skiing was being added to his repertoire. Meanwhile, skiing and running remained about the same. A steady combination of running, biking, roller skiing and on-snow work prepared him for the 1978 race.

But the single biggest change of all came in the area of food. For the first time ever, skiers were given guidelines for pre-race diet, something that would be commonplace within just a few years. Mark Pearson, of the Telemark Ski School, put together a weeklong pre-race diet to give new skiers and veterans alike an idea of how to prepare their bodies foodwise. "Carbo-loading" became a new key word in skiers' vocabularies.

Out on the course, skiers found much the same food as they had in the past. Body Punch, an energy drink, and oranges were served enroute by a veritable army of workers—volunteer workers who were organized in the first-ever community-wide participation in the Birkebeiner.

"We had always been a little worried about going to volunteer help," said Wise. "We were unsure about how we could rely on local groups for just one weekend. But the food stations were an excellent opportunity for them to get involved and help the race at the same time."

The race had grown to a point where the operation of the food stations was the single largest use of manpower. About 20-30 persons were needed to staff each of nine stations—a huge task force!

With the help of Telemark's jack-of-all-trades Dick Simono, a community-wide effort was undertaken to organize volunteer crews to staff the food stations on the course. Local civic clubs and other organizations from the Hayward and Cable areas were contacted to solicit their support.

Much of the coordination was done through the Hayward Chamber of Commerce. Chamber President Tom Brenholt and Executive Secretary Bob Fairfield coordinated the effort, bringing community groups together.

"At first I think a lot of people were apprehensive," said Dick Weishaupt of the Hayward Lakes Resort Association. "They were all into downhill skiing or snowmobiling. They didn't know what to think about working at a cross country race. They didn't know what it would be like."

The enthusiasm quickly built, though. Group by group, more came into the fold—each organization taking responsibility for running a food station on the course, and many setting up their own concession stands at the Kortelopet and Birkebeiner finish lines.

"Overall, the reaction was outstanding," recalls Simono. "And each and every group fulfilled all of the responsibilities that was entailed!"

It was an amazing group of volunteers, so diverse in interests and pursuits that one had to wonder how it would all come together. There were Boy

Coming out of the OO food station.

The trail opened up a bit near OO before a long, steady uphill to the midway point.

With ice on his beard and hair, a skier gobbles down an orange at a food station.

Local civic groups manned food stations on the course in the race's first organized volunteer effort.

Nancy Davis, wife of Telemark Academy Director Peter Davis, grabs a cup of ERG at a food station.

Scouts and Cub Scouts, resort owners and civic club members, snowmobilers and water skiers, Jaycees and more.

Literally overnight, the story of the Birkebeiner became the volunteer army. And it was tremendously important to the operation of the race itself. The food stations were a crucial area—no one in the entire race organization would spend more time with skiers during the entire Birkebeiner week than the volunteers at the food stations. The impression they left on the skiers would be what was remembered.

Very much in army-like fashion, three training sessions were scheduled for group leaders at the Hayward National Guard Armory. "It was a typical National Guard operation," recalled Hayward's Connie Miller, then a member of the chamber board. "I'll never forget the roller skiers from Telemark that came down to train us. They skied round and round the Armory and everyone practiced running alongside of them with cups!"

Whether it was their expert training or just their dedication, they were outstanding. Volunteers were up and around as early as 5 a.m. on race morning, heading off into the woods with huge new garbage cans full of Body Punch and cases upon cases of oranges—ready for the onslaught of skiers a few hours after dawn.

The day in the cold snow wouldn't fatten their wallets any. Their payment was a Birkebeiner staff stocking cap, a pass good for skiing and pool privileges at Telemark, and words of thanks from a few thousand skiers.

They stayed throughout the day, passing out thousands of oranges and hundreds of gallons of Body Punch until the sun finally set over Lumberjack Bowl. "Afterwards we were amazed," said Weishaupt. "It was really exciting! It did something to you—it was fun, not really work. And we began to look forward to it each year."

By 1978, the race had definitely become a year-round operation. A lot had been learned in the short history and it was all put to work. The operation flowed very smoothly with regular meetings months before the race.

Costs were escalating, as well. For the first time officials put a serious effort into finding sponsorship for the Birkebeiner. The race had outgrown the financial capability of NorTur, which had sponsored the race in 1976 and 1977. In January, officials announced a new sponsorship with Silva Ski Company, a small company in itself but backed by its parent of several years, Johnson Wax Associates.

OO was rapidly becoming **the** spectators' gathering spot on the course for a glimpse of skiers striding through the midway point of the Birkebeiner.

Johnson Wax Company President Sam Johnson, who owned a considerable amount of property near Telemark, was a friend of Wise and other Birkebeiner officials. It was a natural combination for a new sponsorship.

One of the major interests in Silva, as a sponsor, was the media coverage of the race. Even by 1978, nearly a hundred stations and publications were covering the race in person and literally hundreds of others were detailing it over the air and in print. National news carried film of the impressive mass start and photographs were flashed around the world on the news wires.

Without question, the Birkebeiner was the most visible ski event in North America!

During Birkebeiner Week the elite foreign racers became the central attractions of photographers outside the Lodge. They amazed onlookers as they, very nonchalantly, skied from Telemark to Seeley in a quick hour-and-a-half training run. And they added that international flavor that was to become so much a part of the race in years to come.

By Birkebeiner day, everyone was expecting an incredible race—but no one could have dreamed how incredible it would actually be.

As hundreds of skiers converged on Telemark Friday evening, snow began to fall. Grooming crews were anxious but their anxiety was quickly squelched. There was little question about what had to be done. It was apparent from the start that they were in for some all-night grooming.

Through the night snow continued to fall—a half foot blanketing the woods and covering the neat tracks that had been meticulously laid on the 15-foot-wide trail earlier that day. The groomers did their best but still racers would face some slow going out on the course.

That morning, vehicles flowed rapidly into Telemark, the new traffic patterns working perfectly. Not all went so well with the buses, though. The 8 a.m. buses from Hayward were delayed in bringing their charges to the start—some arriving as much as 15 to 20 minutes late!

Tom Allar, who would later become chief of race, was in charge of buses for the first year in 1978. A year earlier, only about 300 skiers had taken the buses the morning of the race. Based on the expected increase in the race, officials were counting on around 500 riders that morning and increased the number of available buses accordingly.

But after the traffic jams a year before, many more skiers decided to park in Hayward and ride up—in fact, *twice* as many as officials had expected!

"We had a heck of a morning," recalled Allar. "I remember frantically calling Spooner [Wisconsin where the local Jelco bus line was based] trying to get more buses."

Starting time moved closer and closer, with several hundred skiers still in Hayward waiting for buses. Haywardite Jim Ledvina, a stocky old man who had nearly 20 years of experience working for Telemark under his officials cap, was helping coordinate the buses in Hayward. Needless to say, the skiers were getting a little antsy. "Don't worry," he told them, "they'll hold the race for you!"

Monday after the race, at the annual critique meeting, Chief of Race Jerry Berard looked slyly over to Ledvina. Berard didn't have to say a word. His slick little grin let everyone know what he was up to. All Ledvina could do was turn several shades of red and say "Well, I had to tell them something."

As 9 a.m. approached officials paced nervously, hoping and praying that the skiers would stand fast on the line. There were no PA announcements of any kind as the start approached, only high tempo military music, capped off by the traditional Olympic theme.

At 9 a.m. sharp Berard gave the sign, the cannon blast went off, and 2,472 skiers headed up Valhalla. About 500 race officials and workers breathed a collective sigh of relief!

On top of Morgedal, a huge crowd of photographers were poised—one digging his wooden skis into the hill to keep from sliding down into the masses, which he eventually did.

Much to everyone's surprise, little-known Audun Endestad, a Norwegian who had been spending his winter at Telemark, led the pack up the hill. "Go Vestar," shouted someone from the crowd, obviously aware of Endestad's affiliation with the famous Norwegian club.

Volunteer groups from Hayward and Cable took over the food stations in 1978. Through 1981 one of the most popular sights was the Hayward Civic Club's mobile home food station just a few kilometers before the finish.

Stillwater, Minnesota, skier Kevin Brochman was a two-time Kortelopet champion, winning in 1978 and 1979.

Endestad had spent several winters in the states in the past. But his winter at Telemark in 1977-78 won him over to the American racers. If there was a sentimental favorite in the pack for Birkebeiner officials and racers who knew him, it was the "Duner."

Right behind Endestad going up the hill was the pack—a huge group that never broke up until well into the race. The heavy snow in the track slowed the racers considerably as most of them alternated the lead in a gentleman-like fashion, each of the leaders taking his turn busting through the powder in the track.

At 23 kilometers, the pack began to break up. The tough Europeans, who had raced many times against each other, picked up the pace and "got serious" as U.S. Ski Team racer Randy Kerr explained.

At 50 k's, Sweden's Sune Asph was in the lead, but soon Pauli Siitonen took over. Just seconds separated them as they headed across the lake. With nothing but flat lake to go, Kaelin finally broke ahead into the lead. Kaelin hadn't exactly won a lot of friends that morning as he held back letting the others break trail. But now, it was his race and he never faltered through the finish.

As they headed down the final hundred meters through Historyland, spectators couldn't believe their eyes. What a finish! Kaelin, Chiocchetti, Siitonen, Arvnes and Asph—literally crashing into the timing building about 50 feet past the line. The crowd was absolutely stunned for a few moments. Nothing like that had ever been seen before. In fact, even in the hotly-contested races of the Euroloppet, such a close finish was rare.

It was two-and-a-half minutes before the next skier came across the line. Endestad, who had led the pack up and over Morgedal, was seventh. He was a little anxious in those early days of his long-distance career—often charging out fast at the start. He was to have a great career ahead of himself.

Randy Kerr picked up the top American spot, finishing eighth in 3:14:32.12 and winning a trip to Norway. Less than a minute back was Sten Fjeldheim, then a collegiate racer at Northern Michigan University, who skied one of his best Birkebeiners ever, narrowly missing a chance to return to the land of his birth. Right behind him was Duncan McLean, also skiing one of his best races ever.

But one of the most stunning finishes of all came at 3:41:30.66, only 31 minutes after the first finisher, when 47-year-old Valborg Østberg, a Norwegian grandmother from Gjøvik, came striding easily across the line as the first woman.

It was a sight that few will ever forget—and a moment that was as happy as any in the long racing history of grandma Østberg. She stood high and

With just seconds between him and the pack, Alfred Kaelin comes crashing across the finish line, trying to snowplow before hitting photographers and the timing building straight ahead.

proud, on top of a picnic table in the makeshift awards area, grinning from ear to ear, or horn to horn—a Viking helmet perched on her head!

Back at County OO, a group of racers from the new Telemark Academy were whooping and hollering over their domination of the 26-kilometer Kortelopet. The Telemark Academy had been founded that season by Tony Wise and Peter Davis. Davis, a former Olympian and noted eastern coach, had assembled quite a crew of junior racers.

One of those racers, Kevin Brochman of Stillwater, Minnesota, took the race by nearly two minutes in 1:32:42.66. Terese Maznio of Cable, another Academy racer, led the women in 1:58:10.66. There were 578 skiers starting the Kortelopet with 576 finishing, according to race records.

In the Birkebeiner, Denise Green, a 25-year old Telemark Academy skier, won the Norwegian trip as top American woman. Mitch Mode, a popular skier from Rhinelander, Wisconsin, was the top citizen racer. Officials couldn't have hand-picked two more deserving skiers.

Green, who had a limited racing background that included two years at Northern Michigan University, was working in the Telemark Lodge laundry that winter. A trip to Norway and her international racing debut was a fitting climax before whe returned to her summer job with the U.S. Forest Service in Escanaba, Michigan.

Mode, 28, became an instant celebrity in his hometown of Rhinelander, which up until then had been more famous for its publicity-gathering hodag statue in town. The tall, bearded skier was sent off to Norway at a huge commemorative banquet in Rhinelander the week before he left for Scandinavia.

Nineteen seventy-eight was also my first year as a full-time Telemark employee. Although I had worked at several previous races as a photographer, it's a totally different perspective when you're completely involved in the event.

You feel a lot of emotions when you're a part of the Birkebeiner—not unlike those you feel as a part of the masses going up Valhalla. In the post-race *Birch Scroll* that year I tried to collect some of those feelings.

"Well, it's all over for another year. And what a race it was. American-Birkebeiner VI was about as exciting as you could possibly hope for.

"It's funny how in the weeks leading up to the race when the work for the Telemark staff and officials seems endless, everyone says to one another, 'Boy, I can't wait until it's over and things return to normal!'

Silva Ski President Gunnar Lewander smiles after finishing the Birkebeiner. Silva was the major race sponsor in 1978 and 1979.

Valborg Østberg acknowledges her amazing victory.

Seconds after Alfred Kaelin crossed the finish, Renzo Chiocchetti looks over his shoulder to check Pauli Sittonen and Bjørn Arvnes behind him.

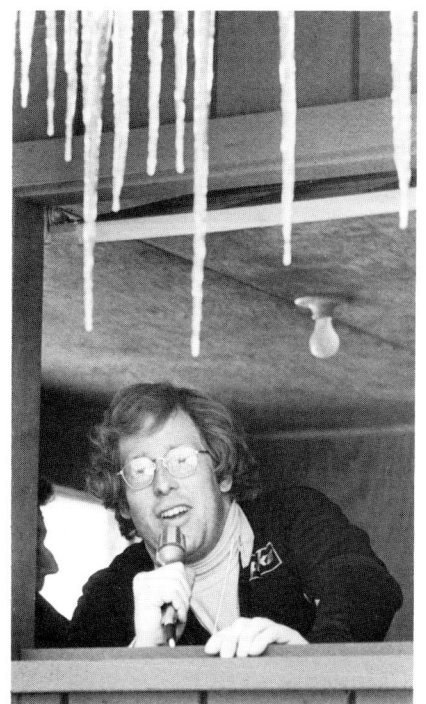

Race announcer Peter Graves was in his second year of calling the action at the Birkie. Graves, who had previously worked for both the U.S. Ski Team and Telemark, was then working as public relations director for NorTur, Inc.

"But as I stood on top of Morgedal Saturday morning, it was sad, in a way. Watching the mass slowly inching its way up the hill like a giant cloud moving across the sun, I could only think that it would be a whole year until I could be a part of the spectacle of the American-Birkebeiner again. And as racer after racer came across the finish line in Hayward, I just couldn't tear myself away to head back to Cable.

"But who were these racers? There was nobody special left to cross the line. It had taken these skiers hours longer than the champions to finish.

"But these weren't ordinary skiers. They were champions. American-Birkebeiner champions—each and every one of the 1701 finishers. Even George Entwhistle who finished dead last was a champion that day.

"There wasn't a laurel wreath awaiting them at the finish, but there was the satisfaction of finishing and having that medallion, heavy as it may have felt after 55 kilometers, displayed proudly around their necks.

"The American-Birkebeiner VI meant a lot to a lot of people. Here's just a few of our thoughts on the race—the memories that will have to last until Ameri-can Birkebeiner VII.

* * *

"Finding ways to communicate with skiers from other lands. And exchanging gifts with the foreign skiers—an exchange of pride between two nations.

* * *

"Introducing our foreign guests to various American customs, and seeing the excitement in their eyes at the Indian Pow Wow.

* * *

"Watching, with a sigh of relief, as the gun fired at exactly 9 a.m. and nearly 3,000 skiers inched their way up the hill.

* * *

"Seeing the tremendous look of accomplishment on the faces of Randy Kerr, Mitch Mode and especially Denise Green. Telemark couldn't have selected three finer people to represent us at the Norwegian Birkebeiner.

"Finally, the beaming smiles on the faces of skiers wearing their Birkebeiner and Kortelopet medals around the Lodge Saturday night. And for some reason, nobody even looked tired."

Kortelopet class winners line up in the Laukka Theatre of the Telemark Lodge for their awards presentation.

CHAPTER VII
Year Of The Mystery Champion

It was a bright, sunny morning in Hayward. Peter Graves and Harry Mayer took their places in the announcer's booth at the end of Main Street in Old Hayward. It was a new look for the Telemark/Silva Birkebeiner (the one-year name change was part of a sponsorship agreement with Silva Ski) finish, a much more "European" atmosphere than the wide open setting in Lumberjack Bowl, which had been used since 1976. Colorful long banners of the World Loppet nations, much like Wise had seen earlier that season at the Austrian Dolomitenlauf, lined the corridor into the finish.

    Graves was the veteran of the two-man announcing corps, having called the Birkebeiner since 1977. Mayer, a marketing director for the Black & Decker company in Vienna, Austria, was one of the announcers for the Dolomitenlauf and was at the Birkebeiner for the first time.

    Sound technician Dan Cinkowski, owner of Dancin Sound in Minneapolis, popped in a cassette and music filled the air. A few spectators had already begun to gather, but the racers were still far away—a tight battle was being waged by the 55-kilometer elite as they approached the midway point at OO. Meanwhile

A solid sea of skiers start up the hill.

A huge Telemark/Silva Birkebeiner welcome banner greeted skiers as they came through Cable.

at Telemark, Kortelopet skiers were just getting underway—their start coming at 10 a.m., an hour after the Birkebeiner cannon had been fired.

Reports were coming in to Hayward on Telemark's two-way FM radio communications network. The names of the leaders changed as fast as they were broadcast. The field was stocked with the World Loppet elite—gunning for points in the heated battle for the championship in the League's first season.

As race officials sped to Hayward following the start, their radios bristled with reports of the lead changes. Graves and Mayer relayed the information to the growing crowds in Hayward. "Our reports now have Canadian Ernie Lenne in the lead, taking over from American Fritz Koch," Graves shouted. Back and forth it went, Norway's Per Knotten and Bjørn Arvnes, Swede Matti Kuosko and Austrian Rudi Kapeller.

Those who thought the down-to-the-wire finish a year earlier would never be repeated were beginning to wonder. "Ladies and gentlemen, can I have your attention please," announced Harry Mayer in his continental English. "This is fantastic, we have 20 or 30 skiers all skiing together!"

At the early to mid-stages of the race, Mayer's estimate was definitely no exaggeration. In fact, even to Lake Hayward there were still ten skiers within seconds of each other. The track was hard and fast, and it seemed like no one was dropping back from the pace.

As the finish neared, on-course position reporters had problems just picking out bib numbers because of the pack. Numbers were frantically called into the announcer's booth as Graves, Mayer and I kept whipping through start lists trying to keep track.

"They're coming across Lake Hayward right now, ladies and gentleman," screamed Graves. "This is going to be an unbelievable finish! We thought we would never see a finish like this again after last year but we just might have another close one today."

As the clocked ticked to 11:47 a.m., they came into view on the edge of Lake Hayward. Seven skiers, all in a line, not quite as tightly packed as a year before. But it was still anybodys race as they sped off the lake onto Old Hayward's Main Street and skated to the finish.

"Here they come, ladies and gentlemen, look at this," announced Graves. "Who is that?" shouted Graves, covering his microphone. Mayer and I frantically went up and down our sheets, there was simply no number 578 on our start lists.

"Look at them skate," said Graves, "and here they come across the finish line. The champion of the Birkebeiner . . . who is it?" Graves asked us again, in vain. All we could do at that point was throw up our hands—we just didn't know. And as quickly as he had called the champion across the finish, Graves added, "and right behind him is Bjørn Arvnes."

At that point, none of us even saw the next five skiers that came across in the following 11 seconds. Nor, for that matter, did we catch the next half dozen after them. Most important of all, we had absolutely no idea who the skier was that had won!

Needless to say, it was one of the most embarrassing situations in the history of the Birkebeiner. The computer start lists that were given to us by Control Data did not include many late entries—that updated list would come later as last-minute entries were keyed into the computer. This had been known, so bib numbers of all elite racers were carefully noted in advance so the printout wouldn't even have to be used for the first few skiers.

Bib number 578 was issued late in the week to Arnt Haarstad, a shy 22-year-old lumberjack from Rennebu, Norway. He was a member of one of several Norwegian ski clubs that were competing in the race. And although his Norwegian credentials were impressive, race officials had been unaware of him until he came skating down Main Street, almost slipping and falling once, but coming across the finish line, not only in record time but also to become the youngest Birkebeiner champion ever.

The frustration of the missing name was but a small foreshadowing of the race itself. The most positive way to look at Birkebeiner VII was that race officials learned many things, and much was changed by the time Birkebeiner VIII was at hand.

While Haarstad was skating to a six second victory over 1977 champion Arvnes, elite Kortelopet racers were weaving their way through the slower Birkebeiner racers who had started an hour before them. Thousands of Birkebeiner and Kortelopet racers alike were ganged together in long lines at the major hills patiently, and impatiently, waiting as long as 20 to 30 minutes to take their turn at the top and, one-by-one, make their schusses, frequently waiting until the track was completely clear of fallen skiers. And for the length of the course, many entrants jammed onto the double-tracked trail with little opportunity to ski a steady pace until after OO.

Despite the horrendous conditions on the trail, over 90% of the skiers who started the two races completed the distance making all the cutoffs. The finishing rate for the Birkebeiner itself was just over 87%, only about one percentage point lower than the past two races (the Birkebeiner rate would hit 92% in both 1980 and 1982). Despite headlines and rumors about the 1,500 skiers who did not finish, only around 350 Birkebeiner racers and just a handful of Kortelopet skiers failed to complete the course.

A total of 3,948 skiers started the Birkebeiner and Kortelopet races, with 3,567 finishing.

Timewise, though, it was awful. The fact that record winning times were set in virtually all classes was of little consolation to the rank and file skiers. If you were normally a five hour skier or slower, you were in for a long afternoon.

When the public Birkebeiner Trail was initially proposed in 1975, it was designed to handle more than 2,000 skiers. Although there had been some indications that the trail was too narrow the previous year, race officials did not hear many complaints from racers.

Nearly 2,500 skiers had started together in Birkebeiner VI, which was one of the smoothest-running races in history. But in planning for this year's Birkebeiner, officials expected a big increase in numbers. (Looking at the increase in terms of percentage, however, the increase was one of the smallest gains since the inception of the race.) And after studying the effect of 2,500 skiers on the trail from the 1978 race, they decided to split the Birkebeiner and Kortelopet into two separate starts, an hour apart. Around 3,000 skiers were anticipated to start the Birkebeiner and another 1,100 the Kortelopet. With an hour between the two, it was felt that the trail could easily handle the race.

Another reason for moving the Kortelopet back, according to Chief of Race Jerry Berard, was to allow Kortelopet skiers to ski their own race, without having to be mixed in with the Birkebeiner racers. No one ever dreamed that the trail would not suffice in its present form.

Besides the change in the Kortelopet start, few other race changes were made. For the first time, though, women's classes and awards were equal to the men's. A wax tent was also erected near the start and more buses were added to the race day bus system.

The biggest race change was in the name. The small sponsorship of Silva Ski a year earlier had mushroomed into a major involvement by the LaPorte, Indiana, ski distributor. Through its Johnson Wax parent company, Silva became *the* major sponsor of the newly-named Telemark/Silva Birkebeiner.

There had been much discussion about the name change between Silva and Birkebeiner officials. Naturally, Birkebeiner officials were reluctant to change the name of the six-year old race, but sponsorship money was becoming more and more important and necessary. The race itself had reached the point where it was costing nearly $200,000. Entry fees, which ranged from $17 to $35, picked up only about 60% of the total race cost.

Working with Silva was a new experience for many race officials. As a Johnson Wax Associates company, Silva was definitely big business. Major boardroom strategies were drawn in the Racine, Wisconsin, offices of Johnson Wax and at the firm's Chicago public relations firm, Carl Byoir Associates, one of the world's three largest PR firms at the time.

Bill Deeter, director of public relations for Johnson Wax Associates, headed the Silva team, planning promotions and strategy carefully to provide Silva with the maximum amount of exposure from the largest ski event in the United States. Jim Herringer, of the same department, assisted. Media work was coordinated through Denis Quinlan, a vice president of the Byoir firm.

National television made a big mark on the race. Here Tom Jarriel, of the ABC Sunday Evening News, interviews Norwegian Bjørn Arvnes in a snowstorm just a day before the race.

Inside the Lodge, by the warmth of the fireplace, Eric Burns of NBC's Today show, talks with Silva Ski President Gunnar Lewander about nordic skiing and equipment. The national television coverage was coordinated by Silva's international public relations firm in New York and had a dramatic effect on bringing the word of the Birkebeiner to millions of Americans.

Meetings were held in Racine, Chicago and at Telemark to map out the promotion. A special T-shirt was developed by Silva, with proceeds going to the U.S. Ski Team. Sponsorship announcements were timed for maximum media exposure and to, hopefully, attract more lower-level sponsors to help defray race expenses.

The most significant contribution from the involvement of Silva was the nationwide publicity generated by working with an international public relations firm like Byoir. The New York office provided direct media contact that had been fruitless in the past—generating national television, radio and magazine coverage that was the best ever for the Birkebeiner, and would not be duplicated for years to come.

At the same time, though, officials of the Birkebeiner began to feel the constraints of working together on a race that, in the past, had been totally theirs. But the corporate wheels, while not as quick to act as Birkebeiner officials had been used to, were turning out more nationwide interest than had been seen before!

Nineteen seventy-nine also marked the first year for both the World Loppet League and Great American Ski Chase. The World Loppet had been chartered at a June, 1978 meeting in Uppsala, Sweden. It was already proving to be a strong race series and a finely-developed racing series.

Reservations from foreign tour groups were starting to come in even before the series had been finalized. Annelies Waneck, from Köpf-Sport-Riesen in Munich, was the first to make her plans. Waneck, who had been a leader in cross country ski travel in Europe since the early seventies, reserved 50 beds for the Birkebeiner on June 1.

Interest in expansion was already seen as Michael Brady, a noted ski author, suggested that the Australian Paddy Pallin race be included someday.

But while the World Loppet was moving full speed ahead, progress on the inception of the Great American Ski Chase was slow. The Ski Chase was a creation of the United States Ski Association's new marketing division. Under the direction of Harry Brown, a former USSA Eastern Division official, a series of six races in the United States was proposed for the new series.

In relation to the Birkebeiner, none of the proposed Chase races had developed to any great size. The initial races, as proposed by USSA, were the

Tony Wise presents Dolomitenlauf President Robert Steiner with an Indian headdress on the eve of the first World Loppet race in Lienz, Austria.

Some of the first Americans to ski in the World Loppet were Haywardites, from left, Bob Bergum, Darrell Thompson and Carol and Tom Duffy.

Birkebeiner; the Minnesota Ski Marathon in Bemidji; the Hennesey Cognac American Ski Marathon in Brandon, Vermont; the Fleischmann's Marathon in Waterville Valley, New Hampshire; the Ranch Creek Chase in Devil's Thumb, Colorado and the Mora Vasaloppet in Mora, Minnesota.

A preliminary meeting was set for Telemark on July 31, 1978. At that time, initial proposals were put down for the Great American Ski Series (later changed to Great American Ski Chase). Among the attendees at the first Marathon Commission Organizational Meeting were representatives from all sites, Brown, Marty Hall, Jock Soper and Howard Peterson from the USSA, John Lindstrom representing the FIS and Budd and Dolores Hagen of *Sports Spectrum* (later to be renamed *Skiweek*) magazine.

One of the big selling points used by USSA officials was the new USSA News Bureau that had been established at the USSA-Marketing offices in Brattleboro, Vermont. A computer had been purchased that would provide resulting services to races. Sites would be able to use the mass-purchasing powers of their numbers to get the best buys on bibs and other race supplies in the future. An equipment van with a sound system would go from site to site. All in all, it was one of the most complete plans ever laid out for skiing in America. The pricetag—$10,000 per race, not really a bad deal for the services.

But Wise and Birkebeiner officials were very reluctant about joining the Chase. Wise was concerned about the new series compromising his already-established World Loppet League. And he just wasn't sure the investment would gain the Birkebeiner enough in services or materials. But at the July meeting, Wise agreed to join. Later, he changed his mind.

USSA officials considered the Birkebeiner to be a key event in the series since it was the largest race and the focal point of cross country skiing at the time. So when Wise finally turned down membership in what was still known as the Great American Ski Series in early September, USSA officials were very disappointed. The Birkebeiner wasn't the only race to turn down the initial offer. The Mora Vasaloppet, which was on the verge of becoming one of America's great national races, just couldn't justify the expense.

Brown did his best to convince Wise, but to no avail. For Brown, who had spent a great deal of time putting together the race series package, it was extremely frustrating. There is no question that at the time the package proposed by USSA appeared outstanding. In the history of skiing in America, there has probably

A new event was initiated in 1979, the Special K Race. The short sprint, which consisted of several laps around the new finish area on Historyland's Old Hayward Main Street was run on Thursday afternoon and featured the top international elite skiers.

never been a finer overall working plan than the one Harry Brown put together for the Great American Ski Chase's inception. There just wasn't enough support from races to make it work at the time.

By October of 1978, USSA officials had pretty much given up hope on bringing the American Birkebeiner into the Great American Ski Chase. But in December, after much persuasion and dealing, Wise finally gave in, and the American Birkebeiner became a part of the Great American Ski Chase.

The World Loppet, on the other hand, had one big factor in its favor that the Chase did not enjoy. The World Loppet League consisted of already-established events—the *smallest* being Canada's 1,000-skier Riviere Rouge Race. Even in 1979, two-thirds of the World Loppet races were over 4,000 participants. Two were topping 10,000!

One of the League's early difficulties was getting the word out to skiers of the world. But the strength of the races themselves quickly led to a huge growth in interest.

If you had to pick one race to kick-off the new international series, that race would be the Austrian Dolomitenlauf. And that's exactly where the World Loppet League officially began—at 9 a.m. on January 21, 1979.

There were but a handful of Americans in Lienz that weekend, a far cry from the 40 to 50 United States skiers that would be starting each European race just a few years later.

Lienz, the home of the Dolomitenlauf, is located in the East Tyrol region of Austria, an hour or two east of Innsbruck. The city of 12,000 is everything you would expect from an Austrian village, right out of the storybooks—from Leiderhosen-clad Tyrolean bands to mountainside farms, towering alpine peaks and bells ringing in century-old church steeples.

Tony Wise and I arrived in Lienz around 6 p.m. Friday evening after an afternoon drive through the Italian Dolomites from Venice. It was nothing short of spectacular. Along the route we passed through Cortina d'Ampezzo, site of the 1956 Winter Olympics. To the west, over two rugged mountain passes, were the valleys of Fiemme and Fasse—where a week later over 5,000 skiers would slosh through the slush and rain in Italy's Marcialonga.

That evening in Lienz we experienced our first taste of what the World Loppet League had to offer. Race officials, local dignitaries and honored foreign

Austrian ice sculptor Engelbert Hattenberger made his debut in 1979. Tony Wise had met Engelbert at the Austrian Dolomitenlauf in January and invited him to Telemark. In the coming years, Engelbert became an important part of the pageantry of the Birkebeiner.

guests, such as ourselves, gathered at the Hotel Traube for the traditional pre-race dinner, compliments of the honorable Burgermeister Hubert Huber, mayor of the city of Lienz.

The World Loppet League was indeed in its infancy at that point. Nevertheless, the Austrians were proud of their role as a World Loppet nation. Dolomitenlauf President Robert Steiner raised a toast to Tony Wise that evening, a toast that was joined in by representatives from the World Loppet nations gathered in Lienz—a toast that was to bind those nations even closer together in new-found friendship. Wise, in turn, presented Steiner with a colorful Indian war bonnet.

As the sun crept up and over the snow-covered peaks Saturday morning, city workers dumped load after load of snow on the city streets. Saturday shoppers scurried about in the Hauptplatz or city center, tip-toeing through the snow with their shopping bags.

A huge waxing tent was erected along the fence near the start.

Seconds after the cannon sounded, the masses began to spread out from the start of the Telemark/Silva Birkebeiner. An hour after the 2,994 Birkebeiner skiers departed, another 954 started in the Telemark Kortelopet.

Skiers filed in and out of the many ski shops, checking the prices on the racks of skis lining the sidewalk. Foto Baptist did a brisk business in film and postcards. Languages from all corners of the continent could be heard on almost every street corner.

In the middle of the Hauptplatz, right at the finish line, a spectacled gentleman with a furry hat was chipping away at a huge ice and snow figurine. With just his bare hands he sculpted and molded while skiers posed in front for pictures as he worked.

The man was Engelbert Hattenberger, a 58-year-old local master of metal work whose snow and ice figures were a very serious hobby. As he worked away on the finishing touches early that afternoon, Tony Wise stopped to talk. He had been compiling an endless list of ideas for the Birkebeiner and the ice figures were high on that list.

Hattenberger spoke virtually no English. But Wise's German was good enough to communicate and an afternoon meeting was setup in the nearby Hotel Traube with Luise Rubner, a local journalist. An invitation was extended to Hattenberger to visit America and to create a sculpture for the upcoming Birkebeiner.

The Austrian didn't know what to make of the invitation at first. He had never been to America. And despite the fact that his ice had been displayed all around central Europe, including the 1976 Olympics in Innsbruck, he considered the invitation to come to America quite an honor.

2,994 Birkebeiner starters move slowly from the start, up and over Morgedal. Little did they know that it would be the last time that the route over Mt. Telemark would be used.

The biggest problem for Hattenberger was time. He was a very hard-working craftsman and his metal work left him little spare time. But an invitation to come to America—that was too much to turn down. He accepted! Little did he know at the time that his work would become a focal point of the American-Birkebeiner in years to come.

That evening, under bright lights and brilliant stars, with trumpets echoing from high on the balconies lining the Hauptplatz, colorful long banners of nations were hoisted high and the World Loppet League was about to be born.

Sunday morning, about 2,500 skiers gathered in a huge field just outside of Lienz. Nearly a hundred Austrian soldiers stood tall and fast along the starting line, manning huge gates with Fischer banners that would be raised at the sound of the cannon at 9 a.m. Along the course, which follows a river through a very flat valley between two mountains, townspeople were preparing oranges and soup for the racers. In Nikolsdorf, near the 40-kilometer mark, a local Tyrolean band was tuning up its instruments.

It was strange to look over the starting list as 9 a.m. approached—so many unusual names! But glancing down the entry of elite racers we saw a few names that we did recognize. Bjørn Arvnes was there as was Albert Giger of Switzerland, who had been a part of the initial World Loppet League meeting at Telemark a year earlier. Most of the others, though, were mysterious names to us—names like Matti Kuosko, Rudi Kapeller and more. Little did we realize, at the time, how close we would become with these skiers in the years ahead.

At 9 a.m. the cannon echoed back and forth between the mountains, a helicopter buzzed overhead, and 2,500 skiers headed out in a spectacular sea of color—heading first for Tristach, five kilometers away, down the valley to Oberdrauburg, back to Nikolsdorf and Tristach again, before passing through Amlach and on to the finish line of the Dolomitenlauf in Lienz—60 kilometers from the start.

For the handful of Americans in the Dolomitenlauf, the race was even longer. Two of the Americans who started that day would complete 587 kilometers during the next two seasons to become among the first to earn the World Loppet League medallion.

At the finish line that afternoon, Kuosko outskated Soviet Ivan Garanin. Kuosko and other elite racers knew little about the World Loppet League

Sidestepping and herringboning, skiers head up Morgedal.

The thrills of Stormoen in the past became more spills in 1979. The downhill was the scene of crash after crash forcing race officials to finally eliminate the up and over of Mt. Telemark beginning in 1980.

One skier who did manage to handle Stormoen with relative ease was Judy Rabinowitz of the U.S. Ski Team.

at the time—it was a new concept for everyone. That would change considerably over the course of the season for Kuosko, who was to go on to win the elite championship that year and the next.

Later that evening, an hour or so after darkness had fallen over the city, thousands of skiers and townspeople gathered in the brightly-illuminated Hauptplatz. It was nine hours after the start, and skiers continued to trickle down the track to the finish. Then, slowly, the crowd began to chant, "Nichts mehr, nichts mehr," ("no more, no more") as the final skier approached the announcer's stand.

Harry Mayer, Jr., and his father, led the crowd in the chant and the Dolomitenlauf drew to a close. Earlier that afternoon, the young Harry Mayer had spoken to me in English over the public address system, urging me to come forward for an interview as a representative of America. He phrased my initial ques-

A three-skier pileup throws up a cloud of snow on the far side of Stormoen.

The scene of 954 skiers starting the Kortelopet seemed many times bigger than the Birkebeiner itself just a few years earlier.

tion first to the crowd in German, then translated to English for me and awaited my reply. Mustering what little I could of my college German seven years earlier, I answered back, not in English, but in German—much to the total surprise of both Mayer and the crowd. "Ladies and gentleman, I ask him in English and he replies in perfect German!" Harry exclaimed. Well, it wasn't quite perfect.

It was a little sad that evening—sad that the Dolomitenlauf had drawn to a close. To the staccato beat of the drums and high-pitched tone of trumpets, the flags that had been raised the day before were slowly lowered, until the next Dolomitenlauf.

Tony and I came back from Austria with a notebook full of ideas. There was plenty of work to do—both for the World Loppet and the Birkebeiner, now not much more than a month away.

Race week was a hub-bub of activity at Telemark. Hundreds of skiers admired the hard-working Engelbert Hattenberger in front of the Lodge. The thing that amazed them the most was that he worked with his bare hands. In fact, so many people began asking him questions that a sign was made: "My name is Engelbert Hattenberger. I do not speak English. No, my hands are not cold!"

Dan Danielson of Wayzata, Minnesota, grabs a cup of ERG from a young food station attendant at OO.

In an effort to spotlight the new era of the World Loppet League, a new event was held on Thursday, two days before the Birkebeiner. Late that afternoon, the top elite racers came down to the finish line for the first "Special K" race, which was to become a traditional opening rite of Birkebeiner weekend.

All of Hayward was encouraged to come to the new finish line on Main Street in Old Hayward to see the finest long-distance skiers in the world ski a one kilometer race. It would make Birkebeiner officials quite proud, a few years later, when a handful of the European World Loppet races added their own versions of the "Special K" race (despite obvious rumors to the contrary, Kellogg's has never been involved in sponsorship of this race!).

It was, indeed, an impressive field of racers. Matti Kuosko, who was leading the World Loppet, Arvnes, Swede Tommy Jonsson, Norway's Per Knotten, Italian Ulrico Kostner and more.

One of the biggest names on hand was Norwegian Magne Myrmo. Myrmo, who was reaching the end of his national team career in Norway, was one of the most noted ski racers in Norwegian history. Unfortunately, he never made it to the starting line for Birkebeiner VII. An illness kept him in bed during most of his stay—a not so unusual affliction of ski racers who have to mix long-distance travel with long-distance racing.

"Here you are sir," says this young food station worker at OO as he passes a cup of energy-restoring ERG to elite racer Phil Peck.

Friday afternoon the Birkebeiner was officially opened. The first opening ceremonies in the race's history drew a crowd of several hundred. Racers from around the world were introduced and the new World Loppet banner, brilliant yellow-gold with the shield of nations emblazoned in the middle, was unveiled.

As time ticked on that night, racers from around the nation and around the world converged on Telemark. Dr. E. Rutledge Gish, a friendly old doctor from Missouri, was slowly making his way to Telemark. Dr. Gish had taken up skiing just a few years earlier, traveling to Germany and the Georg Thoma Ski School. (Thoma was a very famous nordic combined skier in the sixties.) His worldwide exploits had also taken him to the glaciers of New Zealand.

Storms out of the Rockies delayed Gish's plane from St. Louis and his scheduled 7 p.m. arrival in Duluth became 10 p.m. Naturally, with just 11 hours before the start of the race and a two-hour drive ahead of him, his skis, boots and poles didn't arrive at all. A couple of women entrants on the flight were fortunate enough to have their skis, but not their clothing bags.

Being the gentleman that he was, Dr. Gish sent the women on to Telemark and volunteered to wait for the later flight. Sure enough, everything arrived by 1:15 a.m. Over ice-covered roads and with a light snow falling, he headed out in a rented Olds Cutlass for Telemark, arriving at 4:30 a.m., leaving the women's clothing at the Lodge and deciding to catch some sleep in the car rather than drive the 35 miles to his motel.

He braved the sub-zero cold wrapped in just about everything he had and caught a good hour and a half of sleep. Rising early, he warmed his feet up on the soft, warm carpet of the Lodge, put on his ski clothes in the Lodge Health Center, finished off a small bottle of North Central Airlines wine, ate an orange, an

Madison, Wisconsin, Police Chief David Couper literally throws a cup of ERG down his throat in the 1979 Telemark/Silva Birkebeiner.

apple and two granola bars, went for a short walk and headed off to the starting line—a true case of Birkebeiner Fever if there ever was one!

It was, indeed, a cold Saturday morning. It had dipped well below zero during the night, freezing the rain-softened track hard and fast. Temperature by racetime had warmed up considerably, but was still in the low to mid-teens. Slowly, skiers made their way to the starting line, which was setup similar to the year before with lines for international elite racers, 25% Club members, USSA classified competitors and, finally, the remainder of the Birkebeiner field. Kortelopet skiers would file into ranks after the Birkebeiner start.

Meanwhile, snowcats and snowmobiles rushed cameramen around the area. Bunk Kofal, a giant of a man from the local Namekagon Snow Groomers and Patrol snowmobile club, rounded up his charges and mapped out last minute planning at a group breakfast in the Laukka Theatre.

Minute-by-minute schedules had been drawn up to insure that the national media crews got every inch of footage or frames that they needed.

Network crews from NBC's Today Show and the ABC Sunday Evening News clamored for position alongside photographers from numerous national magazines. NBC's crew was worried about camera freeze-up on top of Morgedal. Someone from that crew still has my portable hair dryer I gave them at the last minute! All told, over a hundred media persons were on hand to record the largest ski event in North American history.

At the sound of the cannon, the race was on. The 2,994 Birkebeiner skiers pointed their skis up Valhalla and Morgedal. Behind them, 954 Kortelopet starters awaited their turn at the same ritual an hour later.

The icy snow on Stormoen made for plenty of early-race excitement—although not exactly the kind of excitement most of the racers had wanted. Marty Hall, who had to be talked into wearing a heavy helmet camera for NBC, staggered under its unstable weight. He was hoping that the shot coming down Stormoen from a racer's perspective would be worth it. A crew member grabbed it from him at the bottom, not wanting to tell him right then that the camera hadn't even started. He found out later, anyway!

The widened trail from Stormoen out to the open fields along the Cable-Union Airport quickly jammed with skiers. All along the trail, huge jam-ups

Nils Meland of Oshkosh, Wisconsin, who went on to become a ten-year Birkebeiner founder, grabs a cup of ERG as another skier crashes to the snow behind him. 1979 was the second year of participation by volunteer groups from Hayward and Cable at all food stations.

forced skiers to hold in line at the top of hills, waiting their turn to slide down the slick tracks. Some skiers tried walking through the woods but quickly found that to be even more difficult because of the deep snow.

As Haarstad crossed the finish line and was besieged by the television and newspaper crews, reports of the trail conditions filtered back to officials at Old Hayward. But there was little that could be done then. The fast track conditions that day, compared to a much slower course a year earlier, had indeed shown that the track was not up to handling 3,000 skiers.

Twenty-three minutes after Haarstad had finished, the news media was still gathered around him as the first woman, Judy Rabinowitz, came across the finish line. The young U.S. Ski Team racer, who would wed Audun Endestad a few years later, was the first American to win since Jana Hlavaty in 1976.

Kevin Brochman, of the Telemark Academy, won the Kortelopet for the second straight year. Wendy Brown, of Burnsville, Minnesota, won the women's race. Brochman's 1:30:38.05 stood as the best 27.5-kilometer time in the first ten years of the race, as was Wendy's 1:44:20.70.

As 1:15 p.m. neared, race officials prepared to pull the cutoff fence across the Birkebeiner track at OO. Several hundred skiers were still out on the course, including San Francisco racer Harry Cordellos.

Cordellos had been the subject of much media attention during the week. The 41-year-old Cordellos was a well-known athlete, having competed in literally hundreds of major running events. The Birkebeiner was the first major ski event in his career. The only thing that separated Harry Cordellos from the thousands of other Birkebeiners was the fact that he was blind!

Led by guide Einar Odden, a Norwegian student from the University of Wisconsin-River Falls, he decided to make the Birkebeiner his next challenge. Odden and Cordellos started 15 minutes late to stay out of the mass pack. At the two kilometer mark, Cordellos was beaming—having skied up and over Morgedal without falling. Odden was by his side the entire time, calling out "hill ahead, stay to your left, skier ahead" and other instructions.

Matti Kuosko of Sweden went on to win the World Loppet League title.

A new finish area was used at Hayward in 1979. In order to have the use of more permanent buildings, the finish was moved from Lumberjack Bowl to Main Street of Old Hayward in Historyland. Colorful banners and fencing lined the streets and skiers crossed one large finish line at the head of Main Street.

The bearded face of Roy Carlsted has been a familiar sight to any skiers who could keep up with the St. Paul racer.

No one really knew who he was at first, but Arnt Haarstad didn't let that bother him as he skied to victory and proudly paraded in front of the crowd with the laurel wreath around his neck. Haarstad, just 22, became the youngest champion in history. Sadly, a problem with exercise-induced asthma put a damper on the young Norwegian's career for a few years.

Five hours later, after waiting in line time and time again at hills he easily handled, Harry and Einar reached OO, only to find a fence across the trail. "We're both disappointed about the outcome of the race," he said later, "but for the most part, we look back on it as a positive experience. We had a lot of fun meeting people, and I particularly enjoyed the challenge of skiing on such a difficult course. I'll be back next year. I not only want to be the first blind skier to complete the race, I also want to end up with a pretty good finishing time."

Fifty-seven-year old William Grainger of Prince George, British Columbia was about an hour or so ahead of Cordellos. Grainger was an enthusiastic skier. He had skied several other long-distance races that season and had been looking forward to the Birkebeiner for quite some time. His big goal was also to have a Birkebeiner medallion around his neck that evening.

It was not to be. He had made it past the OO cutoff before the fence had been drawn across the trail and was about four kilometers past the midway point when he was stricken with a heart attack.

Within minutes, a nurse and EMT personnel were on the scene. A few minutes later, Dr. John Ragan, a physician from Minneapolis who was skiing the race, happened on the scene. Cardio pulmonary rescucitation (CPR) was carried out from the moment the first crews arrived, just three minutes after he collapsed. Dr. Ragan assisted in efforts to revive the stricken skier.

Ironically, portable defibrillators (medical equipment that uses electrical impulses to initiate heartbeat in heart attack victims) had been added to the first aid crew equipment just that year. One of the defibrillator units was immediately dispatched to the scene, but not even that was of help.

While first aid efforts continued, he was rushed to the Hayward Area Memorial Hospital where he was pronounced dead of a heart attack.

Skiers continued to stream in by the hundreds in Hayward when announcer Peter Graves put out an announcement to locate Grainger's wife Joan.

One of the many emotions that Joan Grainger experienced that night was one of sadness for her husband, who would never receive the medal he had come to race for and win.

That night there were tears in many eyes and sadness in many hearts as Birkebeiners observed a moment of silence at the awards banquet. The medal that Bill Grainger did not receive was presented posthumously in his honor, the medal later mailed to his widow. A large floral wreath of roses was sent, on behalf of all Birkebeiners, to the family.

A year later, on the eve of Birkebeiner VIII, Joan Grainger reflected in a letter of how much cross country skiing had meant to her husband, expressing her thanks to all Birkebeiners for their support and best wishes for a successful Birkebeiner, 1980.

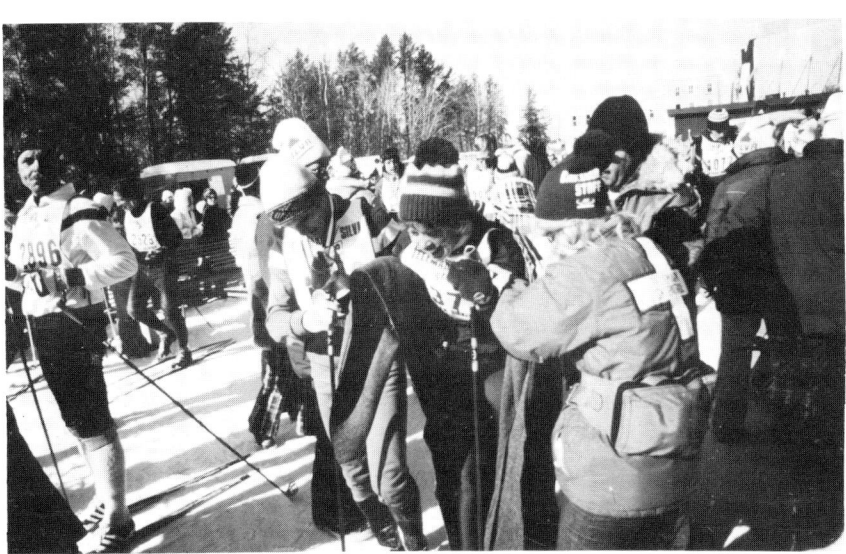

First aid worker Ree Primley helps a skier at the finish line.

Even before the final medallion had been draped around the neck of Carl Stoner, the trailsweeper for 1979, Birkebeiner officials were hard at work planning improvements for the next race. There was little question that the changes would have to be dramatic—in many areas. The Birkebeiner had outgrown yet another era, and was about to reach its full maturity.

Within 72 hours, Wise was in front of the Sawyer County Forestry Committee with plans for widening the 15-foot-wide trail to 30 feet. Substantial changes by Telemark in the start, plus the widening, would mean a trail that would accommodate as many as 12,000 skiers.

A survey of area banks indicated that the race was bringing well over a million dollars into the region of northwestern Wisconsin on race weekend alone. In an economically depressed area where one of the biggest industries is a short three-month summer tourist season, an event like the Birkebeiner is of extreme importance to the many communities involved. The committee gave their support and, once again, the search for funding was underway.

Major changes in the start were made, including completely eliminating the climb over Mt. Telemark. The climb up had become a trademark of the race, and many racers were very critical of eliminating it. But the downhill on Stormoen was becoming more dangerous than could be tolerated. Unfortunately, there was no way up without going down!

The Kortelopet was to be moved to Friday, a move that was discussed at great length by race officials. (Fortunately, the eventual trail widening and start changes were such a success that it was never necessary to go to that Friday start.)

It was a frantic spring for race officials who had double duty. First, there were apologies and procedures to take care of from the race just completed. High on that list was awarding Kortelopet medals to Birkebeiner skiers who missed the OO cutoff because of trail crowding. Second, major plans had to be outlined for 1980. All of this, including race results, had to be prepared for the spring edition of the *Birch Scroll*.

But the major change was the trail itself. That spring, the Sawyer and Bayfield County boards put their final stamp of approval on the new trail plan. In May, approval was received to submit the proposal to the Upper Great Lakes Regional Commission for possible funding of the public portion of the trail.

American Bob Treadwell was jubilant about finishing tenth, took top U.S. honors, winning a trip to Norway.

Robert Gibbs from Minneapolis catches his breath at the end of the Birkie.

Ice and snow hangs from the beard of Tom Rutlin of Madison, Wisconsin.

Frost on a beard and a medal around your neck became a symbol of victory for many.

Carl Stoner of Chicago rests his arm on his bronzed broom after finishing dead last in the Telemark/Silva Birkebeiner.

In mid-May, the *Birch Scroll*, with complete plans for 1980 and appropriate apologies and explanations for 1979, was published, and was generally well-received by the thousands of skiers who had raced that February.

Amidst the frustration of the Telemark/Silva Birkebeiner in 1979, though, was a continuing camaraderie between skiers. The Birkebeiners are a curious breed. They are very vocal, to be sure, but much of that is because they have such an attachment to the sport and to the Birkebeiner itself.

Rolf Kjaernsli, a professor from Lillehammer, Norway, who wrote the history of the Norwegian Birkebeiner-Rennet from its origin in 1932 to 1972 (with a supplement detailing 1973-1981), was on hand for his first American Birkebeiner in 1979. He knew nothing specific about the American race in years past, but had been one of those who had strongly supported better ties between the two races in the early days of the American race.

At the awards ceremony following the Telemark/Silva Birkebeiner, Kjaernsli presented Tony Wise and the Birkebeiner with replica of the two original Birkebeiners and summed up, very well, the spirit of the Birkebeiners.

"You are now the bearers of a great tradition. As you know, the Birkebeiner story goes back to more than 400 years before the landing of the pilgrim fathers at Cape Cod, Massachusetts.

"As it happened, the eighteen-month-old Prince Haakon, who was carried across the mountains, became king, and under him Norway had peace and a heyday in the Middle Ages.

"However, the great thing is that the Birkebeiners made a ski trail, which became a challenge to skiers and to organizers of skiing events.

"Skiing in different parts of the world has given me a vision of the ski trail, a lonely trail crossing the wilderness, finally uniting people and communities. Being a Norwegian I like to imagine that many of these trails started in Telemark, Norway. It may be hard to visualize a ski trail across the Atlantic, but can't we see it in the wake of the Viking ships, thus conquering the New World and eventually making skiing into a great sport on this continent.

"I would like you to know that we in the Old Country are impressed with the way you have taken care of that trail, with what you have achieved over here. I am grateful for your generosity in inviting me over to experience and be part of all this. I congratulate you upon your well-prepared trails, your efficient and friendly organization, and the wonderful weather you laid on for us.

"Good luck for the future—and thank you."

Judy Rabinowitz smiles as Tony Wise presents her with the Skade Trophy—women's champion in the Birkebeiner. Rabinowitz was the only American citizen to win the title from 1977 through the tenth running in 1982.

CHAPTER VIII
A Trail For The Future

It was shortly past 1 p.m., Saturday, February 23, 1980. An hour and a half earlier, a smiling Norwegian forester named Per Knotten had set a race record that will probably never be broken in winning American Birkebeiner VIII.

The hub-bub of news photographers clicking away at the elite champions and the tangle of video cables as the television crews clamored for a few words with the top American woman Jennifer Caldwell, who had broken a hand earlier in the race, was just subsiding. The phones were buzzing as results were rushed to the news wire services to be spread around the globe.

Out on Lake Hayward, 45-year-old Carol Duffy of Hayward sprinted like she had never sprinted before. Since the inception of the Birkebeiner, Carol had always been one of the top citizen women. She had won the short women's race in its first year and has always been near the top of her Birkebeiner class.

But this was a special day for Carol. Skiers like her usually talk about knocking a few minutes off their personal best. On that day, Carol knocked a whole hour off her previous best Birkebeiner as she finished the last of 587 very grueling kilometers to become one of the very first to finish the original nine races of the World Loppet League.

4,374 skiers—Birkebeiner and Kortelopet combined—made American Birkebeiner VIII the biggest starting field at that time.

Former U.S. coach Marty Hall checks final trail work on the huge widening project with his detailed course map. Telemark Academy Director Peter Davis (right) looks on.

As Old Hayward came into view her legs kept pushing—harder and harder. From deep inside, her arms and shoulders reached and tugged as she double-poled down the track—passing skier after skier as the colorful banners of the World Loppet nations on Historyland's Main Street seemed to melt into a blur.

And, as she sailed underneath the finish banner, the long, hard trek seemed all worthwhile. The disappointment with her opening race a year before in Austria, the drenching downpour and sea of mud at the Marcialonga, being forced to ski a preliminary 85-kilometer Vasaloppet just two days after completing the 75-kilometer Finlandia just because she was a woman, and the struggle of climbing and climbing in Norway with a 12-pound pack—suddenly, it all came back, but in a flash of victory.

She had finished the Birkebeiner in a remarkable 4:06:38:50. Two minutes behind was her husband Tom. Together, they had conquered the World Loppet League and stood proudly together amidst hugs and tears from a quorum of their 11 children who were there to cheer them. Spring bouquets of flowers in hand, they had never stood prouder!

But Carol and Tom Duffy were but a pair of many of the "Heroes of Telemark," as the *Birch Scroll* labeled them that spring. Birkebeiner VIII had been dubbed the "Citizen's Olympics"—in keeping with the spirit of the Lake Placid Olympic Games, nearing their conclusion a thousand miles to the east—as 4,387 Birkebeiners took off from Telemark that morning.

If there was ever a Birkebeiner with more than its share of citizen heroes, this was the one. Six skiers, including four Americans and a pair of Swedes, completed the World Loppet League series that day. On his second try, blind skier Harry Cordellos finally made it and 77-year-old Tommaso Defrancesco, his smile never leaving his face, became the oldest skier ever to complete the Birkebeiner. He, too, would finish the World Loppet two years later at the age of 79!

There had never been a better year to promote the Citizen's Olympics. Tony Wise's dream of an international ski series for citizen skiers had matured in only its second season. Because of scheduling, this was the first year that anyone could complete all nine races. And because of the way most of those leading the pursuit for the gold medallion arranged their schedules, the American Birkebeiner was destined to be the site of the first finishers.

However, an international crisis of sorts was brewing thanks to the weatherman. This was Canada's year to experience problems because of the lack of snow. The scheduled February 3 Riviere Rouge Race near Montreal simply could not be held and was postponed to March 2.

But the postponement wasn't that simple. Much like what would happen a year later with the Birkebeiner, some concessions were requested by European racers who were unable to rearrange their travel itineraries at such a late date. To accommodate them, a substitute race was provided on Wednesday, February 5, in Morin Heights, Quebec, north of Montreal.

Snow conditions were better in Morin Heights, where the first World Masters Championships were being held. A 30-kilometer race was held as part of that event, which was as close as officials could come to duplicating the 55-kilometer Riviere Rouge distance. A handful of Europeans, mainly Swedes, took part. A number of West Germans, who had planned to make the trip, decided instead to wait for the postponed Riviere Rouge Race itself.

The decision to approve the new site was one of the most critical thus far in the three-year term of Wise as secretary general of the World Loppet League. Wise had just returned from the Italian Marcialonga where he sensed some disfavor from a number of League representatives.

Wise's liberal manner of storming ahead was not well understood by many of the typically more conservative Europeans. "It was very, very important to me that the World Loppet hang on to the original ideals for which it was established," said Wise. "Although the Europeans were very much in favor of the World Loppet concept, there had always been some disfavor about having to come over to North America. The European citizen skiers that had made their plans to come to the Riviere Rouge Race had to be taken care of. It was a decision that had to be made quickly and I just hoped, at the time, that the decision I made to honor the 30-kilometer race was in the best interest of the World Loppet. In retrospect, I still believe that it was."

A unique tree-shearer was used to quickly fell trees up to 15-inches in diameter. The machine simply grabbed the small trees, sliced them and neatly set them along the trail. The entire widening project took only two months.

One of the skiers taking part in the shortened race that February was Gunnar Sarring of Sweden. (At the Birkebeiner, officials also thought that Swede Lennart Håkansson had taken part.) The Duffy's, along with Americans Steve Fossett of Chicago and Robert Vangene of Minneapolis, had completed the Riviere Rouge the year before so their plans of finishing the World Loppet at Telemark were not jeopardized. West Germans Heinrich Popp, Friedrich Hartmann and Eckehard Wille all opted to wait for the postponed race on March 2, not wanting to accept what they felt was a compromised Canadian race. (Håkansson also opted to wait but, in the confusion, was ultimately awarded his World Loppet medallion before he actually completed the Riviere Rouge.)

On the day of the Birkebeiner, all five (plus, in effect, Håkansson) would complete the World Loppet. Wise was about to find out that the prestige of a low-numbered medallion was more strongly sought than even he had originally thought.

The first across the finish line that afternoon, much as expected, was Sarring. The 38-year-old Swede was an excellent skier and was always one of the top citizen skiers in World Loppet events. He finished in 3:21:38.40.

But the next finisher was a big surprise. Carol Duffy probably skied the best race of her life, beating everyone else to become the second World Loppet finisher across the line. She was followed two minutes later by husband Tom. Vangene, 56, was next in at 4:26:38.10. After him were Håkansson, 65, a retired SAS airlines employee in 4:40:45.30; and finally Fossett, a commodities broker who had become somewhat celebrated a year earlier when he flew overseas every weekend to race, finishing in 5:12:47.20.

Fosset was the type of person who loves a challenge. He hadn't done much skiing before tackling the World Loppet, but it certainly wasn't the first time he had undertaken such an adventure. Among his accomplishments were climbing the Matterhorn and swimming the Hellespont and Bosporus. He even swam around Alcatraz once and was also an avid marathon runner.

The Duffys were promoted most often by World Loppet officials because of their attachment to the Birkebeiner itself and the unusual fact that they were parents of 11 children (although it wasn't until more than a year afterwards that Carol Duffy began getting the acclaim she so much deserved). Fossett's escapades in life made him a central publicity figure also.

Vangene hadn't attracted as much initial publicity himself. The Minneapolis skier took up the sport in the early seventies, competed in the Birkebeiner since 1975, and had become quite involved with biathlon, a natural outgrowth of his tremendous interest in marksmanship. In fact, Vangene had been working as a biathlon official at the Lake Placid Olympic Games until just a day before the Birkie.

A few weeks earlier at the König Ludwig Lauf, he demonstrated the type of skier he was by skiing an extra ten kilometers to make it an even 100. "I had always wanted to do a 100-kilometer day and figured this was the best chance," he said. So after he finished the 90-kilometer race, and despite hitting the wall severely at 74 kilometers, he kept right on skiing.

Trail crews cut fallen timber near the Phipps Firelane intersection as work continues on widening the Birkebeiner Trail.

Carbo-loading began to be looked upon with more and more significance each year. In 1980, the Creamette's Company began its traditional Friday evening spaghetti buffets.

Thousands of racer packets hang from hooks in the Red Arrow Room of the Telemark Lodge, site of race registration.

The traditional Friday evening waxing clinic began in 1978 as a fundraiser for the Telemark Academy. The clinic continued in 1980 with Canadian Darrell Frank, who was coaching the academy skiers that year, providing expertise, along with Swix Wax officials. After the closing of the academy following the 1980 season, Swix continued to provide the annual clinic.

John "Buffalo Bill" Benson put his horse team and sleigh to work hauling skiers from the outer parking lots to the Lodge and the start.

"Bob Vangene always gives that extra effort!" said a friend, Dr. Irv Lerner of Minneapolis, at the awards ceremony Saturday evening. Dr. Lerner, his wife, and a group of Vangene's closest friends from Minneapolis made a special presentation to him that night—an engraved sheet of brass with the names, dates and distances of each and every race!

But there was trouble that evening, as well. Six gold World Loppet medallions were lined up for presentation. Each was numbered on the back. The medallions would be presented to the finishers in the order they came across the finish line. A serious situation arose when several of the finishers questioned if the 30-kilometer substitute race used by Sarring should count. Should Gunnar Sarring be declared the first World Loppet finisher or was it really Carol Duffy?

"It was an unfortunate incident," recalled Wise. "It was a situation where I could have given in to Carol because of my affection for the family. But I had to consider all facets of the problem in an impersonal manner. It was a shame that the Riviere Rouge wasn't held on schedule. Then there would have been no problems. As it was, I had to be fair to nine countries and I just hoped that I was."

Several of the skiers did not feel Sarring should qualify because he did not ski the real Riviere Rouge Race. In fact, he did not even ski near the proper distance. But a decision had already been made weeks earlier to accept that race because of the last-minute change.

After much discussion with the Duffys, the Swedes and other World Loppet finishers, Wise put together a compromise. Carol Duffy would receive medallion number one and Gunnar Sarring would receive number zero.

But many skiers weren't concerned about a nine-race international schedule; they worried about getting through Birkebeiner VIII. The severe trail crowding in 1979 had upset numerous skiers and race officials were hopeful that their quick action to insure future improvements would be evident to all concerned.

The number of entries for Birkebeiner VIII did not increase much from the previous year. In fact, it was the smallest percentage increase since the race's beginning.

The major project of the year was widening the public Birkebeiner Trail. Unlike the original construction, which took nearly two years from planning in 1975 through construction in 1976, the widening in the summer of 1979 went much quicker.

Ironically, despite the crowding on the trail in 1979, a number of skiers wrote that they did not want the trail to be widened, fearing it would destroy the in-

Bruce West (rear), of West's Hayward Dairy, and his son Brett fill bucket after bucket with ERG.

Hundreds of skiers congregate around the waxing tent near the starting line.

With the start just minutes away, skiers put a few finishing touches on their wax. By 1980, wooden skis were quite rare.

tegrity of the scenic trail. Some actually claimed later that it did, but most were ecstatic about the new trail and how well it blended into the northern Wisconsin forest.

The concept of the widened trail was born just hours after the 1979 race, when Wise announced at the awards banquet that work would begin immediately to alleviate the problems, suggesting that widening the trail might be the answer.

Planning began in earnest the very next week when Wise made an initial appearance before Sawyer Country officials to lay the groundwork. To show the race's effect on the entire region, deposit totals were checked in Hayward, Cable and Drummond banks for the Birkebeiner weekend. The survey found that deposits were up over $1-million compared to a normal weekend.

"We had always felt that the race had a very large economic impact on the area," said Wise. "Now we had proof!"

In early April, the Sawyer County Conservation Committee forwarded a resolution to the Sawyer County Board regarding support of the proposal to widen the trail. That resolution was quickly passed and work began to find funding. The response of the Upper Great Lakes Regional Commission (UGLRC) was extremely favorable. The UGLRC considered the project one of their most successful ever in terms of economic impact on a region. County officials sought supplemental funding of $60,000 through UGLRC, with an additional $14,000 basic federal grant-in-aid from LAWCON (Land and Water Conservation), which had also been involved in the original project, and $18,000 in county funds.

Wisconsin Department of Natural Resources officials had overseen the original construction for LAWCON but rejected the new plan indicating that the period of LAWCON funding had expired and the suggested improvements (widening) were not necessary for normal use of the trail.

But the UGLRC was still in favor of providing funding, so on May 31 the Sawyer County Conservation Committee forwarded another resolution to the County Board to allot an additional $12,000 to replace the LAWCON funding, which had been anticipated. That resolution passed and in late June a final application was made to UGLRC for $60,000 in funding, in addition to $30,000 in county funds.

Meanwhile, efforts were renewed to bring Bayfield County into the fold. In the original project in 1976, Bayfield County gave an easement to Wise to use about five kilometers of the proposed trail that would pass through Bayfield County Forest. No funds were requested from Bayfield at that time and a one kilometer segment was paid for by Telemark, connecting to a town road. In 1979, how-

Thousands of skiers head for the starting gates in 1980.

ever Birkebeiner officials gained the support of Bayfield County to participate with $4,000 in funding for the portion of the widened trail on its land.

The original plan in 1976 had the Bayfield County portion of the trail connecting to the Telemark trail system at what was then about the 10-kilometer point in the Birkebeiner and running out to the Bayfield/Sawyer county line, about five kilometers away. From 1977 through 1979, the course ran out on the Telemark trails to around the 10-kilometer mark and connected instead to existing town roads and then to the trail itself.

Now, with the support of Bayfield County, the trail could finally be constructed as planned. The one kilometer segment that Birkebeiner officials had

In consideration of safety, the up and down over Mt. Telemark was eliminated beginning in 1980. Instead, skiers went partway up the flat bottom section of Valhalla and Morgedal. The jog underneath the chairlift did pose somewhat of a bottleneck, but the new start greatly reduced the number of injuries that had been suffered on Stormoen.

The newly-widened trail allowed skiers to spread out quicker than in recent years and avoided the nerve-racking back-ups of 1979.

1980 was Audun Endestad's year as he tied for the title in the Great American Ski Chase with Jan Bjørkheim.

cut in 1976 was widened to 30 feet, and the remaining section in the Bayfield County Forest was finally constructed, 30 feet wide.

(Following completion of the new segment through Bayfield County, actual kilometer marks were redone to reflect changes in the start and about the first 15 kilometers of the race. A very accurate survey was undertaken the summer of 1980, after it was determined that the 1980 race had been only 52 kilometers. The newly cut section in the Bayfield County Forest ran from the 6.5-kilometer point to the Timber Trail Road intersection at 10.5-kilometers. The trail intersected the Bayfield/Sawyer county line at 11.5-kilometers. Distances were again changed when the course was reversed in 1982.)

As the summer quickly passed, it seemed like once again the trail might fall victim to government bureaucracy. Finally, on August 3, approval was received from the UGLRC. Only three days later bids were opened and approved by the Sawyer County Board. Bob Thomson of Exeland, Wisconsin, who had worked on several segments of the original construction project, was awarded the bid for the majority of the trail. Work was to begin the first of September.

With less than three months to finish the job, Thomson brought in a unique tree shearer which utilized a vise-like device to grip trees up to 15 inches in diameter and sheer them off just above the base, setting them down alongside the trail. Bulldozers then finished the clearing, carefully smoothing the trail to avoid erosion. Marty Hall, who had helped lay out the original trail in 1976, supervised much of the project, working much more closely this time with the crews to insure that the trail kept its character.

"The trail crews have done a superb job," said Hall late in October, as work was nearing an end. "I can't believe how well they've retained the integrity of the trail. The new trail lets you see much further down the track and there's less of a feeling of enclosure. It gives you a much better look at the surrounding scenery.

"What's really amazing is that the trail did keep all its little undulations and dips, despite being twice as wide!"

Snow came early that season, hampering crews who were reaching the end of their work. On October 22 and 23, over seven inches fell on parts of the trail. One person who will never forget the snow was Telemark Cross Country Manager Harold Treland, who was awakened from sleep early that morning to be out on the trail just after sunrise for publicity photos. The next day, a photograph of Treland skiing on the newly-widened Birkebeiner Trail appeared in newspapers from coast-to-coast.

The trail itself wasn't the only change, though. After years of thrills and spills on Stormoen, the up and over Telemark was eliminated from the start. Skiers would be directed partway up Valhalla, across the lower section of Valhalla and Morgedal, then down and across what was then the Exhibition Slope (renamed Jerry Berard Run in December 1980), and out behind the Lodge. At that point, skiers would use the 50-foot wide Nordmor Road to a trail along the east-west airport runway, connecting to a power line which would lead to the new Birkebeiner Trail. All in all, it gave skiers a 50-foot wide trail for about the first eight kilometers of the race (later resurveying would indicate that it was to about the seven kilometer mark).

With construction well underway, registration personnel were literally bombarded with race applications. A record 279 were received on one day alone in early October! Although that record was to be nearly tripled within just a year, the total put entrants several hundred above the previous year just a few months into the registration period. With a fee schedule that ranged from $20 to $50, skiers were beginning to take advantage of lower fees for early registration.

Promotion of the race had become centered around the *Birch Scroll*. The first edition had been published in 1974, promoting American-Birkebeiner III. By 1979-80, the *Birch Scroll* had become the backbone of the race. It was the one way in which race officials could reach skiers with information and to encourage new skiers to enter the race.

The newspaper, which was published in fall, late-January and again in the spring, was mailed to around 5,000 former Birkebeiner finishers and about 7,000 other skiers. Those numbers would grow even larger in the coming years.

Race advertising had been used for several years. Ads appeared in both of the two major cross country publications, *Nordic Skiing* and *Nordic World*, along with regional publications such as *Skiweek* (or *Sports Spectrum* as it was known for a time). But the prime medium for promotion was still the *Birch Scroll*.

A professional graphics firm was contracted to produce advertising materials for 1980. After much discussion, it was decided to use an enlarged birch bark legging, to symbolize the race, along with an inset photo of the historic rescue of the Norwegian baby prince. Barbara and Patrick Redmond Design of Minneapolis designed and produced the ad, which ran in major cross country publications. A similar poster had also been planned, but instead, because of cost considerations, a colored rendition of the rescue of the child prince was designed by local artist Lyle Nelson. Nelson, a native of nearby Solon Springs, Wisconsin, was a veteran Hollywood set designer. He had been working at the Lodge on a number of projects and was pressed into service to design the poster for 1980.

Posters had become a tradition of the race since Fran Howard's trail map poster the year before.

Race officials were without a major sponsor in 1980. Silva Ski had dropped out of its sponsorship role following the 1979 race. It was a tremendous financial blow to the race organization, but one that Wise felt had to be taken. "We had a very good relationship with Silva," said Wise, "but we reached a point where we felt that we would have to give up too much of the race to them in return for their investment. We didn't feel we could compromise the race in that way."

Telemark Academy skier James "Mac" Read, of Marine on St. Croix, Minnesota, was first across the finish line in the Kortelopet.

OO chief Bob Murdock directs a beaming Kris Storm, Burnsville, Minnesota, across the finish line after her victory in the Kortelopet.

Flags are flying as skier after skier comes into the Kortelopet finish.

With dusty snow clinging to his knickers and sweater, Harland Hesselberg of Deforest, Wisconsin, comes across the Kortelopet finish.

Although there was no single major sponsor, a number of companies became involved in the race in 1980 in other ways. Several ski shops, including Sitzmark and Ski Haus in St. Paul, Morrie Mages Sports in Chicago, Petrie's Sports in Madison, Wisconsin, and Haugen's Sport & Cycle near Milwaukee all became "Official Birkebeiner Ski Shops."

The select ski shops were promoted as sites where skiers could obtain registration materials and special information about the race. In January, special newsletters were sent to each shop detailing race information that would appear in the Birch Scroll several weeks later.

Woolrich, in conjunction with 3M, manufacturers of Thinsulate, donated parkas to race officials. The Creamette Company became the "Official Pasta of the Birkebeiner" with the first pre-race spaghetti feed. Stokely Van Kamp contributed Gatorade, while General Mills supplied 25,000 Nature Valley Granola Bars. River Bend California oranges were provided for food stations through Super Valu stores. While there was not a major race sponsor, contributions by companies such as these allowed race officials to get by without major financial support, other than entry fees.

Computer services had been purchased the past three seasons from Control Data in the Twin Cities. Race officials had become increasingly disappointed with the service and cost and began to look into other systems for 1980. Through the help of Minneapolis ski promoter Skip Sponsel, Minnesota Micro Systems (MMS) was contracted for computer services for Birkebeiner VIII.

MMS had developed special programming, which fit quite well into the needs of the Birkebeiner. Less than two months prior to the race, arrangements were completed for MMS to handle its timing and results.

The unique aspect about the MMS system was that it was a totally on-site system. The company utliized Vector Graphic micro computers, small computers that were similar, although much more sophisticated, to the popular small home computers that began hitting the market about that time.

In the past, when Control Data was used, there was only a computer terminal and output unit at the race. The computer itself was located back in Minneapolis. All instructions and operations were accomplished by feeding the signal between the terminal, computer and outputter through a phone line. The system had worked relatively well, with skiers even able to pickup time slips with rank and 25% Club indicators at the Historyland Depot.

While that method of computer operation certainly had not become outmoded, there were certain advantages to having complete control over the system right at the site. Technology had progressed to the point where the on-site micro computer could handle a much greater volume of work than even a much bigger computer could just a few years earlier.

There were disadvantages, too, which were very evident to race officials that year. The first micro system was somewhat slow due to limited storage capability. This, however, was rectified by 1981. There were also problems, as might be expected, just because it was the first year for the programming.

But officials were very pleased with the overall result of using the new system. "It was much easier dealing with a group that was more sensitive to our special needs," said Wise.

Officials in all areas began to realize the complexity of providing accurate times and results. It seemed like every time someone turned around there was another small item which had to be taken care of. In 1979, for instance, officials had not considered the idea of separate finishing chutes. But because of the huge backups on the trail, skiers were also terribly bunched as they crossed the single finish line, often making it nearly impossible for timing crews to accurately pick out each finisher.

By 1980, that had changed. Three finishing chutes on each side of the timing building easily accommodated the thousands of skiers. Each chute was timed separately with times and bib numbers typed into the computer. The computer then collated all of the times together to produce the final results.

Probably the most crucial point in the timing of the 1980 race came in the first hour of the race when MMS officials, who were just arriving at the Hayward finish line, found that a leaky roof was about to wreak total havoc with the sensitive micro computers. The roof was quickly patched!

The Kortelopet, meanwhile, was not yet to make its computer debut. Times in the shorter race, which consisted of about a thousand skiers, were done by hand, much as in the Birkebeiner of the past. Times were matched with bibs at the OO finish area, and relayed up to Telemark using a telecopier, a device that transmits pages of data to a receiving unit over a phone line.

At Telemark, workers then took each transmitted page of data and fed them into the Telemark Lodge's new IBM OS-6 information processor, which was normally used as an office word processor. The OS-6 was not capable of actual calculation, but it could sort in order of time. That was certainly sufficient to handle the basic results requirements of the Kortelopet. (It wasn't until 1982 that the shorter race finally became totally computerized.)

Nineteen eighty also marked a significant change in race leadership. Jerry Berard, who had been chief of race since 1976, had resigned from Telemark that fall. In his place, Tony Wise took over the key leadership himself. He was assisted at the start by Don Plante of Hayward, who had been hired in November.

The expertise in actually running the race itself came from Marty Hall and Harry Brown. Both Hall and Brown had been involved with the USSA in organizing the new Great American Ski Chase a year earlier. Hall had worked very closely with Telemark in the past few years on a variety of projects in addition to the trail widening. At the time, Hall was also still involved with the Chase.

Marty had become even closer to Telemark before being abruptly dismissed as head coach for the U.S. Ski Team following the 1978 season. Hall then began freelancing as a cross country consultant, working on a host of projects.

Brown, on the other hand, had resigned from his USSA-Marketing position that fall. He still worked closely with Hall, however, and the two of them provided the technical assistance that was needed to coordinate the ever-growing Birkebeiner.

By 1980, race officials had a great pride in the Birkebeiner. There was intense disappointment a year before when the race had not gone smoothly. But officials were ecstatic about the changes in advance of Birkebeiner VIII and eager to show skiers how well they could respond.

Letters from skiers like Doug Riske, a five-year Birkebeiner veteran at the time and a 2:29 marathoner, brought a special feeling of pride to everyone on the Birkebeiner staff. "With the Birkebeiner being touted as the Boston Marathon of X-C skiing, people are putting the shoe on the wrong foot. Boston's organization, rather, should strive to merit the accolade—the Birkebeiner of marathon running. Your people are tops!"

Nineteen eighty saw a tremendous increase in volunteer support, as well. With two races under their belts, the volunteer crews at the food stations were getting more and more in tune with cross country ski racing. Working the Birkebeiner had become something that most groups looked forward to for an entire year. To solicit even more support several volunteer meetings were held in Hayward and at Telemark. The main purpose of the meetings was to find persons in the community who might not have ties with a specific civic organization, but were still interested in helping.

The 1980 race would be a very special Birkebeiner, workers were told. The spirit of the Lake Placid Olympic Games brought a new feeling about skiing to the American people. In a way, the American Birkebeiner would be on a world stage alongside Lake Placid as the Citizens Olympics.

Ten days before the Birkebeiner, a torch was lit in a small outdoor stadium just outside of Lake Placid, New York. The eyes of the world were focused on this tiny town and the 1980 Winter Olympic Games.

The Birkebeiner was well represented that day. Tony Wise was in Lake Placid as a guest of the U.S. Ski Team. Jerry Berard, although no longer actively working on the Birkebeiner, was chief of electric timing for cross country. Harold Treland was his chief of start. Lars Kindem, who had acted as the Birkebeiner's first official technical delegate in 1976 and again in 1977, was chief of timing. Peter Graves, the "Voice of the Birkebeiner," was now the voice of ABC Sports' cross country coverage team. And I served as a press assistant in cross country. There was a lot for all of us to learn at Lake Placid. In terms of the race operation at Lake Placid, you couldn't have asked for a more professionally-run operation! The best experts in the country had been assembled to make the races

It was an all-Norwegian victory stand with Per Knotten first, Arnt Haarstad second and Jan Bjørkheim third. It was Bjørkheim's first Birkebeiner after being named an All America selection four years straight at the University of Utah.

Norwegian Gry Oftedal holds her skis high after winning her first long distance race ever! Anna Bjørgan was second, followed by American Jennifer Caldwell. It was a tough race for Caldwell, who fell and broke her hand at 17 kilometers but continued to ski.

Swede Lennart Håkansson was one of six skiers to be awarded World Loppet medallions after the 1980 Birkebeiner. He later became the first skier ever to complete all ten World Loppet events, including the French Transjurassienne which was not a part of the series until 1981.

go like clockwork. The overall organization of logistics, however, did not go nearly as smoothly. Coordination of lodging, access, bussing and other areas did not impress those of us who were working there.

In both the good and bad, however, we learned a lot. From the opening ceremonies to the cross country scoreboard; from handling the media to bussing, we took back literally hundreds of ideas, many of which were incorporated into the Birkebeiner that very next week.

Wise returned after three days at Lake Placid. I came home 48 hours later—just five days before the Birkebeiner. The next few days became the incredibly hectic time that everyone in the Birkebeiner organization has come to know and love. Last minute preparations, developing new ideas and trying to cover every possible angle filled every second of every day.

Saturday morning, it all came together. Outside the service entrance to the Lodge, pancakes sizzled on a portable griddle. Lodge manager Dave Howard and head chef Andreas Sellner, dressed in whites and down coats, flipped flapjack after flapjack for hungry skiers in the Lodge's Namekagon Room, which had been turned into a breakfast buffet. By 7:30 a.m., the sound of high-tempoed military march music filled the air as thousands of skiers began decending upon the start. It was a new start that year, divided off into honor rows where skiers seeded themselves by their anticipated finish time. Special cards were stapled to bibs at registration to permit skier admittance into the start area of his choice. The honor system of starting was an idea that was bantered back and forth among officials. Originally after the 1979 race, officials had set the date of the 1980 Kortelopet for Friday, a day prior to the Birkebeiner. In the months before the race, however, it was apparent the new trail, and especially the new route out of the start and onto the course, was even better than anticipated. It was then decided to move the races back together again. The honor system of starting position was then devised to, hopefully, seed skiers into their respective ability classes right at the start.

In its first season, the honor system was an unqualified success. If anything, skiers appeared to be conservative about their seeding. In later years, the system would be less successful.

Carol and Tom Duffy embrace at the finish line after wrapping up their World Loppet experience—skiing 587 kilometers together in two years!

Swede Gunnar Sarring was the first World Loppet finisher across the line. He was later awarded medallion number 0.

As the clock ticked closer to 9 a.m., a crew of about 30 students from Bayport High School near Green Bay, Wisconsin, held wooden barriers to keep the skiers in line. The group was put together by Cheryl Treland, sister of Harold.

The students were a little nervous that first year, wondering just what would happen when they would raise their barriers and stand firmly in place as over 4,000 skiers came screaming off the starting line—right at them!

Despite their apprehensions, the start went smoothly. And other than a few pinches on the rear suffered by some of the female students, there were no injuries and an incredible experience was gained!

The only near serious problem at the start was the fact that the crew manning the cannon forgot to remove the muzzle cover. And while a shell didn't go whizzing through the canvas, the canvas did take a short flight and the blast of the howitzer wasn't quite what it could have been!

It was sad, in a way, as the skiers headed up and across Valhalla and Morgedal, coming down between trees protected by hay bales and mattresses. A small crowd of spectators stood at the top of Morgedal surveying the scene below. For the four years previous, that mass of humanity had climbed and gritted up Mt. Telemark and come screaming down Stormoen. There was a little piece of the Birkebeiner missing in 1980 without the hill.

The stretch from the start to behind the Lodge went like clockwork. Out on the trail it was much of the same. There were some delays, of course, in the early going. But skiers were learning that it was part of the game—certainly a far cry better than a year earlier!

Near the eight kilometer mark, Phil Rasmussen, owner of The Lakewoods resort, checked the temperature in a huge vat of Gatorade. Dozens of station workers from the Great Divide Resort Association, the Cable Boy Scouts and Drummond High School AFS (American Field Service) Club began pouring the liquid into cups, as hundreds and hundreds of sliced River Bend oranges were spread on serving trays. It would be just minutes before the skiers would hit, and not much longer before they would all be gone.

At the Great Divide's second food station, near the 17-kilometer mark on the Seeley Fire Tower Road, Fred Gall helped unload over 7,000 cups in preparation for the work ahead. Several hundred gallons of Gatorade were warming, and even that wouldn't be enough. Not even 10 cases of oranges would feed the hungry skiers at the second station.

At OO, two complete food stations began to take shape. Roy Powers, from the Sunrise Resort on Round Lake, coordinated the effort for the Hayward Lakes Resort Association. Birkebeiner skiers passing through OO would keep his crews busy until after 1:30 p.m.

Next to the Hayward Lakes group were the Hayward Lions Club and Hayward Cub Scouts. Their Kortelopet finish line station would be busy until even later in the day, serving nearly 2,000 Nature Valley Granola bars in addition to over a hundred gallons of Gatorade.

The second half of the course is always the most critical for skiers. At 35 kilometers, Linda Plante, whose husband Don was working on the race staff, coordinated a crew from her Hayward High School Debate Team. Besides the food, caps and mittens were in big demand. In fact, one skier offered $100 for a warm, dry pair of socks. They were happily provided, at no cost!

One Italian came up to Hayward Scoutmaster Tony Kerner at the Boy Scouts' 41-kilometer station at Mosquito Brook Road and told him about the fried chicken and wine they served at the Marcialonga. And while chicken and wine were not available, donuts were and they became very popular by late in the race. Over 2,000 were served at the Boy Scouts' station alone.

By the 48-kilometer station, the last on the race course itself, the requests of racers were more exotic yet. Not wanting to disappoint one hungry skier who craved a piece of chocolate cake, the Hayward Civic Club happily provided some of their own from Allen Heinkel's motor home, which had become a familiar site over the past two seasons.

And while the Hayward Jaycees and Jaycettes served up oranges, Gatorade and granola bars at the finish, the Hayward Girl Scouts found out just how strong the blueberry soup was. "I think we should have some longer spoons

Austrian race announcer Harry Mayer made his second appearance at Telemark, this year handling the bulk of announcing chores as Peter Graves was away at the Lake Placid Olympic Games. Mayer worked with former local radio announcer Gary Wernlund.

Steve Fossett of Chicago points at his hard-earned ski stickers after completing his ninth and final World Loppet event at the Birkebeiner.

With frost on his beard, Jim Limbach, Fremont, Wisconsin, finishes American Birkebeiner VIII.

next year," said Mrs. Rhoda Poreda after the race. "The skiers took one look at our hands and thought we had squeezed the blueberries ourselves!"

On-course first aid continued to be one of the strongest areas of the Birkebeiner organization. This year there wasn't nearly as much work for the crew of 80 trained first aid personnel under the direction of Don Primley and Rick Anderson of Hayward. Forty-five skiers had required hospital treatment a year before, but only five made the trip in 1980!

Paramedics were on the crew in 1980, equipped with a defibrillator, as the year before, plus drug kits and procedures for obtaining off-site doctor's authorization as required by Wisconsin state law. Several Minnesota paramedics, who could not administer drugs under Wisconsin law, were on hand to assist in whatever way was necessary.

One of the most noteworthy additions to Primley and Anderson's crew was a staff of 20 National Ski Patrollers from Michigan, Minnesota and Wisconsin. It was the initial year for National Ski Patrol participation and the first of many to come.

To say it was a fast course in 1980 was an understatement! For the fourth straight year, a klister or skare base topped off with extra-blue or something close was the ticket. But in 1980, the icy speed of the tracks left spectators' mouths gaping at the fast finish.

Per Knotten set a torrid pace. As media crews filmed the skiers at the halfway point on OO, few took real heed of their watches. After the Birkebeiner leaders came through, it was only minutes before Telemark Academy skier James "Mac" Read, of Marine on St. Croix, Minnesota, won the Kortelopet in 1:17:15.14. Kris Storm, Burnsville, Minnesota, took the women's race in 1:25:17.63. It was an incredible pace!

Media staff members yelled and screamed at reporters and photographers to get back in their escorted vehicles to make it to Hayward in time. Listening to the live coverage on WRLS-FM and WHSM radio on the way to Hayward, it was evident that Haarstad's record of the year earlier would be butchered. Haarstad was in the running himself, trying to become the first skier to win two in a row. Pacing him was Per Knotten, another Norwegian who had begun to make real waves in the World Loppet League that year, winning the König Ludwig Lauf.

The thrill of victory!

Dozens of skiers await the presentation of their medallions or pins.

The international field in 1980 was not quite as good as had been hoped. Even until just days before the race, Finn Pauli Siitonen had been expected. Instead, he opted to ski his nation's own Finlandia. Sweden's Ola Hassis, who had won the Dolomitenlauf that year, also chose to stay in Europe despite an invitation to the Birkebeiner.

Although skiers competing for the World Loppet elite title had to ski in North America, the concept hadn't achieved the significance it would by 1981.

Matti Kuosko took great advantage of this situation in 1979 and 1980. Although he had been a top skier for years, he saw the World Loppet as an opportunity to gain real recognition. That he did, winning the series both years.

Out on the course it was a two-way battle. Knotten and Haarstad had moved out in front of Kuosko, Audun Endestad and Norwegian Jan Bjørkheim, a former four-time All America at the University of Utah.

On Highway 63, it was a race to Hayward for spectators and media. Press buses pulled up in front of Historyland with barely minutes to spare as photographers jostled for position in a pen in front of the timing booth.

Ron Meyer of Metabasis, a Madison, Wisconsin, film production company, stood ready and waiting at the finish. The remainder of his 20-person film crew were at points around the course. Meyer was producing a film for the Educational Communication Board in Madison for future showing on public broadcasting. He and partner Tim Ellestad, along with Dave Conyer and a crew from the Telecommunications studio at the University of Wisconsin-Stout in Menomonie, had worked for nearly a year on the project. They would eventually produce an excellent 30-minute feature which was shown dozens of times nationwide in the next few years.

One of the hottest shows on television in 1980 was a new program called *Real People*. *Real People* was on hand for the Birkebeiner, as was a *PM Magazine* crew from WCCO-TV in Minneapolis. Both of them were victims of the fast finish, having to duplicate tapes from very cooperative colleagues at another midwestern television station later that day, running the dupes from tape machine to tape machine right outside the Clark House at the finish line.

As the photographers who arrived in time secured their positions, Knotten and Haarstad came sprinting across the lake. Austrian Harry Mayer and local radio announcer Gary Wernlund called the action in the absence of Graves, who was still in Lake Placid.

There was no question about the winner this year. Knotten led Haarstad across the finish in 2:24:55.80 for a four second victory, but setting a mark that

David Jesh holds a can of beer after finally completing the Birkie in darkness to earn the title of trailsweeper for 1980.

77-year-old Tommas Defrancesco of Italy was the oldest competitor.

Per Knotten has an armful of trophies at the awards banquet Saturday evening.

World Loppet representatives, from left, Fritz Lang of Germany, Robert Steiner of Austria and Eugen Peter of Switzerland proudly wear their new cowboy hats.

Local favorite Gary Kramer of Cable won the men's citizens' trip to Norway.

will probably never be broken. Although the course is recognized today as only 52 kilometers, the time was still an incredible achievement!

Always the jokester, Knotten quipped after the race, "I even called to him [Haarstad] to come up and lead for awhile, but he was tired, he said! A different time and it could have been another guy to win. But today, it was my day."

It was the first Birkebeiner for Bjørkheim, who is without question one of the friendliest skiers ever to compete. Bjørkheim was third, just over a minute back from Knotten after leading for much of the early going. He had devoted his season to the Great American Ski Chase, which he eventually won in a close battle with Endestad.

Although Norwegian Birkebeiner women's champion Anna Bjørgan had been favored in the women's division, it was another 21-year-old Norwegian that stole the limelight. Gry Oftedal, a striking, blond racer from an Oslo suburb, broke the three-hour barrier in 2:53:48.20 to take first in her very first long-distance race ever, finishing 51st overall. (Ironically, Gry went back and won the 1981 Norwegian Birkebeiner and also the 1982 American Birkebeiner for a perfect three-for-three record in long-distance races.)

But another of the heroes of the Birkebeiner was yet to cross the finish line. Twenty-one-year-old Jennifer Caldwell, daughter of former U.S. Olympic coach John Caldwell, took a nasty fall at 17 kilometers. The fall broke her hand and left her bloodied and sore especially since she, as a habit, did not wear gloves in a race to keep her hands from sweating. Regardless, she pressed on, finishing just over two minutes behind Oftedal for third place in the women's race and 60th overall. A fiberglas cast allowed her to represent the American Birkebeiner at the Birkebeiner-Rennet just two weeks later.

Also representing the United States was Duncan McLean, who became the only skier in the history of the race to win both the citizens' trip (1976) and as top American elite skier (1980). Gary Kramer of Cable won the citizens' trip, which had been inadvertently announced as going to Duluth skier Tom Haas. Haas, who had won the trip in 1977, had initially been listed as the citizens' winner due to an oversight, but was a USSA classified competitor in 1980 and therefore not eligible.

Gabriele Andersen, a tough skier from Sun Valley, Idaho, won her second straight American citizen women's title. Andersen, who began skiing in 1977, was a native of Switzerland. She came to the United States in 1974 as a tourist, met her future husband, and settled down in the states. Her citizenship became final just a short time before she won the 1979 crown.

Amidst all of the heroes of the Birkebeiner the smiling face of 77-year-old Italian Tommaso Defancesco, as he crossed the finish line, is one scene that few of us will ever forget.

So very often, by 3 or 4 p.m., media crews have long since departed the finish line. Spectators are usually thinning out by this time, as well. The *PM Magazine* and *Real People* crews were still around, however, when at 3:53 p.m., blind skier Harry Cordellos crossed the finish line.

As I rushed from the media center to the awards area after seeing Harry come across, I couldn't help but think back a year-and-a-half earlier when Einar Odden called. He wanted to know what we could do to help a blind skier ski the Birkebeiner.

In retrospect, we weren't all that accommodating, at first. We agreed to assist the two with lodging but balked at allowing them to start early or to have any special concessions in the race. We did what we felt we could without compromising the rules of the event.

What Harry Cordellos accomplished on the tracks between Telemark and Hayward was his. In many ways he was no different than the thousands of other skiers on the track. His will to succeed brought him back a year later after just missing the cutoff at OO.

The *PM Magazine* feature, which aired nationwide a year later, captured the heroes of the Birkebeiner in many ways. But none were more heartfelt than Harry Cordellos' victory. Every inch of Harry Cordellos' tall body sensed the easing of a red, white and blue ribbon over his head and the weight of the Birkebeiner medallion on his chest, as Stan Knutson, the grandson of old Carl Hanson, made Harry's Birkebeiner championship complete.

Several hours later, just a handful of race officials remained. Jack Reed and Leon Wirth of the Telemark sales department paced around in the timing building, where they were patiently awaiting their final timing duties of the day. Out on the lake, the tiny light of a snowmobile weaved its way across the frozen ice.

The radio crackled as the ski patrol radioed in to the finish line. There was still a skier out on the course. Officials had kept a close watch on the final skiers. One reason was for the obvious safety reasons, but the other was for the Bronzed Broom Award. Since its inception in 1978, officials had become more and more worried about skiers "trying to win" the award for last place. Frankly, it was an easy honor to win. A rules interpretation left it to the discretion of the officials at the finish. The Bronzed Broom Award was not necessarily for the last place skier any longer, but for one of the final skiers who best typfied the spirit of the Birkebeiner.

In 1980, there was little judging necessary. David Jesh, Long Prairie, Minnesota, skiing his first Birkebeiner, was last by around four minutes without really trying. As he came across the finish line, ice in his beard and an Old Milwaukee in his pack, he threw up his arms in victory and proudly accepted the Birkebeiner medallion.

Each year virtually every race chief and worker is asked, "How can you work so long and so hard? Skiers like Harry Cordellos, Tommaso Defrancesco, Carol Duffy, Robert Vangene and thousands of others are why.

After the race, Jesh wrote a letter to Tony Wise. It's feelings like this that epitomize what the Birkebeiner really means to us.

"Four of us fellows from Minnesota came over and entered your Birkebeiner race and we are all very happy about it, but that is not why I am writing you, sir. I want to thank you for the spirit you gave me in particular.

"You have given time, money and maybe the better part of your life for the enjoyment of your fellow man. I hope you are rewarded a hundred fold for your efforts, here and after.

"I think the real champion of the race never put the skis on, and that being you, Mr. Wise. You have no idea how happy you made me, and I'm sure many other people this year and before. I salute you, Mr. Wise.

"Tell the Norwegian skiers about our 55 mile an hour speed limit."

Your last place finisher,
THE SWEEPER
Dave Jesh

"See you next year."

In a moment that brought tears to many skiers' eyes, Harry Cordellos accepted a special award from Tony Wise after the blind Cordellos finished the Birkebeiner on his second try.

Race official Dick Simono (left) presents Gabriele Andersen with her cup as the top citizen women.

CHAPTER IX
Sixty-Five Degrees And Sunny?

Tony Wise rode alongside Canadian Ski Marathon official Cor Westland, racing from point to point in Westland's Jeep. It was a cold, sunny, crisp February morning in southern Quebec. The Canadian Ski Marathon, the longest ski event in North America, was in its second day as skiers wound their way through the 160-kilometer wilderness course. I was winding up my own 26-kilometer portion of the marathon (skiers choose their own distances to ski) around mid-morning, meeting Wise and Westland near Lac Long, about a half-hour drive east of Ottawa.

The drive back to Ottawa that morning was filled with praise for the Marathon and the organization of the Riviere Rouge Race, held a week earlier. There, American Bill Koch had suffered a tough loss to Finn Pauli Siitonen, but at least there had been a race. A year earlier a frantic postponement of the Riviere Rouge had left the field scattered. Foreign diplomacy within the World Loppet was seriously tested as weather forced a substitute race, only 30-kilometers long, to be offered to Europeans who could not return for the rescheduled race. The Canadians were much relieved now, in 1981, to see snow blanketing the Quebec countryside.

Slowly the huge mass of skiers moved away from the start and the Norwegian American Birkebeiner was underway—even it if was two weeks late.

At Westland's Ottawa apartment, I called back to Telemark. "It's a beautiful day if it were May," Public Relations Assistant Karen Gibson told me. "I hate to say it, but it's getting pretty bad."

Winter had been slow arriving in 1980-81. The mid-December Gitchi Gami Games ski races at Telemark were nearly cancelled before a decision was made to create a drastically-modified course around the man-made-snow covered slopes of Mt. Telemark.

Early-January snowfall left the northwoods wintry and white, but a mid-January thaw turned that to slush. Continued mild weather wiped out every trail before an early-February blizzard restored hope and confidence to Birkebeiner officials. That confidence was buoyed by frigid temperatures going into mid-February. "Just to be safe, we built a mountain of man-made snow," said Chief of Race Tom Allar. "We had some excellent snowmaking weather. It would have taken a total disaster to stop the race, we felt."

From a helicopter huge tracks of mud can be seen on the Monday prior to the scheduled Birkebeiner. Conditions looked hopeful at the time, but the weather simply got worse by the minute.

The ninth American Birkebeiner was to be the biggest in history. Over 7,000 entries had been expected. Actual entries were on target for that goal much of the pre-season until poor snow victimized most of the nation.

A huge sponsorship by the Norwegian Ski Council, an association of eight American distributors of Norwegian ski products, brought a new look and a new name to the race: the Norwegian American Birkebeiner.

All in all, it was shaping up to be the most spectacular ski race in North American history. And in may respects, one of the most thrilling ski events in the world.

It was an ominous Friday, February 13, when Wise and I took off from Hayward enroute to Ottawa, Ontario, for the Canadian Ski Marathon and to make a Worldloppet presentation to an international recreation conference in the Canadian capital. Temperatures had been rising over the past two days but there was no hint of a serious problem.

Beneath the thin layer of white was more mud than race officials could deal with. This section just a few kilometers from the start was especially bad.

Flying at 4,000 feet to Minneapolis, however, we could actually see the warm front moving in from the southwest. It was awesome. We could literally see a line of heat moving across the sky. But we still never really felt anything was in jeopardy.

The report from Telemark that Sunday afternoon after the Marathon prompted a quick return for us. Still, plans for the race were in full progress. On the flight back, details for the elaborate opening ceremonies and huge Birkefest Saturday night were finalized.

But on the final leg of the flight, over the fields and forests of northern Wisconsin, it was becoming increasingly apparent that there were difficulties ahead for the race. There was hardly any snow to be found. I thought I would wake up Monday and everything would be fine. But it wasn't.

It had been a weekend of hope—hoping the weather would change, hoping for snow, hoping for cold, or just hoping for clouds to hide the sun. But there was no luck.

Monday, then, became a time of action. Somber race officials met at Telemark that morning and quickly hit the trail to survey its condition.

By 11 a.m. most of the officials were back. There was little to see outside. Maps were produced and ideas tossed back and forth as to the best way to accurately survey the situation.

Chief of Race Tom Allar took charge. There was no question that an alternate route was needed. One that, perhaps, had escaped the heated stare of the sun. Calls went out as far away as Madison to get a helicopter on the scene. Finally, a Bell Jet Ranger was dispatched from the Twin Cities.

By 2 p.m., the chopper was on location. Allar, Technical Advisor Marty Hall, Assistant Chief of Race Tim Dechant, photographer Ginny Peifer and I took to the sky. Officials saved themselves some aerial time by limiting their inspection to the first half of the course. It had already been determined that the race could not go all the way to Hayward. Lake Hayward was nearly under water and virtually all of the open fields in the last ten kilometers were barren of snow.

"It was a sad sight," said Allar, "but we felt we had a fighting chance. There were a lot of possibilities."

While cameras clicked away, documenting the dwindling base of snow, Dechant, Hall and Allar had the helicopter go back and forth—picking out trails on the map and hoping to find them as ribbons of white.

Officials were cautiously optimistic as they met in early evening, trying to pin down a legitimate course.

Local outdoorsman Andy Depta, a Telemark employee since 1947, suggested several little-known roads through the forest—sheltered enough to hopefully protect the snow.

After hours of laboring over maps, a course was drawn stretching from Telemark to OO and back. Some parts of the Birkebeiner Trail were used, especially on the first half. Some parts of the trail would be used twice, out and back. It totaled 45 to 50 kilometers. Would it work? Well, there was no alternative at this point, it had to.

But help was needed. First of all from the weatherman and secondly, a source of snow to spread on bare spots was essential. Quick calculations showed that the towering pile of man-made snow wouldn't be nearly enough to repair the course, which was rapidly turning brown. And the weatherman offer no help, either. Meanwhile, calls began to pour into the Telemark Lodge. "Is the race on?" "Yes," was the reply, "but the course will definitely have to be changed."

From the start, officials endeavored to avoid rumors. Nothing was to be given out except stated facts issued in regular dispatches from race officials. As of Monday, the race was on. It would not run to Hayward. But conditions were changing and skiers were urged to check back in a day.

Media were called and special news bulletins were sent across the nation. Ski shops were notified, as well, and soon the weather at Telemark was attracting national and international attention.

"If there was any gratification that entire week it was in the support and offers of assistance we received," Wise said. "Local businesses and individuals offered trucks, shovels, manpower and more. Total strangers called to see if there was anything at all they could do!"

Marty Hall was out early Tuesday, driving the back roads looking for snow, hoping to find a sheltered lake hidden from the persistent rays of the sun. He was back by mid-morning with little success.

Meanwhile, even the newly-proposed trail began to deteroriate badly. More alternatives were needed, and there weren't many to be found.

Race officials were ecstatic to finally have Bill Koch enter the Birkebeiner, but were disappointed not to see what he could do. Heat exhaustion took Koch out of the elite race after several strong laps.

Hall was soon back on the road, heading north with *Ski Racing* journalist Paul Robbins, hoping for better luck in the Hurley-Ironwood area 70 miles northeast of Telemark.

The Hurley (Wisconsin) Chamber of Commerce quickly offered help. They didn't have as much snow as usual in 1981, but they did have some. Hall even suggested racing in Hurley, but officials felt that it was not practical from a logistical standpoint. It would not have been the Birkebeiner which skiers had come to know. And although there was indeed snow in Hurley, hauling enough to the Cable area was simply impossible.

Back at Telemark, the search went on while crews continued patching areas of the trail in anticipation of Saturday's race. Conditions changed, literally, by the minute. And just as soon as snow was tossed on the trail from the woods, it seemed like another patch melted under the sun.

A 24-hour phone crew was organized with eight lines setup to handle calls. Thousands were received during the week.

Late Tuesday afternoon, as darkness began to settle, Allar and his crew put together one last-ditch course, similar to Monday's but not going all the way to OO. Instead, it would wind more to the east by Smith and Rock Lakes, east of the Telemark Road.

"It's going to work," said Dechant. "I think we're gonna be able to do it. But we need every shovel and able body in the area."

Don Dorak, executive director of the Hayward Chamber of Commerce, had been sitting by his phone for two days waiting for the call. So had dozens of others. Everyone was waiting to pitch in. Dorak quickly organized the entire city of Hayward—even though the race wouldn't even reach their city! Cable was organized as well with everyone possible mustered into service for a Wednesday morning "Save the Birkebeiner" operation.

Bulletins went out from WHSM radio and WRLS-FM in Hayward. Local school systems, while not specifically calling off school, agreed to allow students to help. Buses were organized for the morning rescue effort, box lunches were prepared and everything looked "go."

By midnight it was evident that the support was staggering. It appeared that at daybreak over 300 persons would be on hand to shovel snow from

Bruce Cranmer, like most skiers, had his racing suit unzipped to get as much cool air as possible as temperatures soared to near 65 degrees in the elite race on Friday.

Jean-Paul Pierrat sloshes through a puddle on his final lap in the grueling elite race held a day before the regularly-scheduled Birkebeiner, which had been postponed for two weeks. Pierrat had a big lead winning the race—somehow handling the heat and strenuous course with relative ease.

Sven-Åke Lundbäck needed the Birkie to keep up his battle for the World Loppet title, which he eventually won. He admitted that he had never skied a more difficult race after finishing third in the elite event.

Norwegian Marianne Hadler, then residing in Vermont, was smiling after her victory in the elite race but only after the intense pain of skiing up and down Mt. Telemark had subsided. Never had a championship been earned more.

the woods out onto the trail. But while the workers slept that night, the rains came. Not just sprinkles or freezing rain. Not just a simple shower. But torrents, pouring down on northern Wisconsin. The course never had a chance. The buses never left Hayward.

At 1 p.m. Wednesday, just three days before the scheduled race, a press conference was called at the Lodge. Tony Wise presented a statement that no one had ever thought would be considered. The Norwegian American Birkebeiner IX would be postponed until Saturday, March 7. A special race for elite skiers from abroad, foreign tour groups and other skiers from outside the midwest would be held on Saturday, February 21 on the man-made snow covering the Mt. Telemark downhill runs.

Instantly the news was flashed to the media. Within a matter of hours, most of the ski world heard the word. The widespread news coverage was amazing. I remember calling Bjørn Arvnes in *Norway* to tell him the news and he had already heard about it.

As was expected, the phones rang non-stop into the evening. Operators manned their stations around the clock. And while calls dropped off during the graveyard hours, over 40 calls were received in one strange 60-minute stretch between 3 and 4 a.m.

Skiers for the most part were extremely understanding. One couple even comtemplated rescheduling their honeymoon in the Bahamas. Some skiers were understandably disturbed about the changes in the race, but it was a situation totally out of human control.

"For those of us who worked year-round on the Birkebeiner it was an empty feeling," said Allar. "I know it was one of the saddest and most frustrating experiences any one of us has ever gone through, and I'm sure it was the saddest day in Tony Wise's life!"

No one thought things could get worse, but they did. Although more rain was not in the forecast, even warmer temperatures were. It was evident on Thursday that even Saturday's shortened races were in jeopardy. Changes were quickly made and bibs issued to eligible skiers—about 60 for the elite race and 120 for foreign competitors. Officials couldn't chance waiting until Saturday. The races were now set for Friday, February 20.

Abbreviated course maps were drawn and distributed to skiers. It would be a tough, demanding trail up and down, up and down, looping a six-kilometer course around Mt. Telemark.

After a day of near 50-degree temperatures Thursday, the worst thing that could happen was sub-freezing temperatures that night. And much in the pattern of the week, it got very cold Thursday night.

The six-kilometer loop soon became a mountain of ice. The Friday, 8 a.m. start was moved to 9 a.m. and then even later in hopes that the track would soften a bit. There was no way the skiers were going to risk their lives on the icy, steep and harrowing course.

By 11 a.m., the ice had begun to break. Clear, sunny skies and temperatures in the high 30's to low 40's greeted skiers at the start. The tiny starting field, reminiscent of the scene eight years earlier on Lake Hayward, gathered at the base of Valhalla. Photographers perched on top of the Morgedal lift building, awaiting the first of what would eventually be four 1981 Birkebeiner races.

As the clock ticked down to starting time, Sweden's Sven-Åke Lundbäck jumped off the line early, the rest followed, and the chase was underway. It was a surreal scene, this small pack of skiers winding their way up Mt. Telemark and then back down, weaving back and forth to make up distance and slow their descent down the faces of Morgedal and Valhalla.

From below one could barely make out the leaders—Bill Koch and Frenchman Jean-Paul Pierrat, in their blazing red Peugeot/Rossignol Team suits, and a pack of skiers hot on their trails.

For a lap or so it was really quite a race with a group of nearly a half-dozen skiers juggling the lead. But with temperatures soon pushing 65 degrees, it didn't last long. Koch, suffering from near heat exhaustion, pulled off after several laps into the eight-lap race. It was all Pierrat, the short, compact Frenchman didn't seem to mind the heat in the least.

Racing suits were soon zipped down from top to bottom. Hats and gloves were discarded. ERG was quickly consumed at food stations and one by one, skiers dropped from the heat. The temperatures were virtually unbearable. Sweat poured from skiers' bodies, caking in a huge, white salty mass on the fronts of their suits. Heads of hair were matted with moisture, and mouths gaped for more oxygen. Up and down they went, skiing across in front of the Colosseum, stopping at the west end for more wax, and then up and over the Jerry Berard slope. Behind the hill they climbed—up and up to the top of Mt. Telemark. It was only 1,750 feet above sea level at the top, but the 370-foot climb felt like climbing Mount Everest.

"I tell you, the only one thing that kept me going was knowing that the race would count, that I wouldn't miss a Birkebeiner," said Ironwood, Michigan, skier Duncan McLean, who had been in every Birkebeiner or Kortelopet since 1973.

U.S. Ski Team veteran Alison Owen, who was retiring from active competition following the race, tried to keep the pace but couldn't last. Up-and-coming marathoner Muffy Ritz of Wayzata, Minnesota, skied a strong race but couldn't quite keep up to Marianne Hadler of Norway. Hadler's husband, noted nordic author Michael Brady, was there to greet her as she collapsed into a deck chair outside the Colosseum.

Nearby, a sizeable crowd of spectators sipped on wine or beer and basked in the sunlight. Children played in the sand as skiers passed just feet away. After the week of disaster and misfortune, it was actually a very relaxing afternoon of racing—if you were on the sidelines.

Meanwhile on the course, Pierrat kept clicking off the kilometers. When he needed the extra little kick, he just reached one ski on top of the other to dab on a little more klister, which he had conveniently applied just ahead of his bindings on the top of each ski.

Three hours and nine minutes after he started, Pierrat skated easily across the finish line, snapped out of his bindings, held his skis high and took a long sip of champagne. Norwegian Jan Frode Bjørkheim was four minutes back; eventual World Loppet champion Sven-Åke Lundbäck another two minutes off in third.

In mid-afternoon Friday, around a hundred foreign citizen skiers started off on their version of the Norwegian American Birkebeiner—a 42 kilometer up and down course that took many into nightfall.

1973
Thirty-five skiers line up on Lumberjack Bowl for the first running of the Birkebeiner, Saturday, February 24. Race Chairman Bob Treland (with bullhorn on dock) gives the final instructions.

On a tiny logging road near Seeley, nineteen women and juniors get ready for their short version of the Birkebeiner. On the right is Duncan McLean who won the 22-kilometer race.

1974
Don Quinn had a slight lead over his brother David early in the race, although Dave went on to win American Birkebeiner II. Crowds eagerly await the first finishers in front of the old Telemark Base Chalet.

1976
Previous year's champion Chris Haines and new American citizen Jana Hlavaty pose in their bicentennial bibs.
1977
The black and yellow Norwegian ski suits dominated the starting field.

1977
American and Norwegian skiers strided side-by-side in American Birkebeiner V. Over 400 Norwegians took part.

Tightly-packed waves of skiers hit the wooded trail early in the race.

A group of Norwegians relax around a food station table at the Hayward finish line—not far from where the Birkebeiner began four years earlier.

1978
A group of skiers kick up snow along the trail in American Birkebeiner VI.
1979
As starting time approaches skiers begin to converge on the Telemark Lodge.

1979
It was a chilly morning as breath from the skiers indicates.
Like a sea of centipedes, thousands of skiers herringbone their way up Morgedal and Valhalla for the last time. A year later, the race would only skirt the lower portion of the hills.

1979
A skier hits the snow.
It's a close race as the leaders pass through a short downhill near the end of the wooded trail.

1979
The pack is very tight with the elite leaders skiing tip to tail as they exit the woods and begin the long loop of Lake Hayward that leads to the finish.

All afternoon, huge lines of skiers poured into the Old Hayward finish line during the Telemark/Silva Birkebeiner VIII—trail crowding didn't allow skiers to spread out as much as usual.

Zooming in on a Birkie finisher.
1980
Skiers congregate at the start; talking over their strategy and putting on those last few layers of wax.

1980
With spectators lining the fences, skiers break away at the sound of the cannon to begin American Birkebeiner VIII.

1980
Snow is falling as skiers come into the finish in Old Hayward.
Hundreds of medallions wait for their recipients at the Birkebeiner finish line.

1980
As the sun sets over Lake Hayward, two first aid snowmobiles light the way for Bronzed Broom winner David Jesh.
1981
Racers snowplow down a wide, steep downhill.

1982
A colorful hot air balloon soars overhead as thousands gather in front of the Telemark Colosseum for the opening ceremonies.

Since his first visit to America in 1979, ice sculptor Engelbert Hattenberger had always wanted to carve an Indian. He finally had his chance this year—a native American greeting a Norwegian Viking warrior. In addition, Tony Wise presented Engelbert with his own headdress; an honor reserved for the most important dignitaries.

1982
Skiers crowd around the wax benches prior to the start.

Just moments before the start, entrants in the largest ski event in North America wait anxiously for the firing of a skyrocket that will begin American Birkebeiner X.

1982
Hayward's Iowa Avenue was ablaze with color as nearly 6,000 skiers strided down the main street.

1982
After the luxury of more than a hundred tracks on Lake Hayward, skiers had to do a little funneling as they crossed Wheeler Road near the first food stop.

A massive display of fireworks brought Birkebeiner X to a close, as seen in this double-exposed photograph of the Telemark Lodge.

Antonio Cosulich (left) flew from Italy only to find the Birkebeiner postponed. Through his pleading officials decided to add a third race on Saturday. Couslich and Mora (Minnesota) Vasaloppet official Glen Johnstone skied through a driving rain to finish at dusk.

Bjørkheim, who admits to being fond of skiing hills, could only shake his head. "It was so tough out there today," he said. "And what was really hard is that I had lost track of my laps. I thought someone told me I had one lap to go but when I came through they said 'go one more.' I thought I was going to die."

Sven-Åke Lundbäck, one of the greatest skiers of all time, said it was the hardest race of his life! "Any other race I would have quit" he said, "but I desperately needed this race to qualify for the World Loppet championship."

Of more than 60 who started, only 30 survived. And it was truly a race of survival! As the elite skiers staggered in—some more than five hours after they started—over a hundred European citizen racers charged off on the same course from the middle of the Jerry Berard slope in front of the Colosseum, and Birkebeiner IX-B was underway.

"The biggest problem we had at this point was the impending darkness," said Allar. The citizen's version of the race was changed to only a seven-lap, 42-kilometer event—still proper marathon distance but shorter than the elite.

The European skiers handled the course with expertise, turning in very impressive performances. And as darkness began to fall, those left on the course were shuttled to a smaller loop and given revised lap figures to complete their 42-kilometers. Norwegian Per Lokas, who covered the 42 kilometers in 3:22:13.91, was the champion.

Spirits were higher in the Lodge that night. At least part of the Birkebeiner had been held. But a little piece of the hearts of everyone associated with the race was missing that night. There was no Swix waxing clinic that night, crowds didn't jam into registration, and the aroma of spaghetti sauce didn't wind its way through the Colosseum. All in all, it was a pretty quiet evening, certainly not the way it was supposed to be.

But the Birkebeiner weekend was not over yet. There were still more skiers who desperately wanted to race—skiers from around the nation and even from around the world who had arrived on Friday, unknowing of the troubles that had beset the race.

No one knew what to expect at the postponed Birkebeiner. From ground level, at first, it didn't appear to be a big group. But from the air, and as the skiers broke from the start, it was official—there really was a Birkebeiner in 1981. An estimated 3,400 skiers started the race, about half as many as might have started two weeks earlier.

Around 3 p.m., a gentleman walked into the Telemark Sales Office. Frances Wise, like most all race officials, was relaxing a bit now—happy that at least something had been run that weekend, and thankful, too, that it was all over for two weeks. But not quite.

"Please," pleaded Antonio Cosulich of Genova, Italy, "I must have a chance to race." "I almost fell out of my chair," said Frances. "Here was someone who had traveled by plane and bus for 3,000 kilometers just to race. We had to have another race!"

An emergency meeting was held to decide what to do. "There was no way we could turn them down," said Tony Wise of the last few skiers who wished to race. But the weather was not looking good. Rain was predicted for Saturday and it was only a question of how long it would hold off. So plans were made for one final race that weekend—Norwegian American Birkebeiner IX-C.

Saturday, February 21—planned as the day of the largest ski event in the history of North America. 7,000 skiers were to be on hand for the start. The only history made at all that day was that a ski race of any kind was held.

It didn't look good in the morning as skies turned gloomy. The six-kilometer course from a day earlier was gone, the heat taking its toll. All that was left was a 1.83-kilometer loop and it would take 23 laps to make an official marathon of 42 kilometers.

It was a dark, messy, awful day. That anyone even bothered to race was a real credit to them. Nineteen skiers made it through to the finish, and it actually materialized into the best championship battle of the weekend.

Brattleboro, Vermont, skier Hank Lange led most of the way but received a strong bid from Palm Springs, California, competitor Sam Simakis. But as each lap wore on, Simakis wore down. Lange increased his lead and finally crossed the finish line alone in 4:07:47.28—about nine minutes ahead of Simakis.

But the real struggle came over two hours later. Darkness was moving in. The small crowd of spectators had long since departed. And in the late afternoon the skies opened and rain began to fall. And it kept falling and falling. Only a

The skiers head through the trees between Morgedal and Jerry Berard, alongside the Telemark Colosseum and out onto the trail.

Skiers are strung out for the length of the trail as the race runs alongside the Cable-Union Airport and Namekagon River just a few kilometers from the start.

handful kept the vigil, including race announcers Peter Graves and Austrian Harry Mayer and *Skiweek* publisher Dolores Hagen.

In the pouring rain, skier after skier managed to cross the finish line. After what they had already gone through that day, no one cared to quit! Six hours into the race four skiers still remained on the course. Among them was Antonio Cosulich. Antonio won the hearts of those at the finish line. Another was Glen Johnstone, an official of Minnesota's Mora Vasaloppet ski race and a five-year veteran of the Birkebeiner.

With chants of "forza, forza" Harry Mayer cheered on the Italian each time he passed in front of the Colosseum. It was the only thing that kept him going. "Uno, due, uno, due," "one, two, one, two," Mayer chanted. And every time he passed a food station, interpreter Kathy Ramsted urged him on in Italian.

Six hours and 22 minutes into the race, Antonio Cosulich crossed the finish line. As proud as any Birkebeiner finisher has ever been as his medallion was draped around his neck. And a minute later, he was joined by Johnstone who was greeted with a big hug in the pouring rain by Dolores Hagen, who had braved the rain so that each and every skier had someone to welcome them across the line.

It wasn't the Birkebeiner IX that it had been planned to be. But in a way, for that small group of skiers who had the opportunity or misfortune to have to ski the rugged hill, it was a Birkebeiner experience that meant even more. The medallions earned by Cosulich, Johnstone and others in the sleet and rain took on a very special significance.

Even a year later, in all corners of the ski world, they were still talking about the hill, and what an accomplishment it was for those who conquered it.

That night, as what was to have been Birkebeiner weekend drew to a close, the rain turned to snow. And it snowed, and snowed, and snowed—as much as 18 to 20 inches on some parts of the trail. Suddenly, spirits were lifted and life started anew. There were two weeks to go, and nothing was going to stop the Birkebeiner now. One of the best things about the snow was that it was wet. When it accumulated on the ground it packed down like concrete. With a little grooming work that week, there was no way even warm temperatures would take out the snow.

Now officials had to start from scratch. The March 7 race was on, but how many skiers could be expected? Officials had absolutely no idea of what to plan for. It was decided to put together a phone survey. About 200 entrants were selected at random and called to find out if they would be coming on March 7. Officials came up with figures of around 60% who planned to make it. The actual count on March 7 was just under that.

1978 American citizen champion Mitch Mode gets some energy drink and course times from Karhu rep Mike Oliver at OO.

Dan Cronen of Lakeville, Minnesota, became the fourth straight Minnesota Kortelopet champion.

Robin Brown, Apple Valley, Minnesota, followed in the footsteps of sister Wendy and friend Kris Storm as Kortelopet champion.

A huge mailing was sent out to everyone entered in the race, plus ski shops and media around the nation. Word of the rescheduled Birkebeiner spread like wildfire.

Although a vast majority of skiers were understanding of the situation, a few did voice their opinions against it. Strangely, most skiers who complained seemed more disturbed about the race being postponed to a new date rather than cancelled outright.

"We have always maintained a no refund policy on the race," said Wise, "which is much the case with other events like ours. I wish there was more we could do but virtually all of the costs of a race are borne before the event itself. We just hoped that skiers would understand this and know that we would do everything in our power to make the race even better in the future." The original Birkebeiner script, complete with Friday's opening ceremonies, waxing clinics and more, went as planned. Thousands of skiers crowded the Creamette Spaghetti Buffet and Swix waxing clinic that evening.

Saturday, March 7 was an absolutely beautiful, sunny, brisk and welcoming day. Temperatures were looking to be in the high 20's or low 30's, although it actually got much warmer by the end of the day. The track was hard and icy at the start, but warmed with the race. It was definitely a klister day.

About 3,400 skiers, a similar number that had started the Birkebeiner two years previously, went into the starting gate and with the 9 a.m. cannon, were on their way to Hayward, hoping to finally complete Birkebeiner IX-D.

As the crowd of skiers passed across the bottom of Mt. Telemark an unusual silence prevaded the masses. It had been a somewhat strange morning already, with skiers slow to get into the start. On the line it didn't even look like more than a thousand skiers. But when they broke away, it looked more like four or five!

But the silence was almost deafening. There wasn't the usual jovial chit chat and shouting at the start, just the swish, swish, swish of skis on the snow.

"I think that skiers were out there that day just because they felt they had to," said Hayward's Carol Duffy. "It wasn't quite like the Birkebeiner usually is, it lacked that feeling at the start. But you skied along for the first few kilometers and then pretty soon it hit you. 'Hey, this is really the Birkebeiner and it's really happening.' And then you could just sense this change in everyone. Everyone came to life!" It was indeed the Birkebeiner. It was as real as ever and probably one of the smoothest-running and most enjoyable races ever to be skied.

U.S. Ski Team veteran Tim Caldwell of Putney, Vermont, who had been enjoying one of his best years ever, jumped off to the lead and was never seriously threatened. He crossed the finish line in 2:34:16.9. Bjørn Arvnes was three minutes back, while Green Bay, Wisconsin, skier Mark Ernst came in 13 minutes after Arvnes.

Bemidji State (Minnesota) University trainer Muriel Gilman was the top woman, finishing in 3:22:36.8—11 minutes ahead of Wendy Brown of Apple Valley, Minnesota. Muriel was exhausted at the finish, but not nearly as much as she would be a few weeks later in Norway. Riding a late train back to Oslo after the race, she tried in vain to catch a few winks of sleep. She attempted to explain to the Norwegian next to her on the train how she had done. After several minutes trying to bridge the language barrier, his eyes lit up when he heard that she had been fourth in her class!

Brown's younger sister Robin won the girls' title in the Kortelopet. Dan Cronen of Lakeville, Minnesota, was the overall Kortelopet champion.

One of the most impressive performances of the weekend, though, was by Dr. Stephen Harrington of Duluth who took the citizen's title, finishing tenth overall in 2:56:58.5—the best citizen finish since the early days of the race!

The day wore on and temperatures climbed higher. Some bare spots did develop on the course, but nothing like two weeks earlier. The track was sluggish in the late going, but the Birkebeiner skiers pressed on.

As darkness crept over Lake Hayward, the clocks of Northeast Sports Timing kept ticking away in the timing shack. Allar and Dechant talked to first aid snowmobiles as skiers came across the frozen lake one by one. A skier with his shoulder in a cast (he had *started* with a broken collarbone), a pregnant woman and more—all struggling to win their own personal battles.

Tim Caldwell had an easy victory, the first United States winner since Chris Haines in 1975.

Women's champion Muriel Gilman (left), Bemidji, Minnesota, greets Larry Gullingsrud at the finish line. Gullingsrud was head ski coach at Bemidji State University (BSU); Gilman, who won a trip to the Norwegian Birkebeiner, was a trainer at BSU.

"It was one of the hardest times we've ever had determining a winner for the Bronzed Broom Award," said Allar. "We've tried to get away from just automatically awarding it to the last place skier. When I saw David Joseph (who actually finished second from last) coming into the finish I just knew it had to go to him. I had been there two years earlier when he just missed the cutoff at OO and to see him come back again and to make it to the finish was really something."

While Joseph wasn't the absolute last skier, his sweep time of 9:37:43.50 is the slowest on record in ten years! That night at the Birkefest, Joseph accepted the bronzed broom. Other champions accepted their trophies and laurels, as well. But in the true spirit of the Birkebeiner, there were more champions in 1981 than in any year before. From start to finish, week in and week out, Birkebeiner IX became a struggle just to survive—for both race officials and racers alike. And for those that stuck with it, Birkebeiner IX will probably be the most memorable of all!

Tim Caldwell stands tall and proud, along with second-place Bjørn Arvnes and third-place Mark Ernst of Green Bay, Wisconsin.

All afternoon, skiers poured into the finish chutes as workers clad in Woolrich/3M parkas recorded their times.

Wendy Brown, Apple Valley, Minnesota, whose sister Robin had already won the Kortelopet, catches her breath at the finish after placing second to Bemidji, Minnesota, skier Muriel Gilman, who won the citizens' trip to Norway.

CHAPTER X
Greatest Birkie So Far

It was shortly after 9 a.m., Saturday, February 27, 1982. Tony Wise and 106-year-old Herman "Jack Rabbit" Smith-Johanssen stood side by side—atop the balcony on the tower of Hayward's Walker Hotel.

Just moments earlier, a huge boom had resounded through Hayward from the northeast. Suddenly, church bells began tolling and helicopters buzzed ever nearer to the thousands of spectators lining Iowa Avenue.

Wes Lindahl, owner of Lindahl's Sporting Goods, peered down Iowa Avenue from his two-story building—movie camera in hand. Across the snow-covered street in the sidewalk beer garden of Angler's Bar, the stacatto beat of the University of Wisconsin marching band kept the crowd on edge. On a scaffold in the middle of Iowa Avenue, nearly 20 photographers elbowed for position while others were lofted overhead in a hydraulic bucket or squatted in the snow.

It was like ten years of slow motion. Ten years of defeat and victory. Ten years of heartache and joy, ever so slowly coming into view at the far end of town. Ten years and three days earlier, Duncan McLean had become the first skier

Thousands of spectators jammed the sidewalks as thousands more skiers paraded in view in the most spectacular ski event ever held in America.

Marty Hall gives a group of skiers instructions at the annual Birkebeiner Training Weekend in December. Originally introduced by former Telemark Academy Director Peter Davis in 1977, the clinic became a popular early-season training forum.

Huge snowcats and truck after truck of snow turned Hayward's Iowa Avenue into a ski trail several days before the 1982 Birkebeiner.

ever across the finish line, winning the shorter junior race in the first Telemark-Birkebeiner. On this day, it was Duncan's turn to lead the pack through Hayward.

Ten years earlier, when the Birkebeiner first began, Wise had dreamed of a huge parade of skiers—skis on shoulders, marching to the start on Lake Hayward. Ten years later, that parade became a reality.

A lot of pride welled up inside both Tony and Jack Rabbit that morning. Along the length of Iowa Avenue below them, thousands upon thousands of skiers strided in parade, skis in tracks, as they began the greatest Birkebeiner in history. For Tony Wise and the hundreds of staff workers and race volunteers, it was a spine-tingling relief to a two year wait. It was the fitting climax after a frustrating season of little snow and even less good fortune a year earlier.

Jack Rabbit waved his cane in the air, turning often to his daughter Alice in amazement. In his 106 years, Jack Rabbit had brought more to the sport of cross county skiing than virtually any man who had ever lived. That day, he saw the fruits of his labor pass proudly in review.

Birkebeiner day had begun nine hours earlier. Before midnight, Chief of Course Ray McConnell led his crew up the trail, grooming the snow and setting the tracks. At the Telemark finish line, Harold Treland was putting the finishing touches on the timing control gates, while Northeast Sports Timing officials made final checks on their computer system.

In the distance, the flashing blue and orange lights of the huge snow machines and the roar of their engines broke the cold stillness of the night. Like the skiers who would follow them, the snow machines paraded through the woods, pulling their powder makers and track setters behind.

Chief of Race Tom Allar and Technical Delegate Lars Kindem were pacing the boardwalk in front of the Telemark Colosseum. Weather reports from Duluth were not good—two to four inches of new snow was on its way. Even as the race approached, there was no shortage of snow. What Allar wouldn't have given for that same snow a year earlier! But this year he would have just as soon gone home for a few hours sleep rather than worry about too much snow!

Just after midnight Allar called the crews inside for a late night dinner and sent them home to bed. About 3:30 a.m., the snow was getting too close for comfort. "It was time to cash in a few favors," recalled Allar. In the pre-dawn hours, Allar called in the crew, plus anyone he could find to help haul the machines to Hayward in case retracking was necessary. "These guys were fantastic—I don't think there's anything they wouldn't do."

While the heavy equipment was being ferried to Hayward, Terry Johnson was hard at work on Iowa Avenue, laying the tracks for the start—now just five hours away.

While most skiers were still asleep, the grooming crews stood at the ready—waiting for the snowfall that never materialized. Just a short drive to the north, towards Duluth, the weatherman's prediction was coming true. But someone looked with favor on the Birkebeiner that morning, as only a light dusting powdered the tracks.

Dawn broke slowly over Lake Hayward—a gray, cloudy day, threatening to snow at any minute. At Clayton Slack's Edgewater Beach resort, ten minutes east of Hayward, 15 Frenchmen awoke to a huge breakfast.

At cabins, motels and resorts across northern Wisconsin, skiers bounced excitedly out of bed. Outside, many could hear the swish, swish, swish of skis as their roomates did some pre-dawn wax testing. At the public schools in Hayward, nearly a thousand skiers rolled up sleeping bags and climbed into long underwear and racing suits. It was now 5 a.m.

For miles around, men and women from all walks of life picked up skis, gently testing the tackiness of the klister or binder they had ironed in the night before. From the sticky depths of wax kits, thermometers were found and stuck into the snow. By 7 a.m., pancakes were being flipped at over a dozen Hayward restaurants and civic club breakfasts. Bacon and eggs were sizzling on the griddle as skiers stuffed some extra wax into fanny packs and tied the strings of their racing bibs.

Mike Cooper, in his first year as chief of bus transportation, was wringing his hands in front of the Telemark Lodge. Early morning traffic had slowed his buses coming from Hayward. All he could think of were the horror stories Allar had told him about his own first experience in the same job years earlier.

Inside the Lodge, University of Wisconsin band members rolled off mattresses on the floor of the Namekagon Room, tuning up their instruments as others tried to catch a couple more winks. Soon, they would be boarding their Badger buses for Hayward to see the Birkie they had heard so much about.

As the time ticked away, everything fell in place. The early morning traffic woes were quickly ended and buses sped back-and-forth with great haste. The Swix waxing tent behind the school was busy with last-minute waxing and chattering about the new course from Hayward to Telemark. Skiers congregated at the Hayward Middle School and then quickly moved down to the National Guard Armory and out to the starting line.

Only minutes to go and American Birkebeiner X would be underway!

The most frustrating experience for racers, and race officials alike, was having to wait a whole year after the snowless season the year before. All of the

The World Loppet banner was brought to earth by Telemark Nordic Director Kevin Mazzu in a tricky double-canopy skydiving routine.

Hundreds of skiers march behind their respective state or national banners in opening ceremonies before American Birkebeiner X.

"Herman the German," a radio celebrity from Munich, entertains the crowds at the opening ceremonies.

The University of Wisconsin marching band performs inside the Telemark Colosseum to officially kickoff Birkebeiner weekend.

While the American Birkebeiner was celebrating its tenth running, the Norwegian Birkebeiner was preparing for the fiftieth anniversary of its first running.

Early Saturday morning the waxing tents at Telemark and in Hayward were busy with activity.

plans that had been made, the hundreds and hundreds of kilometers of training and the sheer anticipation of the Birkebeiner had been lost in 1981. By the time that February 27, 1982 rolled around, it had been two years since a "real" Birkebeiner had been run.

Many of the plans for Birkebeiner X had been formulated the season before. Now it was simply a matter of executing them. But returning the start to Hayward had certainly *not* been among them!

From 1973 through 1975, the Birkebeiner had begun on the frozen ice of Lake Hayward before the start was moved to Telemark. Although there had been thoughts of someday returning to Hayward, it was never considered as seriously as it was in the winter of 1981-82.

In mid-winter, race officials learned that the Drummond High School, one of several race dormitory facilities and the only facility in the Cable area with showers, might not be available. A music festival had been scheduled for race day. Efforts to move that festival were in vain.

With the ever-increasing demand for accommodations, officials pondered the problem. Accommodating the thousands of Birkebeiner skiers has always been one of the biggest concerns. Many improvements had been made in advance of the 1982 race: A new lodging directory was put together and efforts were stepped up to assist skiers in finding lodging. The dormitory facilities at the area schools had also been heavily promoted. Already, space in both the Drummond and Hayward schools was filling fast.

The idea of moving the start to Hayward was not totally new. It had been thought about before, but never in a very serious vain. One morning in early January, Wise was having coffee with Norm Cooper, owner of the Moose Cafe in Hayward. Searching for any ideas, Wise told Cooper of his dilemma.

"We have to start thinking about the future," he told Cooper. "The facilities here in Hayward are much better for handling the skiers at the start of the race. And we simply have to have more accommodations closer to the start than we do in Cable—especially after losing the Drummond High School."

The biggest advantage of a Hayward start, at this point, was the availability of nearly 1,000 sleeping spaces. In the past, only the small Hayward Elementary School was available. But a new high school, which had opened in the fall, made the old high school available as well. The additional space was more than adequate to pick up the difference lost since Drummond High School was not avail-

In the hour prior to the start, skiers congregate outside the Swix wax tent in Hayward in anticipation of the Birkebeiner ahead, preparing for the trek from Hayward to Telemark.

Tony Wise and Jack Rabbit Johanssen wait anxiously for the first sight of skiers coming down Iowa Avenue in Hayward from their vantage point on the balcony of the Walker Hotel.

Line after line of skiers assemble at the Windigo Village Subdivision starting area on the northwest side of Hayward. Seven years earlier, the last time the race started in Hayward, it was a much smaller group that assembled on Lake Hayward for the race to Telemark.

In nearly perfect single file lines, the skiers proceeded down Iowa Avenue in this view from a helicopter over the course.

able. Cooper's reply to Wise was simple, "Why *don't* you start it down here?" Wise explained that the idea of a Hayward start in the past had been met with disapproval with businessmen. "Let me see what I can do," Cooper replied.

Just a day or so later, Cooper had already rallied the support of the town—from the Chamber of Commerce to the council members. "I really couldn't believe it," said Wise. "We simply couldn't have done it without him igniting the fire." The thought of moving the start to Hayward was a closely-guarded secret among race officials at that time. Few knew of the idea, which was important in the early stages of planning. Wise wanted to be sure it could be arranged before public rumors spread. Like the postponement a year before, it was crucial that all the facts be ironed out before the information was released.

The logistics of moving the start to Hayward were staggering. A large enough starting area was one of the biggest problems. The best location appeared to be either the Hayward Country Club or the adjoining Windigo Village Subdivision. Both had advantages and disadvantages. In the end, it was the Windigo Village area that was selected.

Officials then worked with the Hayward City Council to secure the closing of a number of city streets, including Hayward's main street, Iowa Avenue, which would be covered with 9,000 cubic yards of snow. Permission to cross state Highway 63 was also obtained, while several other landowners were contacted for rights to use their property for the new Birkebeiner start.

"I just was amazed at how well the city responded," said Wise. "In all my life, I've never seen this town work together so well."

As mid-January rolled around, production of the *Birch Scroll* neared the final stages. Nowhere in the publication was there any indication of a change—there just wasn't enough information available yet. But the *Birch Scroll* had to be released, the other information it *did* contain was of crucial importance to the race regardless of where it started. So the paper went out as planned, without mention of the change that was being developed.

"We held off as long as we could," said Wise. "We finally had to make a decision to send it out and then publish a special edition a week or two later when we had some more details."

In the course of the next two weeks, Allar, Race Secretary Andy Meunier and staff artist Carole Duh pored over maps and details with Wise—putting together a completely new race, start to finish. Day after day, well into the night,

In a seemingly never-ending line, skiers stride down the tracks of Iowa Avenue in downtown Hayward.

the new American Birkebeiner X materialized, changing from a southern route to a northern route, as it was later dubbed by a Twin Cities journalist.

The details of the change itself were released to the media in late-January, giving at least the preliminary word to the racers. As expected, calls began to come in by the hundreds, much like what happened at the postponed race a year before.

In the time since the postponed race, much had transpired in the skiing world. With two bad seasons behind it (even more in some regions) the ski industry, on the whole, was not doing well. The sponsorship of the Birkebeiner by the Norwegian Ski Council (NSC) in 1981 did not materialize for 1982—there just wasn't the strength of the member companies or adequate support from their association for the sponsorship. Three of the NSC companies did continue on their own—Nor-Tur and Swix which had been involved with the race for many years, and Normark which had first been involved the year before.

Telemark, itself, which had operated since 1947, was forced into Chapter 11 reorganization that past spring. The effects of the snowless winter of 1981, and the winter before which wasn't much better were too much to handle. The Chapter 11 reorganization allowed Telemark to continue operating as usual, while a federal bankruptcy court worked with the company to reorganize its finances. But there was renewed hope going into the 1982 season. First of all, the odds were heavily stacked in favor of snow. After two years of drought, the only way to look was up. Although Telemark still had a long way to go to make up for the lack of snow the seasons before, things were proceeding even better than hoped with its financial reorganization.

Snow was a little sluggish in arriving that winter, but eventually it provided one of the biggest snow covers in years. The ski industry, although still hoping for better things to come, was rebounding as well. Birkebeiner entries were steady that fall, but a little behind the rate of a year before. Early projections showed race entries would be much the same as 1981.

The Worldloppet entered into a new era the preceding summer as Wise concluded his three-year term as secretary general. Eugen Peter, president of the Swiss Engadin Skimarathon, took over the reins.

By October, everything appeared to be in order for American Birkebeiner X. But as the leaves began to fall from the trees, reports of an on-trail logging operation filtered back to the Lodge. A year before, Marty Hall had warned officials about the problems of logging on the trail.

Skiers string out along Lake Hayward, several kilometers from the start.

Karl Ludzak, a local logger who was also the county supervisor from the Cable area and a member of the Bayfield County Forestry Committee, had secured logging rights in the Bayfield County Forest bordering the Birkebeiner Trail near the 8 to 10 kilometer marks. A year before, he had logged a major section and was working on another now.

"I just couldn't believe it when I first went out there," said Allar. "It was like a war zone."

Legally, Ludzak had every right to log the trail. His permits had been properly issued from the county. Ludzak was firm on his stance. He maintained that the trail was public and he had as much right to secure logging rights in that part of the county forest as any other.

Several years before, Sawyer County had formulated a policy of not selling logging tracts along the trail. In addition, Sawyer County stringently enforced a no motorized vehicle ordinance, which had been adopted in 1972. Unfortunately, Bayfield County had no such ordinances or policies.

"According to his contract, he was required to leave the land he worked in as good, or better, condition than he found it," said Wise. "That's where our biggest concern came. The year before, the trail had suffered extreme erosion damage from the logging. In fact, the grass in the area he had worked on never regrew! That area was one of our biggest problems when we had the snow melt on the trail. "At the time of his logging operation in the fall of 1981, winter was rapidly approaching," Wise added. "If any of the muddy ruts from the equipment were to freeze, it would have been virtually impossible to adequately groom or track the trail."

Skiers crowd the trail on an uphill just past Wheeler Road about five kilometers into the race.

Skiers herringbone up a small hill as they near the first food station on the Hayward to Telemark course.

In the end, neither side won. Ludzak completed his logging section and did clean up the area to the satisfaction of race officials. But it started a new move to get Bayfield County to adopt similar policies as Sawyer had done.

"In a 1982 survey compiled by *Cross Country Ski Magazine,* over 80% of the cross country skiers questioned listed scenery as the main thing they look for in a ski trail," said Wise. "That's an incredible statistic! We have to do everything we can to insure that the trail remains that way."

But autumn's troubles on the trail were quickly forgotten in December. Snow fell across the northwoods and continued to fall—huge snowfalls that locals had all but forgotten about! January turned bitter cold, with temperatures down to 40 below zero and refusing to rise above the zero barrier for weeks. February brought more snow as the Birkebeiner drew ever near.

About the only sure thing in a midwestern winter is an early hint of a spring thaw, just before the Birkie. As mid-February rolled around, temperatures rose and rose. Just like a year earlier, the switchboard began to light up daily.

But unlike 1981, there was little problem. There was more snow than officials needed, and the Birkebeiner couldn't possibly be jeopardized in 1982!

When Birkebeiner Week finally arrived, things really began to come alive. For the first time in a year, race workers were certain that this was it—the Birkebeiner would return. Racer after racer descended upon registration towards the latter part of the week. Engelbert Hattenberger, who had been slowed by the heat a week earlier, was chipping away at two huge replicas of the Norwegian and

U.S. Ski Team racer Howie Bean leads the pack through OO. Behind him is Swede Bengt Hassis, Norway's Jan Bjørkheim, eventual winner Ola Hassis of Sweden, Austrian Rudi Kapeller and Norwegian Dag Bjørkheim. Dag, who was sick the day of the race, dropped out several kilometers later.

U.S. Ski Team racer Todd Kempainen leads a pack of elite racers on the track at OO. Behind him is Kristian Normann of Norway, Sten Fjeldheim, (left rear) and Phil Peck (right rear).

St. Paul Skier Walt Huemmer grabs some liquid at OO.

American Birkebeiner logos. It was the 50th anniversary for the Norwegian Birkebeiner-Rennet, and the tenth running of its American counterpart.

On Tuesday, Mike Gobler and his crews dumped 9,000 cubic yards of snow on the Hayward streets. The job went smoothly—better than ever anticipated. In just a matter of hours, Iowa Avenue was made into a stage for all the world to see.

"It's funny," laughed local businessman Wes Lindahl before the NBC cameras of WEAU-TV from Eau Claire, Wisconsin. "We spend all winter taking it away and in one afternoon put it all back. I think it's great."

The majority of businesses seemed to echo Lindahl's feelings, although some were very concerned about the loss of Iowa Avenue traffic and parking for four business days.

Thursday noon, German tour leader Annelies Waneck grabbed hold of a huge pair of scissors and cut the ribbon to the Telemark Colosseum's replica of downtown Munich—the work of artist Lyle Nelson. Nelson spent several months creating the hallway mural, changing the traditional Telemark Rathskeller into Munich's popular Hofbräuhaus!

Later that afternoon, some of the top elite racers put on a show in downtown Hayward. Hundreds of townspeople were in the streets ringing cowbells at the annual "Special K" race.

Friday afternoon, officials began to see their plans come to life. Just two years earlier, a tiny crowd of 200 gathered around the ice sculpture in front of the Telemark Lodge for the opening ceremonies. But today, the crowd was enormous. Thousands of skiers gazed skyward as NorTur's Telemark Ski School Director Kevin Mazzu followed his skydiving club gently to earth from thousands of feet above Telemark. Brightly-colored hot air balloons soared overhead, while the University of Wisconsin marching band burst into their patented Budweiser song.

Flags of all 50 states were hoisted high on flag poles, while the huge banners of fifteen nations fluttered in the breeze. Behind signs for each participating nation and state, hundreds of skiers lined up proudly—some on shoulders, some waving their own flags. Annelies' group of Germans even wore matching ski caps with their familiar red, black and gold flag emblazoned on the front. Bengt-Åke Mohlin's Swedish tour group was prominent in yellow and blue.

It was every bit as impressive as the Lake Placid Olympic opening ceremonies! But instead of watching it from the bleachers or on a television screen, thousands of Birkebeiner skiers themselves were marching, heads held high, into the Telemark Colosseum.

Rusty Scott of Jackson, Wyoming, skis strongly through OO.

Peter Davis, formerly director of the Telemark Academy, grabs some energy drink from Brad Sellew at OO.

Telemark's Gary Crandall passes some liquid to citizens champion Steve Harrington of Duluth.

Inside, Norwegian dancers from Minneapolis and the local Lac Courte Oreilles Ojibwa Indians, bridged the ocean with their native dances. Jack Rabbit Johanssen and local Ojibwa medicine man Chief Running Elk joined hands and smoked a peace pipe.

It was like a fairy tale come true. In fact, some wondered just how to top the magnificent opening on Friday. That came easily on Saturday.

At the sound of the exploding rockets Saturday morning, 5,793 skiers burst out of the starting gates, their thoughts set on Telemark—55 kilometers away, or the Kortelopet finish at OO, 29 kilometers from the start.

And what a race it was!

Although the top ten of American Birkebeiner X were still predominantly European, the race marked a dramatic step forward for American skiers. The strength of "factory" ski teams, plus a newfound interest in marathon skiing by the U.S. Ski Team, made for some interesting results.

Twenty-five-year-old Wolfeboro, New Hampshire skier Howie Bean had never been a real notable on the U.S. Ski Team. But he was a good, solid skier. In 1979, Bean had finished 12th in the Birkebeiner—quite an accomplishment for his first shot at the long distance race.

He had made the early-season European squad in 1982, though, and struggled through a somewhat disappointing European World Cup swing in January. Bean returned late that month to make his mark on the Great American Ski Chase, including a victory in the Traverse City (Michigan) Vasa two weeks before the Birkebeiner.

"Beaner's here to win," said U.S. Ski Team's marathon coach Gary Larson before the Birkie. Larson wasn't kidding.

The skiers were tightly packed throughout the early stages of the race, the lead changing often. But Bean was consistently up front, and as they crested the knoll coming into OO, it was Howie Bean in the lead—skiing strong as he headed the pack down the trail.

Surprising at the time was the fact that Norwegian brothers Jan and Dag Bjørkheim were right behind. Dag, a 31-year-old medical intern from Oslo, had only skied a handful of long distance events that year, including a victory in the Italian Marcialonga. He had broken a hand at the König Ludwig Lauf three weeks before and had come to America earlier in the week with a very bad cold. It was surprising to see him since the night before he hadn't planned on racing at all! (Although he was in contention at the time, he finally dropped out a few kilometers later, his illness finally taking its toll.)

His younger brother Jan, who had struggled to second in the crazy elite Birkebeiner a year before, had picked up his brother's cold and wasn't feeling much better. Like Dag, he felt an obligation to at least try to race after being invited to the Birkebeiner. He had certainly never expected to be so close to the lead!

The sleeper of the group was Bengt Hassis, the younger brother of Ola Hassis. Bengt, 25, had come over earlier in the month to ski for Rossignol's factory team on the Great American Ski Chase. Although his results in Europe had been impressive, he still had not been considered a likely contender by race officials.

The pace through OO was somewhat slow. It had been expected that the direction change of the course would result in slower times. But it had been anticipated that the times for the elite skiers, especially racers like the Bjørkheims who thrive on uphills, wouldn't vary much. But the slight dusting of powder that morning slowed things considerably.

In the final half of the course, Jan Bjørkheim and Ola Hassis pulled away—leaving their brothers behind. It was a nip-and-tuck battle through the rolling power line section of the trail. Both skiers knew the other well, having competed side-by-side in Europe on many occasions. As they came in behind the Lodge, it was Bjørkheim in the lead—about two or three ski lengths ahead of Hassis.

With just 400 meters to go, both skiers looked ready to drop at any instant. Their energy had been sapped and their senses drained. Neither one could keep a steady stride in the tracks as they approached the downhill into the finish area. Down below, in front of and inside the Colosseum, thousands of spectators were anxiously waiting. Just a few meters away, I ran alongside the two—all alone, almost unthinking that these two skiers were actually vying for the championship of the Birkebeiner.

Ben Dodge of Deer River, Minnesota, took the Kortelopet.

Hayward skier Brenda Bergum, whose cross country skiing career had begun just two months earlier, was the top woman in the Kortelopet.

Skiers spread out across the width of the 30-foot-wide trail.

Gatorade cups litter the snow as hundreds of skiers pass through a food station on the course.

A food station worker passes a plate of oranges to hungry skiers.

Evenly, very evenly they strided along, and I shouted my report over the wireless microphone to the public address system. When they came into the stadium, Peter Graves took over. Stride-for-stride, Hassis stayed right on Bjørkheim's heels—waiting for just the right moment.

Then, as they traversed the Jerry Berard Slope, the Swede made his move, skating around Jan, who was helpless to defend his position. Suddenly, I saw them coming into the finish, it was Ola in front—waving his arms high, winning American Birkebeiner X in 2:42:09.

In the finish area, public relations assistant Lea Justice tossed me a bottle of champagne. Hassis did the honors, spraying the dozen or more photographers who were clamoring for photos. With the laurel wreath proudly hung around his neck, he skied his victory lap in front of the Colosseum.

In the excitement of the finish, Howie Bean was not forgotten. He came across the finish line strong—just 18 seconds behind Hassis—the best American finish against the Europeans since John-Mike Downey's second place in 1977!

In the women's class no one was surprised when Gry Oftedal, the young Norwegian racer who had made her mark two years earlier, finished in 3:04:20—four minutes ahead of second-place Jennifer Caldwell.

As she took her own victory lap, she also took a little pinch—some Happy Days supplied by U.S. Tobacco, one of the sponsors of the Great American Ski Chase.

Leading the champions through the jam-packed Colosseum to the press conference was incredible. Thousands jammed the outdoor boardwalk and the inside of the Colosseum. All of them chanting and applauding for Ola Hassis and Gry Oftedal! Ola turned to me and said, "This is amazing, I've never seen something like this before!"

Nearly two hours earlier, at the Kortelopet finish along OO, Ben Dodge of Deer River, Minnesota, came across the line in 1:40:53 to become the tenth Kortelopet champion. A short time later, Brenda Bergum of Hayward, whose father had finally convinced her to give skiing a try during Christmas vacation two months earlier, took the woman's crown.

At Telemark, the parade of skiers continued. Dr. Stephen Harrington, the young Duluth doctor who had won the citizen title a year earlier, became the first male skier ever to repeat. Harrington, who had attracted acclaim from Marty Hall at the Birkebeiner Training Weekend a year earlier, was 23rd overall.

Tim Wonser of Menasha, Wisconsin, rests for a moment with a cup of Gatorade.

Dozens of small tins of Swix wax are readied for skiers wishing to rewax at the on-course waxing stations.

Ola Hassis double poles into the finish as Jan Bjørkheim tries fruitlessly to muster that last bit of energy to catch Hassis, who had just passed him.

Ola Hassis (left) and Jan Bjørkheim embrace smiling at the finish line.

The line of skiers continues all afternoon as thousands complete American Birkebeiner X.

The citizen champions have always been difficult to predict. While Harrington was certainly one of the favorites in the men's battle, no one knew who to pick among the women. The 1981 champion Muriel Gilman had become a classified racer so wasn't eligible, and all of the other well-known women were classified as well.

Computer problems at the finish line delayed most of the results for nearly 24 hours. Errors early in the race from the electronic bar code bib number readers had thrown some of the results off kilter. Officials decided to spend the extra time to insure that the results were as accurate as possible, going back through each and every time by hand through the night.

While Harrington's title was fairly well confirmed even Saturday, it wasn't until Sunday that a women's citizen champion could be named. Around 9:30 a.m. Sunday morning, Chief of Timing Jim Moe and I pored over the new result outputs. Finally, at 3:40:53 of the race, the name of Ruth Hamilton, Carbondale, Colorado, appeared—just 20 seconds ahead of Patricia Murray of Akron, Ohio. Hamilton was the winner.

Hundreds of skiers converge on the finish line food station, grabbing bananas, oranges, donuts and granola bars.

The finish line is just a few strides away for these skiers.

At the time, Ruth was somewhat of an unknown. She had thought that she might have been the citizen's winner, but wasn't even aware that the prize was a trip to Norway! As the rescheduled awards ceremony at 10 a.m. Sunday was getting underway, Oskar Gnaedinger of Swissair, who presented the Swissair Cup for the top woman citizen racer, found Ruth in the hall and broke the good news to her as she was heading out the door to catch a flight back to Colorado.

Ruth, who was just 25, was cross country racing for the first year ever. Veteran alpine skiers and runners, she and her husband Skip had decided to give cross country a serious shot that year.

Ruth's real ability showed up even more a few weeks later when she was 29th woman in the Swiss Engadin Skimarathon, which sports the best women's fields in the Worldloppet. And she did it despite breaking a pole in the huge mass start! A week later in Norway, she was seventh in her 25-29 year class at the Birkebeiner, not far behind Ruth Baxter of the U.S. Ski Team.

Skip, meanwhile, served notice that he would be a potential Birkie citizen's champ himself. Skip finished the Norwegian Birkebeiner in 3:43:30—nearly beating U.S. Ski Team member Todd Kempainen who had a good race himself! Skip hadn't fared so well in Wisconsin, 'hitting the wall' late in the race and being forced to spend an hour or two in a first aid tent before he could continue and finish the race.

American Birkebeiner X produced some of the most interesting class battles in history. The European domination ended after five classes, with Raimo Ahti, the incredible hulk of cross country skiing, winning his first Birkebeiner class crown ever. Ahti, from Fitchburg, Massachusetts, took the 45-49 year class over Park Rapids, Minnesota, skier Kare Lid.

One of the most gratifying results was in class 7, (men 50-54). Bjørn Lasserud, a Norwegian native living in Minneapolis, finally won his class in 3:30:57.

Two women, Carol Duffy of Hayward and Margareta Lambert of Warrenville, Illinois, won their third straight class titles. Carol's 4:16:38 took the women's 45-49 class, while Lambert, who continually amazes women in her 55 & over class, won by nearly two hours with a 4:36:06, her slowest of three consecutive titles. And 30-34 winner Kaarina Engelbrecht, Winfield, British Columbia, finally did not have to contend with the speed of Gabriele Andersen, who passed up the 1982 race.

Former Haywardite Judy Scheer Hoeschler, a six-time world logrolling champion in the summer, completes the Birkebeiner.

Marion Bradford of Beloit, Wisconsin, limps across the finish line on only one ski.

Skiers search through the hundreds of clothing bags at the finish.

The huge Telemark outdoor pool was heated and opened for a refreshing swim following the race.

The long, hard day is over for a smiling Belinda Hyneman—the trailsweeper for American Birkebeiner X.

But the closest battle of all came in men's 55-59. As he had shown so many times before, George Hovland of Duluth has never been happy with anything but the ultimate in challenges. And he likes to win.

George had decided that 1982 was his year to make the U.S. Marathon Team by trying to win his age class on the Great American Ski Chase. Along with his good friends Tom and Carol Duffy of Hayward, George did the circuit—always on the lookout for Einnar Svensson, a Swede from Seattle, who George considered his toughest competitor.

"Has he registered for the Birkie yet," George asked time and time again. Fortunately for Hovland, Svensson passed up the Chase circuit and the Birkie in 1982, paving the way for George to take the Chase.

George was a two-time Birkebeiner class winner coming into 1982. Both had come in years when he was at the oldest end of an age bracket (1976 and 1981). Hovland had gone into the race gunning for two titles in a row. He had just moved up to the 55-59 class, facing Roy Carlsted of St. Paul and Olavi Seppala of Menahga, Minnesota, as his toughest competition.

Throughout the early stages of the race, Hovland and Carlsted, whose frosty white beard has become a familiar site at many a ski race, went back-and-forth. It was a cat and mouse game for kilometer after kilometer. "Finally, I said to myself, 'let him have it,'" said Hovland. "I just needed a relatively good finish to stay in the Chase lead and second was still good enough."

So Carlsted took off down the trail as Hovland relaxed a little bit—just making sure he would still finish respectably.

As the kilometers passed by, Hovland rounded the corner into the final on-course food station and headed out across the up-and-down of the power line. "I looked down the trail and couldn't believe what I saw," he said. "There was Carlsted just a couple hills down the line."

Hovland figured it was worth a shot, so he gave it all he had. But strength wasn't the key here—it was strategy. "I didn't want to let him know I was still there," said Hovland, "so I snuck up on him, hiding behind other skiers all the way." Finally, with just a few hundred meters to the finish, Hovland had worked his way to within the tails of Carlsted's skis, still hiding behind a group of skiers so that his presence wasn't known. Just as he was about to overtake his nemesis from the Twin Cities, George's fiancee spotted him from the crowd.

"Go George, go—you can beat him!"

"I couldn't believe it," Hovland said. "I was shouting to myself, 'keep quiet, keep quiet.' I just hoped that I had enough left to get by him." All of a sudden, Carlsted turned around and saw Hovland. The two sprinted away, Hovland managing to take him in the stretch.

Earlier that day, two more old friends had been battling it out on the course. Duncan McLean and Roger Pekuri, who had skied together for many years in Ironwood, Michigan, had been among the dozens of perennial Central Division competitors at the Birkie. Few skiers have the Birkebeiner credentials as these two racers, McLean having won two junior races (the forerunner of the Kortelopet) and both an American elite and citizen trip to the Norwegian Birkebeiner. Pekuri had finished as high as sixth and 13th in previous races.

Way back in 1976, Pekuri was having one of his best races ever. In the latter half of the course he had blown by McLean shouting: "To the finish!" He never let him forget it.

Now, six years later, it was Duncan's turn for revenge. Pekuri wasn't skiing as much as he had been a few years before. McLean, on the other hand, had made it all the way to the U.S. Ski Team that year. As Duncan flew past Roger he turned his head and grinned underneath his beard, "To the finish!"

All afternoon the champions came through the finish lines—at OO and in front of the Colosseum. The overcast sky that had clouded the start broke every once in a while to let in a few rays of sunshine. Then, just as quickly, it would turn to light snow.

Hundreds and hundreds of skiers gathered around the finish food station—munching Chiquita bananas and Nature Valley Granola bars after their hard-earned victories.

For the Birkebeiner Founders, American Birkebeiner X had a special significance. These ten skiers had managed to continue the quest they began February 24, 1973: Karl Andersen, Eau Claire, Wisconsin; Fred Constalie, Westby, Wisconsin; John Gannett, Seymour, Wisconsin; John Holmquist, Minneapolis; John Kotar, Houghton, Michigan; Dave Landgraf, Bloomer, Wisconsin; Wayne Lindskoog, Edina, Minnesota; Nils Meland, Oshkosh, Wisconsin, Ernie St. Germaine, Lac du Flambeau, Wisconsin; and Rick Scott, Superior, Wisconsin.

Saturday evening, as skiers continued to struggle and stride over the finish line, thousands converged on the Telemark Colosseum. Birkebeiner officials had been cautiously optimistic that the huge Birkefest smorgasbord and celebration they had planned would be a big success. Tickets were available on a first come basis, all sales in advance. No one really knew what to expect, but certainly no one would have guessed that it would sell out by Friday afternoon!

Two thousand skiers jammed the Colosseum for the huge Birkefest smorgasbord. Even more gathered for the awards ceremony which would begin at 7 p.m., even though the computer problems were obviously going to delay many of the presentations.

At 6:22 p.m., Birkebeiner X finally came to a close. A snowmobile provided the light for one lone skier left on the track. Tom Allar, Tim Dechant and I had been out on the trail behind the Lodge—talking to the final skiers as they wound their way down the hill into the finish.

Finally, the last skier came into view. Belinda Hyneman, 22, had the title of trail sweeper all to herself. Her body strained with every stride—her training program not being what it had been a year earlier. Her eyes weren't quite focusing right as she struggled down the trail under the watchful eye of the ski patrol's snowmobile crew.

A last, the finish line was in sight. A paddle was put behind her bib and a rubber stamp inked—COURSE COMPLETED.

Somewhat in a daze, she was led into the Colosseum—waiting in the wings for the appropriate moment. A wheelchair was nearby, as was a stretcher—just in case it was needed. Finally, little before 7 p.m., the University of Wisconsin marching band struck up a spine-tingling fanfare. Thousands of skiers leaped from their chairs, hands applauding wildly as Harry Mayer called the sweeper out on stage.

Ola Hassis holds his Haakon Haakonssøn trophy high at the Saturday night awards ceremony.

Gry Oftedal proudly accepts the Lillehammer Cup, including a bottle of champagne, from Tony Wise.

Tony Wise hugs a smiling Jennifer Caldwell who was the top American woman.

All of a sudden, the daze of 55 kilometers disappeared from Belinda's face. Her eyes were aglow, her fists waving in the air, proudly hoisting the bronzed broom for all to see—one of the proudest Birkebeiners of the day. And the crowd went absolutely wild!

Such was American Birkebeiner X. It was a fitting culmination to ten years, and a beginning of many, many more.

No one could have been prouder that day, though, than Jack Rabbit Johanssen. Jack Rabbit had been to Telemark once before, at the Gitchi Gami Games in 1979. He attracted a great deal of media attention, as he always does, and shook hands with the several hundred elite skiers gathered for the Games.

But it was different this time around. This was more what Jack Rabbit had lived for. This was the goal of his life's work. He could see it in the eyes and faces of each and every skier who earned a medallion that day.

A few weeks before the Birkebeiner, Tony was searching for yet another attraction for the greatest Birkebeiner ever. Finally, he picked up the phone and called Alice, Jack Rabbit's daughter. "Tony, I just don't know," she said sadly. "He just went to the Marathon [Canadian Ski Marathon] this weekend and I just don't think he's up to another trip. He gets so many requests, you know. And he's just like the skiers in the Marathon—it takes him a few weeks to recover," she laughed. But Wise was persistent, "Check with me in a few days," Alice said. Days went by and finally Jack Rabbit said he would come. He had heard plenty about the Birkebeiner. And he had the deepest respect for Telemark and Tony Wise.

The ten Birkebeiner founders who completed their tenth race in 1982 were honored at the Birkefest Awards Ceremony. Pictured are, from left, Karl Andresen, John Gannett, John Holmquist, John Kotar, Dave Landgraf, Wayne Lindskoog, Nils Meland, Rick Scott, and Ernie St. Germaine plus Eric Ersson, champion of the first Birkebeiner. Missing is founder Fred Constalie.

Two years after his first visit to Telemark, Jack Rabbit spotted Tony Wise from the distance, around the Saturday evening campfire during the Canadian Ski Marathon. "Tony Wise, it's so good to see you again," he shouted—instantly recognizing the man he had known for only a matter of two days several years before.

In the course of one weekend, Jack Rabbit Johanssen became a part of nearly 6,000 skiers' lives. He became a part of the American Birkebeiner saga.

"Tony Wise called me and asked me to come to the race," he shouted loudly to the crowd. "I told him I couldn't come, so he asked me again and again. Finally, I just got mad and said, 'if you come and get me I will come.'

"I have to tell you now, though. In all my 106 years, I've never seen so much excitement as you have here in your Birkebeiner. This is one of the greatest things to happen in the cross county ski sport!"

Carl Hanson, who had put the idea of the Birkebeiner in Tony Wise's head years before, did not live to see its tenth running. But from somewhere above, he looked over the Birkebeiner and a little bit of him was evident in Jack Rabbit that day. "Tony Wise," said Jack Rabbit, "this has been the most exciting day of my life!"

It would have been the most exciting day of Carl Hanson's life, too. After all, a Swede had won again!

Jack Rabbit Johanssen, wearing an Indian headdress presented to him during his 1979 visit to Telemark, and his daughter Alice, wearing a typical Norwegian dress, were honored guests at American Birkebeiner X.

THE FUTURE

Few had any inkling on February 24, 1973, as to what the Birkebeiner would become. Likewise, few can really guess what the second ten years will bring. Skiing has come a long way since 1973. (How many pairs of wooden skis and cane poles do you see today?)

The Birkebeiner offers a level of competition found in very few participant sports. Any skier, regardless of his or her ability or age can find a goal for themselves in the Birkie.

Surely, it will continue to grow and it's feasible that someday there could be as many as 12,000 skiers in the Birkebeiner—much like the Swiss Engadin Ski-marathon or Swedish Vasaloppet. That growth, however, will have to go hand-in-hand with increased race efficiency and technology. More beds will have to be found to accommodate the thousands of skiers, along with continued improvements to the start and entire race course. Skiers are likely to see the race continue to start in Hayward, the size of the event already having outgrown the starting facilities at Telemark.

Ski equipment will continue to change as well. New technology is constantly making its mark in construction of skis, poles, boots and clothing.

Around the world, citizen racing is growing by leaps and bounds. More and more races are seeking to join series like the Worldloppet and Great American Ski Chase. Skiers are looking for new challenges every year.

When you get down to the basics of the sport, however, very little has changed. Outwardly it is much different than it was in 1973. But in the hearts of the thousands who have donned a Birkebeiner bib, the feeling of exhiliration and pride is much the same as it was in 1973. And there will never be a cure for Birkie Fever.

RESULTS 1973-1982

1973
TELEMARK-BIRKEBEINER
(48 kilometers)

Men 20 - 31
1. Kenyon King — 3:33:10 — St. Paul, MN
2. Fred Albright — 3:44:19 — Cable, WI
3. Andrew Houkom — 4:02:11 — Meadowland, MN

Men 32 & older
1. Eric Ersson — 2:48:16 — Aesele, SWEDEN
2. Sven Wiik — 3:15:03 — Steamboat Springs, CO
3. Nels Meland — 3:33:11 — Oshkosh, WI

1973
WOMEN'S AND JUNIOR'S RACE
(22 kilometers)

Men Under 20
1. Duncan McClean — 1:08:33 — Ironwood, MI
2. John Anderson — 1:22:50 — Robinsdale, MN
3. Barry Bolich — 1:33:31 — Ironwood, MI

Women under 20
1. June Rueben — 2:15:30 — St. Paul, MN
2. Dede Strouse — 2:35:06 — St. Paul, MN

Women 20 - 31
1. Alexandra Boies — 2:19:08 — Hopkins, MN

Women 32 & older
1. Carol Duffy — 1:56:21 — Hayward, WI
2. Marlene Tremblay — 1:58:51 — Hayward, WI
3. Bebe Hanson — 1:59:51 — Hayward, WI

1974
AMERICAN-BIRKEBEINER
(50 kilometers)

Men 20 - 34
1. Dave Quinn — 2:59:47 — Cloquet, MN
2. Don Quinn — 3:08:43 — Cloquet, MN
3. Lars Arnesson — 3:10:14 — Cable, WI

Men 35 - 42
1. Tim Knopp — 3:54:50 — St. Paul, MN
2. Nils Meland — 3:59:20 — Oshkosh, WI
3. Rick Scott — 4:28:45 — Superior, WI

1974
WOMEN'S AND JUNIOR'S RACE
(24 kilometers)

Junior Men 19 & under
1. Duncan McClean — 1:06:50 — Northfield, MN
2. Tony Hartman — 1:10:00 — Woodruff, WI
3. Roy Fryburger — 1:14:50 — Northfield, MN

Junior Women 19 & under
1. Wendy Williamson — 1:47:40 — Hayward, WI
2. Jill Hubbell — 2:01:10 — Hayward, WI
3. Julie Hubbell — 2:10:55 — Hayward, WI

Women 20 - 34
1. Frances Wise — 1:35:45 — Hayward, WI
2. Marlene Tremblay — 1:36:00 — Hayward, WI
3. Jean Dick — 1:50:59 — Minneapolis, MN

Women 35 - 42
1. Bev Pfaff — 2:20:30 — St. Paul, MN

Women 43 - 49
1. Nickie Kohler — 2:29:10 — Hayward, WI

1975
AMERICAN-BIRKEBEINER
(55 kilometers)

Men 18 years, 9 months - 24 years
1. Chris Haines — 3:00:34 — Anchorage, AK
2. Dag Anmarkrud — 3:04:47 — Hernes, NORWAY
3. Larry Martin — 3:06:34 — Durango, CO

Men 20 - 34
1. Asbjørn Snekkevik — 3:44:46 — Wausau, WI
2. Thomas Haas — 4:07:13 — Duluth, MN
3. Tom Linderud — 4:11:04 — Somerset, WI

Men 35 - 42
1. Dan Danielson — 4:20:44 — Wayzata, MN
2. Klaus Milinski — 4:39:13 — Milwaukee, WI
3. John Kotar — 4:41:11 — Duluth, MN

Men 43 - 49
1. David Weiss — 4:21:38 — Eau Claire, WI
2. Nils Meland — 4:36:02 — Oshkosh, WI
3. John Holmquist — 5:00:27 — Minneapolis, MN

Men 50 & over
1. Olavi Seppla — 3:48:04 — Menahga, MN
2. John Burton — 4:15:47 — Deephaven, MN
3. Charles Banks — 4:18:25 — Duluth, MN

Junior Men 19 & under
1. Rod Grozdanich — 5:05:25 — Duluth, MN
2. Jon Malkerson — 5:23:05 — Edina, MN
3. Joel Malkerson — 5:23:11 — Edina, MN

Women
1. Vigdis Snekkevik — 5:00:57 — Wausau, WI
2. Jacqueline Lindskoog — 5:31:36 — Edina, MN
3. Patricia Smith — 6:11:31 — Ely, MN

1975
CITIZEN'S RACE
(27.5 kilometers)

Junior Men 19 & under
1. John Moody — 2:07:47 — White Bear Lake, MN
2. John Bing — 2:13:33 — Edina, MN
3. Roy Fryburger — 2:19:00 — Mazeppa, MN

Junior Women 19 & under
1. Betsey Kuntz — 2:44:50 — Edina, MN
2. Jeanne Christie — 2:53:42 — Bemidji, MN
3. Hege Endresen — 3:11:47 — Eau Claire, WI

Women 20 - 34
1. Linda Strande — 2:29:07 — Minneapolis, MN
2. Frances Wise — 2:42:49 — Hayward, WI
3. Marlene Tremblay — 3:06:29 — Hayward, WI

Women 35 & over
1. Solveig Olson — 2:53:58 — Minneapolis, MN
2. Dee Whitlock — 2:54:25 — St. Cloud, MN
3. Bebe Hanson — 3:03:50 — Hayward, WI

1976
AMERICAN-BIRKEBEINER
(53 kilometers)

Touring Men 18 years, 9 months - 34 years
1. Duncan McLean — 3:07:44.49 — Ironwood, MI
2. Trofinn Gjerustad — 3:09:10.28 — Winnipeg, Manitoba, CANADA
3. Stephen Cooper — 3:12:38.76 — Winnipeg, Manitoba, CANADA

Touring Men 35 - 42
1. Ingemar Sundberg — 3:06:09.68 — Gavle, SWEDEN
2. Frank Sikula — 3:40:03.82 — South St. Paul, MN
3. Rolf Carlsson — 3:40:42.63 — Minnetonka, MN

Touring Men 43 - 49
1. George Hovland — 3:41:33.74 — Duluth, MN
2. Nils Meland — 3:56:11.23 — Oshkosh, WI
3. Dennis Tremblay — 3:59:43.28 — Hayward, WI

Touring Men 50 - 56
1. Lars Augustsson — 3:48:26.34 — Minneapolis, MN
2. Sven Wiik — 3:59:11.95 — Steamboat Springs, CO
3. Henry Swenson — 4:03:34.63 — Grand Junction, CO

Touring Men 57 & over
1. Finn Andvig — 3:59:59.66 — Bekkestua, NORWAY
2. Kris Martinsen — 4:35:20.34 — St. Paul, MN
3. Robert Sandager — 6:03:18.15 — Minneapolis, MN

Elite Junior Men 18 years, 9 months - 20
1. Tim Nadeau — 3:34:45.68 — Hugo, MN
2. David Kask — 3:35:54.23 — Minneapolis, MN
3. Tony Hartmann — 3:46:06.18 — Madison, WI

Elite Senior Men 20 & over
1. Audun Kolstad — 2:40:44.14 — Henning, NORWAY
2. John-Mike Downey — 2:40:46.14 — Butte, MT
3. Bjørn Arvnes — 2:40:48.53 — Rykkin, NORWAY

Elite Veteran I Men 25 - 34
1. Asbjørn Snekkevik — 2:59:42.17 — Wausau, WI
2. Jorgen Skabo — 3:00:28.30 — Merrill, WI
3. Phil Rogosheske — 3:18:10.26 — Minneapolis, MN

Elite Veteran II Men 35 - 44
1. Odmar Eriksen — 3:10:28.13 — Karlsted, NORWAY
2. J.C. Williams — 3:19:07.02 — Aspen, CO
3. John Kotar — 3:19:38.38 — Duluth, MN

Elite Veteran III Men 44 - 54
1. Einar Svensson — 2:59:51.72 — Seattle, WA
2. Bjørn Lasserud — 3:10:35.00 — Richfield, MN
3. David Weiss — 3:21:30.53 — Eau Claire, WI

Elite Veteran IV Men 55 & over
1. Rudy Larson — 4:35:45.39 — Chassell, MI
2. Karl Sommer — 4:54:55.50 — Merrill, WI
3. Gustaf Konopnicki — 5:14:36.81 — Grayling, MI

Touring Women 20 - 34
1. Aina Heimdal — 3:56:18.71 — Bardu, NORWAY
2. Denise Green — 4:33:51.84 — Marquette, MI
3. Elizabeth Schluter — 4:33:59.64 — Waukesha, WI

Touring Women 35 & over
1. Solveig Olson — 4:55:10.90 — Minneapolis, MN
2. Judy Rykken — 5:08:34.84 — Bloomington, MN
3. Carol Duffy — 5:17:54.72 — Hayward, WI

Elite Women 18 years, 9 months & over
1. Jana Hlavaty — 3:05:31.12 — Chicago, IL
2. Lynn Vonder Heide — 3:10:28.40 — Anchorage, AK
3. Terry Porter — 3:11:49.17 — Concord, MA

1976
CITIZEN'S RACE
(27.5 kilometers)

Junior Boys 13 & under
1. John Svensson — 2:11:53.74 — Seattle, WA
2. Joe Pete Wilson — 2:33:04.12 — Lake Placid, NY
3. Robert Constalie — 2:38:36.99 — Westby, WI

Junior Boys 14 - 15
1. Tom McElroy — 1:40:45.97 — Minneapolis, MN
2. William Andresen — 2:06:49.69 — Eau Claire, WI
3. Steve Fahs — 2:07:00.61 — Roseville, MN

Junior Boys 16 - 18 years, 9 months
1. Francis Koch — 1:39:37.31 — Bloomington, MN
2. Hilton Bakker — 1:43:58.18 — Ah-gwah-ching, MN
3. Donald Rosenberry — 1:44:10.61 — Walker, MN

Elite Women
1. Birgitta Wiik — 2:10:04.04 — Gunnison, CO
2. Linda Strande — 2:14:35.86 — Minneapolis, MN
3. Mary Wise — 2:31:31.00 — Cable, WI

Junior Girls 13 & under
1. Beverly Klus — 3:09:09.62 — Madison, WI
2. Kathy Klus — 3:25:08.85 — Madison, WI
3. Judy Finch — 3:28:26.28 — Neenah, WI

Junior Girls 14 - 15
1. Susan Bevis — 2:30:44.88 — Minneapolis, MN
2. Laura Whitney — 2:35:02.10 — Duluth, MN
3. Robin Laursen — 2:53:24.47 — Eau Claire, WI

Junior Girls 16 - 20
1. Bonnie Fuller — 2:00:04.97 — Golden Valley, MN
2. Inga Soderberg — 2:28:07.17 — Minneapolis, MN
3. Cathy Wright — 2:38:46.73 — Edina, MN

Women 20 - 34
1. Karin Bunk — 2:30:47.53 — Hartstad, NORWAY
2. Luule Late — 2:39:00.25 — Platteville, WI
3. Marilee Bradford — 2:42:45.48 — Lutsen, MN

Women 35 & over
1. Rigmor Ohlsson — 2:40:57.65 — Cable, WI
2. Carol Davis — 2:41:41.00 — Winnetka, IL
3. Marlene Tremblay — 2:55:07.13 — Hayward, WI

1977
AMERICAN-BIRKEBEINER
(55 kilometer)

Class 1, Men 19 - 34
1. Bjørn Arvnes — 3:00:03.44 — Rykkin, NORWAY
2. Kjell Pettersen — 3:01:47.58 — Boaq, NORWAY
3. John Spencer — 3:05:26.82 — Anchorage, AK

Class 2, Men 35 - 42
1. Mike Gallagher — 3:16:41.41 — Pittsfield, VT
2. Per Gunderson — 3:20:26.38 — Spikkestad, NORWAY
3. Asbjørn Nordheim — 3:22:07.31 — Seattle, WA

Class 3, Men 43 - 49
1. Havard Bjerke — 3:28:24.79 — NORWAY
2. Leif Skaug — 3:29:26.06 — Oslo, NORWAY
3. Egil Borge — 3:31:57.90 — Strommen, NORWAY

Class 4, Men 50 - 56
1. Johanes Kopland — 3:23:09.28 — NORWAY
2. Oddvar Aasen — 3:32:22.26 — NORWAY
3. Einar Svensson — 3:37:31.61 — Seattle, WA

Class 5, Men 57 & over
1. Eldar Hagen — 3:48:19.58 — NORWAY
2. Egil Endresen — 3:57:01.42 — Dramen, NORWAY
3. Hjalmar Brennum — 4:01:00.01 — NORWAY

Class 6, Women 19 - 34
1. Alison Spencer — 3:32:09.36 — Anchorage, AK
2. Terry Porter — 3:32:36.50 — Concord, MA
3. Pat Engberg — 3:47:16.99 — Seattle, WA

Class 7, Women 35 & over
1. Berit Lammedal — 3:29:22.24 — Oslo, NORWAY
2. Suenhild Roiri — 3:40:51.17 — Skarek, NORWAY
3. Astrid Engebretson — 3:50:57.48 — NORWAY

1977
TELEMARK KORTELOPET
(27.5 kilometers)

Junior Boys 13 & 14
1. John Svensson — 1:46:36.87 — Seattle, WA
2. Kevin Marciniak — 2:01:59.23 — Cloquet, MN
3. Donald Kowantz — 2:20:54.29 — Winnipeg, Manitoba, CANADA

Junior Boys 15 & 16
1. Knut Engebretsen — 1:36:08.34 — NORWAY
2. Tor Lillemoen — 1:46:39.43 — NORWAY
3. Jarle Kristiansen — 1:50:19.33 — NORWAY

Junior Boys 17 & 18
1. Bernt Lund — 1:35:46.31 — Oslo, NORWAY
2. Carl Swanson — 1:47:26.59 — West Yellowstone, MT
3. Donald Rosenberry — 1:51:13.32 — Walker, MN

Novice Men 19 & over
1. Glenn Fuller — 2:09:28.44 — Golden Valley, MN
2. John Harju — 2:20:52.50 — Two Harbors, MN
3. Brad Parker — 2:29:49.04 — Cable, WI

Junior Girls 13 & 14
1. Trude Fixdal — 2:29:41.30 — NORWAY
2. Ann Wellnitz — 2:57:51.55 — Bloomington, MN
3. Jill Prange — 3:11:11.35 — Merrill, WI

Junior Girls 15 & 16
1. Kristin Green — 2:46:49.92 — Bloomington, MN
2. Jennifer Mead — 3:01:25.85 — Madison, WI
3. Susan Bevis — 3:01:41.00 — Minneapolis, MN

Junior Girls 17 & 18
1. Susan Kangas — 2:35:47.61 — Ely, MN
2. Eva-Lena Ivarsson — 2:39:45.20 — Eau Claire, WI
3. Inga Soderberg — 2:43:37.97 — Minneapolis, MN

Novice Women 19 & over
1. Gina Regland — 2:18:04.85 — Lillehammer, NORWAY
2. Sylvia Sommerfelt — 2:27:43.42 — NORWAY
3. Turid Kolstad — 2:29:28.07 — NORWAY

1978
AMERICAN-BIRKEBEINER
(55 kilometer)

Class 1, Men 19 - 24
1 Sten Fjeldheim — 3:15:16.23 — Minneapolis, MN
2 Duncan McLean — 3:17:01.97 — Ironwood, MI
3 Pentti Joronen — 3:22:42.61 — Marquette, MI

Class 2, Men 25 - 29
1 Alfred Kaelin — 3:10:04.35 — Staefa, SWITZERLAND
2 Randy Kerr — 3:14:32.12 — Norwich, VT
3 Audun Endestad — 3:14:34.17 — Three Lakes, WI

Class 3, Men 30 - 34
1 Renzo Chiocchetti — 3:10:06.75 — Trento, ITALY
2 Bjørn Arvnes — 3:10:10.79 — Rykkin, NORWAY
3 Sune Asph — 3:10:17.17 — Mora, SWEDEN

Class 4, Men 35 - 39
1 Per Arne Hansen — 3:31:08.92 — Drammen, NORWAY
2 Jan Hansen — 3:39:52.16 — St. Dorothee LA, CANADA
3 Arne Saterhaug — 3:44:38.84 — Trondheim, NORWAY

Class 5, Men 40 - 44
1 Pauli Siitonen — 3:10:08.34 — Espoo, FINLAND
2 Olav Bjerkeli — 3:55:09.54 — Jessheim, NORWAY
3 Brooks Anderson — 4:08:10.31 — Duluth, MN

Class 6, Men 45 - 49
1 Alfred Mueller — 3:35:11.75 — St. Lukas, WEST GERMANY
2 Thor Vikstrom — 3:43:21.45 — Laval, Quebec, CANADA
3 Bjørn Lasserud — 3:48:13.98 — Richfield, MN

Class 7, Men 50 - 54
1 Fritz Frey — 3:51:15.34 — Ketchum, ID
2 Kristian Johansen — 3:59:34.82 — Lommedalen, NORWAY
3 John Burton — 4:07:50.48 — Deephaven, MN

Class 8, Men 55 - 59
1 Norm Oakvik — 4:04:58.67 — Minneapolis, MN
2 Gunnar Movall — 4:28:02.71 — Honefoss, NORWAY
3 Rolf Hauge — 4:47:26.49 — Midland, Ontario, CANADA

Class 9, Men 60 & over
1 Hermodt Jahnsen — 4:38:01.13 — NORWAY
2 Hans Christian Knudsen — 4:50:50.37 — Drammen, NORWAY
3 Trygve Nilsen — 5:01:21.49 — Drammen, NORWAY

Class 10, Women 19 - 34
1 Hjordis Klomteig — 3:51:24.08 — Fosso, NORWAY
2 Denise Green — 3:57:04.21 — Cable, WI
3 Sonya Vodica — 4:05:38.75 — AUSTRALIA

Class 11, Women 35 & over
1 Valborg Østberg — 3:41:30.66 — Gjørik, NORWAY
2 Carol Duffy — 4:59:00.93 — Hayward, WI
3 Betty Bell — 5:13:33.58 — Ketchum, ID

1978
TELEMARK KORTELOPET

Junior Boys 13 & 14
1 Dan Kahan — 1:39:35.06 — Cable, WI
2 Clinton Reece — 2:01:49.83 — Winnipeg, Manitoba, CANADA
3 John Nitz — 2:13:34.15 — Tomah, WI

Junior Boys 15 & 16
1 Albert Leger — 1:39:18.56 — Cable, WI
2 James Read — 1:44:25.09 — Marine on St. Croix, MN
3 Don Konantz — 1:47:28.15 — Winnipeg, Manitoba, CANADA

Junior Boys 17 & 18
1 Kevin Brochman — 1:32:46.66 — Stillwater, MN
2 Oyvind Solvang — 1:34:14.76 — Bjornenatn, NORWAY
3 Don Hangen — 1:35:18.48 — Cable, WI

Novice Men 19 & Over
1 John Tormondsen — 1:35:40.72 — Cable, WI
2 Donald Rosenberry — 1:42:30.23 — Walker, MN
3 Jim Carrabre — 1:48:56.73 — Winnipeg, Manitoba, CANADA

Junior Girls 13 & 14
1 Jill Lindstrom — 2:37:38.14 — Dundee, IL
2 Jill Prange — 2:41:36.57 — Merrill, WI
3 Beckie Fuller — 2:41:43.44 — Golden Valley, MN

Junior Girls 15 & 16
1 Terese Maznio — 1:58:10.66 — Cable, WI
2 Rae Hoisve — 2:36:20.95 — Plymouth, MN
3 Katrina Karpuszko — 2:54:26.93 — Minneapolis, MN

Junior Girls 17 & 18
1 Kerry Jung — 2:22:33.70 — Hastings, MN
2 Ann Christensen — 2:30:37.95 — Golden Valley, MN
3 Sarah Bailey — 2:32:19.38 — Minneapolis, MN

Novice Women 19 & Over
1 Donna Rudman — 2:02:29.71 — Marquette, MI
2 Sirra Siitonen — 2:07:32.92 — Marquette, MI
3 Winky Mass-Protzen — 2:27:52.07 — Minneapolis, MN

1979
TELEMARK/SILVA BIRKEBEINER
(55 kilometers)

Class 1, Men 19 - 24
1 Arnt Haarstad — 2:47:27.92 — Rennebu, NORWAY
2 Tommy Jonsson — 2:47:37.34 — SWEDEN
3 Pentti Joronen — 2:47:43.59 — Kaipola, FINLAND

Class 2, Men 25 - 29
1 Per Knotten — 2:47:39.92 — Meraker, NORWAY
2 Audun Endestad — 2:48:09.25 — Brygga, NORWAY
3 Ernie Lennie — 2:49:22.07 — Fort Norman, CANADA

Class 3, Men 30 - 34
1 Bjørn Arvnes — 2:47:33.09 — Rykkin, NORWAY
2 Rudolf Kapeller — 2:47:35.34 — Bad Schaalerbach, AUSTRIA
3 Ulrich Kostner — 2:48:03.90 — Ortisei, ITALY

Class 4, Men 35 - 39
1 Matti Kuosko — 2:47:46.50 — SWEDEN
2 Heinrich Simon — 2:55:38.33 — WEST GERMANY
3 Jan Hansen — 3:06:48.47 — Laval, Quebec, CANADA

Class 5, Men 40 - 44
1 Asbjørn Nordheim — 3:14:10.18 — Seattle, WA
2 Tore Tangen — 3:22:27.24 — Hejjdal, NORWAY
3 Einar Ostle — 3:22:55.83 — USA

Class 6, Men 45 - 49
1 Kurt Kristoffersen — 3:14:38.91 — Skedsmo, NORWAY
2 Bjørn Lasserud — 3:17:06.35 — Minneapolis, MN
3 Gordon Konantz — 3:33:54.54 — Winnipeg, Manitoba, CANADA

Class 7, Men 50 - 54
1 Thor Vikstrom — 3:16:06.50 — Laval, Quebec, CANADA
2 Fritz Frey — 3:25:28.27 — Ketchum, ID
3 Bert Larsson — 3:28:55.71 — Everett, WA

Class 8, Men 55 - 59
1 Gunnar Ostvold — 3:37:40.04 — Dilling, NORWAY
2 John Burton — 3:38:58.86 — Deephaven, MN
3 Norm Oakviik — 3:39:24.04 — Minneapolis, MN

Class 9, Men 60 & over
1 Hermodt Jahnsen — 4:19:23.00 — Nurdal, NORWAY
2 William Andberg — 5:09:26.29 — Anoka, MN
3 Olav Olsen — 5:11:06.42 — Røsvichi Salten, NORWAY

Class 10, Women 19 - 24
1 Judy Rabinowitz — 3:10:05.08 — Fairbanks, AK
2 Ingrid Christensen — 3:14:37.01 — NORWAY
3 Jennifer Caldwell — 3:18:01.49 — Putney, VT

Class 11, Women 25 - 29
1 Birgit Tennøe — 3:18:29.20 — Oslo, NORWAY
2 Denise Green — 3:34:05.26 — Escanaba, MI
3 Kathryn Freeman — 3:45:40.59 — Madison, WI

Class 12, Women 30 - 34
1 Gabriele Andersen — 3:29:41.24 — Sun Valley, ID
2 Jeannie Thoren — 3:57:15.62 — Marquette, MI
3 Sally Elliott — 3:57:45.36 — McCall, ID

Class 13, Women 35 - 39
1 Ronni Dempsey — 4:16:22.98 — Boulder, CO
2 Solveig Olson — 4:40:16.88 — Minneapolis, MN
3 Win Paulson — 4:46:34.36 — Minneapolis, MN

Class 14, Women 40 - 44
1 Gerda Kunz — 3:43:41.51 — Vienna, AUSTRIA
2 Eunice Carlson — 4:05:41.09 — Houghton, MI
3 Georgiana Hurst — 4:59:15.92 — Marquette, MI

Class 15, Women 45 - 49
1 Matilee Christman — 6:18:11.00 — Des Plaines, IL
2 Coralyn Carl — 6:25:25.68 — Minneapolis, MN
3 Joan Smith — 6:55:50.08 — Duluth, MN

Class 16, Women 50 - 54
1 Betty Bell — 4:12:49.07 — Ketchum, ID
2 Margareta Lambert — 5:43:39.02 — Crystal Lake, IL

Class 17, Women 55 & over
1 Brigitte Sandager — 6:11:08.25 — Minneapolis, MN
2 Mrs. Henry Cowie — 7:47:35.07 — St. Paul, MN
3 Flo Viita — 8:03:15.20 — Saulte St. Marie, Ontario, CANADA

1979
TELEMARK KORTELOPET
(27.5 kilometers)

Junior Boys 13 & 14
1 Tom Dooley — 1:48:32.44 — St. Paul, MN
2 Peter Gallenz — 1:52:26.50 — Rockford, IL
3 Marcus Burkhart — 1:53:54.17 — Olympic Valley, CA

Junior Boys 15 & 16
1 Paget Stewart — 1:45:53.15 — Winnipeg, Manitoba, CANADA
2 John Tuma — 1:47:16.47 — Lakeville, MN
3 Thor Eells — 1:48:22.26 — Great Falls, MT

Junior Boys 17 & 18
1 Grant Yatrezenka — 1:30:53.79 — Shoreview, MN
2 Per Jacobsen — 1:33:40.55 — Lena, NORWAY
3 James Read — 1:38:57.40 — Marine, MN

Novice Men 19 & over
1 Kevin Brochman — 1:30:38.05 — Stillwater, MN
2 Jim Carrabre — 1:43:43.08 — Winnipeg, Manitoba, CANADA
3 Stuart Litchty — 1:55:16.40 — Madison, WI

Junior Girls 13 & 14
1 Jill Lindstrom — 2:12:49.75 — Dundee, IL
2 Elke Bunk — 2:38:11.52 — Harstad, NORWAY
3 Wanda Strangland — 2:56:39.77 — Deer River, MN

Junior Girls 15 & 16
1 Tricia Beth Spurr — 2:09:01.19 — Anchorage, AK
2 Julie Wolny — 2:09:13.96 — Bozeman, MT
3 Debi Dannert — 2:17:54.17 — Wayzata, MN

Junior Girls 17 & 18
1 Wendy Brown — 1:44:20.70 — Apple Valley, MN
2 Teresa Brock — 2:05:10.95 — Lakeville, MN
3 Rae Hoisve — 2:09:32.82 — Plymouth, MN

Novice Women 19 & over
1 Roxanne Triebold — 2:07:32.87 — Glenview, IL
2 Grethe Langsrud — 2:20:41.51 — Lier, NORWAY
3 Linda Strande — 2:36:27.87 — Minneapolis, MN

1980
AMERICAN BIRKEBEINER
(53 kilometers)

Class 1, Men 19 - 24
1. Arnt Haarstad — 2:24:59.50 — Rennebu, NORWAY
2. Anders Lennart Rudolfsson — 2:30:12.40 — Eskilstuna, SWEDEN
3. Phillip Peck — 2:36:45.10 — Stowe, VT

Class 2, Men 25 - 29
1. Jan Frode Bjørkheim — 2:26:07.70 — Salt Lake City, UT
2. Audun Endestad — 2:27:06.10 — Brygga, NORWAY
3. Alois Oberholzer — 2:28:50.70 — Schwyz, SWITZERLAND

Class 3, Men 30 - 34
1. Per Knotten — 2:24:55.80 — Meraker, , NORWAY
2. Arne Holmberg — 2:28:47.30 — Eskilstuna, SWEDEN
3. Rudolf Kappeller — 2:29:45.20 — Bad Schaalerbach, AUSTRIA

Class 4, Men 35 - 39
1. Heini Simon — 2:34:57.40 — WEST GERMANY
2. Alpo Virtanen — 2:40:52.50 — Vantaa, FINLAND
3. Per-Arne Hansen — 2:43:15.10 — Drammen, NORWAY

Class 5, Men 40 - 44
1. Matti Kuosko — 2:26:52.20 — SWEDEN
2. Erkki Harju — 2:56:22.90 — Two Harbors, MN
3. Claude Terraz — 2:57:54.60 — Villard De Lans, FRANCE

Class 6, Men 45 - 49
1. Josef Heufelder — 2:50:49.70 — Scharling, WEST GERMANY
2. Sven Broberg — 3:17:33.60 — Guslausberg, SWEDEN
3. David Weiss — 3:19:13.20 — Eau Claire, WI

Class 7, Men 50 - 54
1. Arvid Krogsven — 3:11:17.00 — Minneapolis, MN
2. Trosten Anders Rudolfsson — 3:20:25.60 — Eskilstuna, SWEDEN
3. George Hovland — 3:27:41.90 — Duluth, MN

Class 8, Men 55 - 59
1. Norm Oakvik — 3:21:58.60 — Minneapolis, MN
2. Charles Banks — 3:26:19.20 — Duluth, MN
3. Olavi Seppala — 3:33:21.50 — Menahga, MN

Class 9, Men 60 & over
1. Jack Wadin — 3:27:18.40 — SWEDEN
2. Aarre Heikkila — 3:48:23.70 — Thunder Bay, Ontario, CANADA
3. Rolf Hauge — 4:13:48.00 — Midland, Ontario, CANADA

Class 10, Women 19 - 24
1. Gry Oftedal — 2:53:48.20 — Baerum, NORWAY
2. Anna Bjørgan — 2:54:25.30 — Leiradal, NORWAY
3. Jennifer Caldwell — 2:56:01.00 — Putney, VT

Class 11, Women 25 - 29
1. Kate Freeman — 3:14:06.60 — Lebanon, NH
2. Pamela Weiss — 3:15:45.50 — Jackson, WY
3. Marilyn Buffinga — 3:23:30.60 — Grand Rapids, MI

Class 12, Women 30 - 34
1. Gabriele Anderson — 3:13:54.80 — Sun Valley, ID
2. Kaarina Engelbrecht — 3:15:11.50 — Vancouver, British Columbia, CANADA
3. Joyce Eidem — 3:29:53.80 — Bemidji, MN

Class 13, Women 35 - 39
1. Veronica Neptune — 3:46:29.30 — Boulder, CO
2. Elizabeth Schluter — 3:53:49.20 — Oconomowoc, WI
3. Joan McNaughton — 4:21:30.10 — Minneapolis, MN

Class 14, Women 40 -44
1. Eunice Carlson — 3:41:38.50 — Houghton, MI
2. Carol Davis — 4:20:42.60 — Winnetka, IL
3. Solveig Lise Olson — 4:33:37.90 — Minneapolis, MN

Class 15, Women 45 - 49
1. Carol Duffy — 4:06:38.50 — Hayward, WI
2. Coralyn Carl — 5:03:24.40 — Minneapolis, MN
3. Matilee Christman — 5:03:50.50 — Des Plaines, IL

Class 16, Women 50 - 54
1. Zeena Novotny — 6:11:31.50 — Eau Claire, WI
2. Delaine Meyer — 6:51:00.10 — St. Paul, MN
3. Mary Gibbons — 7:28:24.90 — Hayward, WI

Class 17, Women 55 & over
1. Margareta Lambert — 4:33:57.60 — Warrenville, IL
2. Brigitte Sandager — 5:11:58.40 — Minneapolis, MN

1980
TELEMARK KORTELOPET

Class 1, Boys 13 & 14
1. Rich A. Patterson — 1:30:21.73 — Winnipeg, Manitoba, CANADA
2. Samuel V. Beberg — 1:32:52.42 — Grand Marais, MN
3. Cordell Prychitko — 1:42:31.13 — Winnipeg, Manitoba, CANADA

Class 2, Boys 15 & 16
1. Steve Schuder — 1:20:07.43 — Cable, WI
2. Carl Ernst — 1:26:35.96 — Green Bay, WI
3. Kjell Bronson — 1:26:52.05 — Cable, WI

Class 3, Boys 17 & 18
1. James Read — 1:17:15.14 — Cable, WI
2. Brad A. Bart — 1:19:18.01 — Minneapolis, MN
3. John A. Tuma — 1:20:09.19 — Lakeville, MN

Class 4, Men 19 & over
1. Randy J. Stewart — 1:20:16.87 — Winnipeg, Manitoba, CANADA
2. Jim E. Carrabre — 1:21:55.57 — Winnipeg, Manitoba, CANADA
3. Alan R. Swanson — 1:22:16.24 — Fridley, MN

Class 5, Girls 13 & 14
1. Terri Pauls — 2:05:49.87 — Excelsior, MN
2. Lisa C. Seefeldt — 2:27:19.10 — Stillwater, MN
3. Christine Helbig — 2:58:34.12 — Detroit, MI

Class 6, Girls 15 & 16
1. Carol Warner — 1:44:55.47 — Excelsior, MN
2. Karen Hammond — 1:49:06.12 — Lakeville, MN
3. Martha Brown — 1:58:19.42 — Bemidji, MN

Class 7, Girls 17 & 18
1. Wendy Brown — 1:28:18.68 — Apple Valley, MN
2. Anita Myhre — 1:30:18.26 — Baerum, Verk, NORWAY
3. Lillian Kirstiansen — 1:37:27.02 — Baerum, Verk, NORWAY

Class 8, Women 19 & over
1. Kris L. Storm — 1:25:17.63 — Burnsville, MN
2. Nancy Stewart — 1:54:30.45 — Winnipeg, Manitoba, CANADA
3. Kristin Dahl — 1:57:50.71 — Winnipeg, Manitoba, CANADA

February 20, 1981
Elite Class
NORWEGIAN AMERICAN BIRKEBEINER
(48 kilometers)

Men
1. Jean-Paul Pierrat — 3:09:19.16 — Veroz, FRANCE
2. Jan Frode Bjørkheim — 3:13:52.20 — Skein, NORWAY
3. Sven-Ake Lundbäck — 3:15:48.25 — Lulea, SWEDEN
4. Pentti Toerni — 3:24:01.62 — FINLAND
5. Per Knotten — 3:26:44.30 — Meraker, NORWAY

Women
1. Marianna Hadler — 3:57:32.42 — Williston, VT
2. Muffy Ritz — 4:09:41.38 — Wayzata, MN
3. Gabriele Andersen — 4:32:28.92 — Ketchum, ID
4. Pam Weiss — 4:36:03.14 — Jackson, WY
5. Karen Henry — 4:38:07.01 — Norwich, VT

February 20, 1981
NORWEGIAN AMERICAN BIRKEBEINER
Citizen's Race
(42 kilometers)

Class 1, Men 19-24
1. Lars Njaastad — 3:41:47.99 — NORWAY
2. Jon Peter Nielsen — 3:47:55.09 — Trondheim, NORWAY

Class 2, Men 25-29
1. Per Lokaas — 3:22:13.91 — NORWAY
2. Joar Hoyem — 3:23:43.35 — NORWAY

Class 3, Men 30-34
1. Knut Forgsgren — 3:24:46.46 — Fauske, NORWAY
2. Stanislav Hrarik — 4:06:45.92 — WEST GERMANY

Class 4, Men 35-39
1. Erik Olsen — 3:42:26.28 — Oslo, NORWAY
2. Dag Aslaksrud — 3:48:34.64 — NORWAY

Class 5, Men 40-44
1. Tor Reiten — 3:23:53.51 — NORWAY
2. Hans Kverneng — 3:31:56.36 — Vestby, NORWAY

Class 6, Men 45-49
1. Terje Sommerstad — 3:44:04.17 — Konnerud, NORWAY
2. Heinrich Zogg — 3:50:03.81 — Embrach, SWITZERLAND

Class 7, Men 50-54
1. Einar Svensson — 3:33:09.27 — Seattle, WA
2. Lasse Virtanen — 3:38:33.83 — Osterskar, SWEDEN

Class 8, Men 55-59
1. Arne Knold — 3:47:27.56 — Valaskjid, NORWAY
2. John Burton — 3:49:15.32 — Wayzata, MN

Class 9, Men 60 & older
1. Osten Segefjall — 4:00:22.71 — Hudiksva, SWEDEN
2. Jakob Schoenach — 4:10:26.00 — WEST GERMANY

Women
1. Randi Someerstad — 4:00:02.60 — Konnerud, NORWAY
2. Joan Lovaas — 4:15:16.18 — Oslo, NORWAY
3. Borghild Kverneng — 4:35:35.42 — Vestby, NORWAY
4. Ursla Bjorklund — 4:49:47.50 — Ingmarso, SWEDEN

February 21, 1981
Citizen's Race
NORWEGIAN AMERICAN BIRKEBEINER
(42 kilometers)

Men
1. Hank Lange — 4:07:47.28 — Brattleboro, VT
2. Sam Simakis — 4:16:37.22 — Palm Springs, CA
3. Mike Fairchild — 4:17:26.54 — Saxon River, VT
4. Doric Creager — 4:33:19.35 — Spokane, WA
5. Donald Christman — 4:36:49.28 — Crested Butte, CO

Women
1. Marit Nord — 6:06:27.56 — Oslo, NORWAY

February 20, 1981
TELEMARK KORTELOPET
(24 kilometers)

Men
1. Stephen Maddock — 2:27:11.00 — Wayland, MA

Women
1. Kathy Maddock — 2:18:12.00 — Wayland, MA
2. Gretge Inagsrud — 2:39:44.60 — NORWAY

February 21, 1981
TELEMARK KORTELOPET
(22 kilometers)

Men
1. Randy Bouldin — 2:47:51.11 — Fairibault, MN
2. J. J. Carani — 4:00:00:00 — Chicago, IL

Women
1. Patricia Kramer — 4:49:48.04 — Benton Harbor, MI

1981
NORWEGIAN AMERICAN BIRKEBEINER
(55 kilometers)

Class 1, Men 19 - 24
1. Mark Ernst — 2:50:21.90 — Green Bay, WI
2. Ulf Kleppe — 2:51:30.70 — Azilda, Ontario, CANADA
3. David Israel — 2:54:48.50 — Tomahawk, WI

Class 2, Men 25 - 29
1. Tim Caldwell — 2:34:16.90 — Putney, VT
2. Borre Fossli — 2:52:47.90 — NORWAY
3. Walt Huemmer — 2:55:44.50 — St. Paul, MN

Class 3, Men 30 - 34
1. Dann Kann — 2:55:10.30 — Rice Lake, WI
2. Roger Pekuri — 2:55:34.30 — Ironwood, MI
3. Stephen Harrington — 2:56:58.50 — Duluth, MN

Class 4, Men 35 - 39
1   Bjørn Arvnes   2:37:15.70   Rykkin, NORWAY
2   David Hilfiker   3:16:21.20   Grand Marais, MN
3   Terry Holm   3:26:16.90   Brainerd, MN

Class 5, Men 40 - 44
1   Martin Hall   3:07:08.49   Hartford, VT
2   Duane Fjelstadt   3:15:09.10   Chetek, WI
3   Roger Block   3:19:56.60   Watertown, WI

Class 6, Men 45 - 49
1   Thomas Hall   3:04:06.60   Traverse City, MI
2   Erkki Harju   3:05:55.00   Two Harbors, MN
3   Raimo Ahti   3:14:00.50   Fitchburg, MA

Class 7, Men 50 - 54
1   George Hovland   3:25:43.50   Duluth, MN
2   Arne Borgnes   3:37:38.60   Bloomfield Hills, MI
3   Arvid Krogsveen   3:43:11.30   Minneapolis, MN

Class 8, Men 55 - 59
1   Roy Carlsted   3:32:05.40   St. Paul, MN
2   Charles Banks   3:32:42.30   Duluth, MN
3   Olavi Seppala   3:51:24.70   Menahga, MN

Class 9, Men 60 & over
1   Arnold Johnson   4:33:43.70   Rockford, IL
2   William Andberg   4:52:07.10   Anoka, MN
3   Rudy Larson   5:18:11.00   Chassell, MI

Class 10, Women 19 - 24
1   Wendy Brown   3:33:54.20   Apple Valley, MN
2   Kristine Danielson   3:41:35.10   Marquette, MI
3   Bonnie Fuller   3:44:24.20   Golden Valley, MN

Class 11, Women 25 - 29
1   Denise Green   3:45:20.90   Escanaba, MI
2   Julia Newton   3:55:21.10   Iron Mountain, MI
3   Jeanne Block   4:05:43.10   Rochester, MN

Class 12, Women 30 - 34
1   Muriel Gilman   3:22:36.80   Bemidji, MN
2   Pamela Schoville   3:42:46.60   Hazelhurst, WI
3   Raylene Kimball   3:51:01.30   Nevis, MN

Class 13, Women 35 - 39
1   Elizabeth Schluter   3:50:39.70   Oconomowoc, WI
2   Tine Thevenin   4:38:15.60   Minneapolis, MN
3   Patricia Grimes   4:42:01.10   Bemidji, MN

Class 14, Women 40 - 44
1   Becky Neumann   4:32:58.00   Marquette, MI
2   Joan McNaughton   4:37:33.70   Minneapolis, MN
3   Abett Icks   4:40:51.80   Cable, WI

Class 15, Women 45 - 49
1   Carol Duffy   4:17:15.60   Hayward, WI
2   Carol Davis   4:24:39.60   Winnetka, IL
3   Arlyn Stertz   5:36:47.90   Altoona, WI

Class 16, Women 50 - 54
1   Zeena Novotny   6:29:56.70   Eau Claire, WI
2   Mary Gibbons   7:20:11.50   Hayward, WI
3   Midge Kremer   8:16:15.50   Bloomington, MN

Class 17, Women 55 & over
1   Margareta Lambert   4:32:31.20   Warrenville, WI

1981
TELEMARK KORTELOPET

Class 1, Boys 13 & 14
1   Simon G. Shepherd   1:33:13.2   River Falls, WI
2   Brian R. Swanson   1:39:32.2   Grand Marais, MN
3   Roger B. Burger   1:41:25.5   Hayward, WI

Class 2, Boys 15 & 16
1   Ben H. Dodge   1:23:14.4   Deer River, MN
2   Peter H. Gallenz   1:24:52.9   Rockford, IL
3   Bruce S. Beckwith   1:25:09.0   Hayward, WI

Class 3, Boys 17 & 18
1   Daniel W. Cronen   1:22:17.8   Lakeville, MN
2   Robert S. Oberbreckling 1:26:54.0   Hubertus, WI
3   Kent O. Anderson   1:29:07.0   Carlton, MN

Class 4, Men 19 & Over
1   Daniel R. Williamson 1:22:19.9   Prior Lake, MN
2   Stephen W. Walburg   1:41:48.7   Chaska, MN
3   Mark A. Folkringer   1:48:18.7   Grand Rapids, MI

Class 5, Girls 13 & 14
1   Kathleen M. Engen   1:52:40.9   Brainerd, MN
2   Cathy M. Quehl   2:19:28.4   Monroe, WI
3   Heide Myles   2:27:23.8   Duluth, MN

Class 6, Girls 15 & 16
1   Carol E. Warner   1:36:06.5   Excelsior, MN
2   Ann M. Rosenquist   1:52:51.9   Grand Marais, MN
3   Susan K. Skrien   2:10:51.0   Grand Marais, MN

Class 7, Girls 17 & 18
1   Robin J. Brown   1:31:03.2   Apple Valley, MN
2   Disa L. Larson   1:48:46.9   Excelsior, MN
3   Megan M. Murray   1:51:38.8   Plymouth, MN

Class 8, Women 19 & Over
1   Verna R. Goltz   2:00:06.6   Rhinelander, WI
2   Carrie T. Hicks   2:04:52.3   Green Bay, WI
3   Linda A. Strande   2:05:09.0   Minneapolis, MN

1982
AMERICAN BIRKEBEINER

Class 1, Men 19 - 24
1   Leif Kagge   2:47:07   Bemidji, MN
2   Todd Kempainen   2:47:37   Minnetonka, MN
3   Brent Lund   2:49:49   Salt Lake, City, UT

Class 2, Men 25 - 29
1   Jan Bjorkheim   2:42:12   Oslo, NORWAY
2   Howie Bean   2:42:27   Wolfeboro, NH
3   Bengt Hassis   2:42:49   Orsa, SWEDEN

Class 3, Men 30 - 34
1   Ola Hassis   2:42:09   Orsa, SWEDEN
2   Rudi Kappeller   2:45:41   Bad Schallerbach, AUSTRIA
3   Mike Devecka   2:51:54   Steamboat Springs, CO

Class 4, Men 35 - 39
1   Arne Hegge   3:09:47   Valnesfjord, NORWAY
2   Per Arne Hansen   3:10:40   Konnerud, NORWAY
3   Tim Schuld   3:13:32   Boulder, CO

Class 5, Men 40 - 44
1   Pauli Siltonen   2:50:01   Espoo, FINLAND
2   Jules Schweizer   3:03:07   Scoue, SWITZERLAND
3   Claude Terraz   3:08:07   Villard de Lans, FRANCE

Class 6, Men 45 - 49
1   Raimo Ahti   3:20:22   Fitchburg, MA
2   Kare Lid   3:24:42   Park Rapids, MN
3   Richard Hunt   3:25:17   Spokane, WA

Class 7, Men 50 - 54
1   Bjorn Lasserud   3:30:57   Minneapolis, MN
2   Joe Csizmazia   3:37:09   Ketchum, ID
3   Sven Broberg   3:40:24   Mora, MN

Class 8, Men 55 - 59
1   George Hovland   3:41:05   Duluth, MN
2   Roy Carlsted   3:41:21   St. Paul, MN
3   Olavi Seppala   3:51:20   Manahga, MN

Class 9, Men 60 & Over
1   Osten Segefjall   4:05:28   Hudiksvall, SWEDEN
2   William Andberg   4:37:43   Anoka, MN
3   Sven Wiik   4:38:01   Steamboat Village, CO

Class 10, Women 19 - 24
1   Gry Oftedal   3:04:20   Baerum, NORWAY
2   Jennifer Caldwell   3:08:20   West Lebanon, NH
3   Joan Groothuysen   3:12:06   Kimberly, British Columbia, CANADA

Class 11, Women 25 - 29
1   Ruth Baxter   3:14:42   Aspen, CO
2   Karen Henry   3:25:57   West Lebanon, NH
3   Ruth Hamilton   3:40:53   Carbondale, CO

Class 12, Women 30 - 34
1   Kaarina Engelbrecht   3:21:56   Winfield, British Columbia, CANADA
2   Kate Freeman   3:35:07   Hancock, MI
3   Molly Higgins   3:36:31   Aspen, CO

Class 13, Women 35 - 39
1   Patricia Murray   3:41:13   Akron, OH
2   Elizabeth Schluter   3:55:37   Oconomowoc, WI
3   Joan McNaughton   4:29:53   Minneapolis, MN

Class 14, Women 40 - 44
1   Veronica Neptune   3:49:26   Boulder, CO
2   Tine Thevenin   4:33:01   Edina, MN
3   Abett Icks   4:43:26   Cable, WI

Class 15, Women 45 - 49
1   Carol Duffy   4:16:38   Hayward, WI
2   Arlyn Stertz   4:53:35   Altoona, WI
3   Charlotte Baertsch   5:02:09   Hayward, WI

Class 16, Women 50 - 54
1   Caralyn Carl   5:13:49   Eden Prairie, MN
2   Joan Smith   5:40:13   Duluth, MN
3   Mary Frey   6:27:49   Marquette, MI

Class 17, Women 55 & Over
1   Margareta Lambert   4:36:06   Warrenville, IL
2   Brigitte Sandager   6:33:59   Minneapolis, MN
3   Helga McNair   7:11:51   St. Paul, MN

1982
TELEMARK KORTELOPET
(29 kilometers)

Junior Boys 13 - 14
1   Jeff Rydland   1:55:58.0   St. Cloud, MN
2   William Beckwith   1:57:26.5   Hayward, WI
3   Nate Engen   2:19:43.0   Brainerd, MN

Junior Boys 15 - 16
1   Koll Fjelstad   1:47:08.8   Chetek, WI
2   Samuel Beberg   1:47:09.8   Grand Marais, MN
3   Roger Burger   1:51:15.8   Hayward, WI

Junior Boys 17 - 18
1   Ben Dodge   1:40:53.3   Deer River, MN
2   Bruce Beckwith   1:44:34.5   Hayward, WI
3   Joe Kelly   1:47:53.8   Woodruff, WI

Novice Men 19 & over
1   Stuart Lichty   1:43:19.6   Wauwatosa, WI
2   Carl Trabant   1:47:43.4   Minneapolis, MN
3   Chuck Phipps   1:48:03.1   LaCrosse, WI

Junior Girls 13 - 14
1   Cathy Quehl   2:25:33.6   Monroe, WI
2   Cindy Gallenz   2:31:52.5   Rockford, IL
3   Lisa Rosenquist   2:47:03.7   Grand Marais, MN

Junior Boys 15 - 16
1   Terri Pauls   2:11:21.1   Excelior, MN
2   Kathy Engen   2:13:10.3   Brainerd, MN
3   Nadine Make   2:26:33.1   Hovland, MN

Junior Girls 17 - 18
1   Brenda Bergum   2:10:35.3   Hayward, WI
2   Stacie Kuff   2:24:31.8   Drummond, WI
3   Amy Krohn   2:31:49.7   Black River Falls, WI

Novice Women 19 & over
1   Judy Swank   2:21:30.6   Rhinelander, WI
2   Susan Barnes   2:22:59.7   Eau Claire, WI
3   Ellen Truax   2:29:08.2   St. Louis Park, MN

PERSONAL BIRKEBEINER LOG					
Year	Time	Class Place	Overall	Notes